LESLIE HOWARD: THE

Leslie Howard
The Lost Actor

ESTEL EFORGAN

VALLENTINE MITCHELL
LONDON • PORTLAND, OR

This revised edition first published in 2013 by Vallentine Mitchell

Middlesex House,
29/45 High Street, Edgware,
Middlesex HA8 7UU, UK

920 NE 58th Avenue, Suite 300
Portland, Oregon,
97213-3786 USA

www.vmbooks.com

British Library Cataloguing in Publication Data

Eforgan, Estel.
 Leslie Howard : the lost actor. — New ed.~
 1. Howard, Leslie, 1893-1943. 2. Motion picture actors and
 actresses—Great Britain—Biography. 3. World War,
 1939-1945—Secret service. 4. World War, 1939-1945—
 Propaganda.
 I. Title
 791.4'3'028'092-dc23

ISBN 978 0 85303 941 9 (cloth)
ISBN 978 0 85303 915 0 (paper)
ISBN 978 0 85303 856 6 (ebook)

Library of Congress Cataloging in Publication Data

Printed by CMP (UK) Ltd, Poole, Dorset, BH12 4NU

To my father, Michael Eforgan,
British Army, Jewish Brigade, 1944–46.

And to my uncle, Barnett Miller,
Lancashire Fusiliers, 1942–46.

Contents

Illustrations

The author and publishers are grateful for kind permission to reproduce the following illustrations: The Inns of Court Regiment: 6, 7, 8, 12, 13; The National Archives: 1, 7, 11; Trustees of the Crystal Palace Foundation: 3; The Bodleian Library: 2, 21, 23; Northamptonshire Imperial Yeomanry: 9; Mrs Barbara Bruce Littlejohn: 10; The British Library: 18; ITV Global Entertainment: 20, 26; The National Archives and Records Administration, USA: 24. The British Film Institute: 25. Film stills reproduced in the book from films originally distributed by the following companies to whom thanks are due: MGM, London Film Productions, British National Films, British Aviation Pictures, Two Cities Productions.

Acknowledgements

I must thank Professor Jeffrey Richards for his guidance, encourage-ment, and exceptional kindness over the years the book was written.

I am greatly obliged for research help to Mrs Jan Pick, who (amongst many other things) found evidence of Leslie's meeting with Paul Kuttner, one of the kindertransport children. It was the start of a long trail for me.

Also to Mr James Oglethorpe, who works miracles from 12,000 miles away, and directed me to Leslie in Ireland, and Leslie's connec-tion with wartime SOE through Hilda Monte and Josette Ronserail, Leslie's last companion. Mr Oglethorpe also helped with a discussion of Leslie's last days in Portugal, and his last flight, although it has to be said we differed in our idea of events.

Others who very kindly helped, without the slightest idea of any reward – Professor Nicholas Cull, Mr Charles Drazin, Mr Andrew Cun-ynghame, Dr Kevin Gough Yates, Professor Philip M. Taylor, Professor Bernard Wasserstein, Senôr José Rey-Ximena.

Grateful thanks to: Mr Guido Coen, Mr Ronald Neame, Mr Paul Kuttner, Mr Gordon Mitchell, Mr Pat Jackson, Mrs Mavis Batey, Mr David Sharp of the BFI, Mr A.R. Chandler, Alleyn's School Archivist, Dr C.H.R. Niven, Alleyn's School Headmaster, Mr Dennis Durkin, Inns of Court Regiment Archivist, Mr Savage, Local Studies Librarian, Upper Norwood, Captain Holtby, 17th Lancers Archivist; also to Mr John and Mrs Laura Wainwright for their Spanish translation and dis-cussion of El Vuelo de Ibis; Mr John Rogers, Mr Allan Lodge, Dr Charles Swaisland, Jamie Copeland and Alan Brown – all from the Bodleian Library who specially helped in various ways; Ms Vanessa Corrick, Head of Reader Services at the Bodleian, was endlessly kind and patient; Miss Isabel Holowaty for her German translation; Mrs Anne Wickham, who allowed me to look round Leslie's old house in Surrey.

To the members of the Leslie Howard fansite, who helped me in various ways, including Miss Elizabeth Adams, who showed me a key letter written by Leslie, in her possession. Grateful thanks to this fansite and its many small helps, kindness and courtesies, from Margaret Sherry King, Laurel Howard, Ivan Sharp, Jeremy Sharp, Sheila Fienes, Jane Schlitz and Mary Jane Sinclair.

To Mr Mark Warby who very kindly helped with the permission for and provision of the Bruce Bairnsfather cartoon, kindly allowed by Mrs Barbara Bruce Littlejohn, daughter of Bruce Bairnsfather. Also Mr Nick Cistone, Ms Linda Townsend and Mr David Mitchell of the Bodleian Imaging studios. Mr John Mason and Mr Peter Higginbotham of OUCS, who saved my life after the disc containing the book was damaged.

And last but by no means least, to Dr Norman Paskin for his very generous help and patience over many years.

Foreword

Among film stars, both in Britain and America, Leslie Howard was unique. For he represented an archetype not generally held to be popular with the mass audience – the intellectual. He consistently projected a romanticized but thoroughly convincing image of the thinking man as hero. The secret of his success in this role lay partly in his appearance and his manner. The sensitive features and blond good looks, the cultured speaking voice, the slightly absent-minded air, the look of dreamy-eyed abstraction offset by the dry, donnish wit – all combined to give the appearance of the 'absent-minded professor' of popular myth. He looked as if he were not entirely of this world, as if his mind were elsewhere, in touch with the spiritual as well as the actual. His success also lay partly in the nature of his acting. He acted for, and not at, the camera, utilizing such economy of gesture and expression that he appeared not to be acting at all. Anthony Asquith, who worked with him on *Pygmalion*, observed admiringly: 'Leslie Howard was wonderful. He'd come on the set, have a quiet walk through in rehearsal and then could repeat a shot again and again – even his eyelashes would be in the same place at any given moment, yet his performance was never mechanical. He had the most wonderfully controlled technique I have ever seen.' He was, however, not successful in parts which called upon him to be demonstrative. When he starred with Norma Shearer in the film of *Romeo and Juliet*, Graham Greene noted that 'Mr Leslie Howard and Miss Norma Shearer spoke verse as verse should be spoken and were very satisfying in the conventional and romantic and dreamy mode (one still waits to see lovers hot with lust and youth and Verona fevers)'.

Leslie's mastery of technique allowed him to accentuate various aspects of his personality to extend the range of his performances beyond that of the thinking man alone. His sense of timing, his wit and well-modulated voice enabled him to play sophisticated comedy, as in *The Animal Kingdom*, *Service for Ladies* and *It's Love I'm After*. Without the humour, he could play the tragic hero of romances like *Of Human Bondage* and *Intermezzo*. But it was his otherworldly quality which enabled him to undertake some of the most memorable roles of his career, roles for which he was uniquely qualified, in *Outward Bound*, *Smilin' Through* and *Berkeley Square*. They were all parts in which he communicated with 'the world beyond'.

But most characteristic of all his roles were his intellectuals, his thinking men who find a cause, his professors humanized – for the discovery of commitment is what brings them to life and down from the rarefied heights of academe. There is Alan Squier in *The Petrified Forest*, the philosophic defeatist and failed novelist who finds purpose in sacrificing his life to save Gabrielle Maple, in whom he sees 'the renewal of vitality, courage and inspiration'. There is Professor Henry Higgins, the arrogant, self-centred bachelor phonetics expert in *Pygmalion* who eventually falls in love with his 'creation', Eliza Doolittle. There is Sir Percy Blakeney in *The Scarlet Pimpernel* whose pose of foppish languor conceals a man of daring, wit and commitment. Finally there are the patriotic intellectuals of the wartime propaganda films: Professor Horatio Smith in *Pimpernel Smith*, the Cambridge archaeologist who rescues artists and scientists from the clutches of the Gestapo in Nazi Germany; R.J. Mitchell, the inventor of the Spitfire in *The First of the Few* and Philip Armstrong Scott in *49th Parallel*, an ethnologist who takes on fugitive German submariners in Canada.

Curiously, none of the aspects of his personality as outlined above was singled out when his obituaries were written in 1943. 'A frank, intensely English quality in Howard's voice, face and bearing must be taken as part explanation of his sustained popularity', was a typical comment. C.A. Lejeune of the *Observer* wrote: 'Howard was more than just a popular actor. Since the war he has become something of a symbol to the British people'. It is clear, then, that Leslie Howard was seen in terms of quintessential Englishness. But what kind of Englishness? He certainly did not incarnate the sturdy assurance and dependability of the 'officer and gentleman' archetype so perfectly incarnated by Ronald Colman, Clive Brook and Herbert Marshall, although he did play that kind of part twice, in *Captured* and *British Agent*. It seems likely that what Howard represented to wartime audiences was the visionary aspect of Englishness, that fey, mystical quality that crops out periodically in English writing and thought. He came to embody the spirit of a gentlemanly nation, a quiet, thoughtful spirit roused to action by an evil more monstrous than the world had ever known. It was what the British believed they were fighting for – the eternal verities. It was an attractive image and it was one which Leslie Howard – dreamer, thinker, wit – was ideally suited to project.

During the 1930s his film career had been largely pursued in

Hollywood, culminating in 1939 in his appearance as Ashley Wilkes in *Gone with the Wind*, a role he detested in a film he disliked but which was destined to run throughout the war in English cinemas. At the outbreak of war, inspired by his love of his country and his hatred of Fascism, he returned to Britain and threw himself wholeheartedly into the propaganda war. Not only did he act in films supporting the war effort, but he turned increasingly to direction (*Pimpernel Smith, The First of the Few, The Gentle Sex*) and production (*The Lamp Still Burns*). He narrated documentaries, served on the 'ideas committee' of the Ministry of Information and broadcast to the United States and Canada. He was on a lecture tour of Spain and Portugal promoting the British cause when the civilian aircraft on which he was returning to England was shot down over the Bay of Biscay by the Luftwaffe on 1 June 1943. *The British Film Year Book for 1945* recorded:

> Leslie Howard, whose presence in England, as a producer, director and actor, constituted in itself one of the most valuable facets of British propaganda, was responsible for many fine British productions. This kindly, intelligent and cultured Englishman did much in his screen appearances to present to the rest of the world the embodiment of the finest qualities of the British people. His dignity, charm and tolerance, as apparent on the screen as off it, were indeed invaluable propaganda assets. He was representative of the finest type of Englishman and his loss ... was one of the tragedies of the war.

In his last major screen role, as R.J. Mitchell, Leslie Howard had pronounced his own epitaph: 'We've all got to pack in some time. It doesn't matter when. It's what we do before that is important.' What Leslie Howard had done for a few short years in the early part of the war was to demonstrate 'why and how we fight', and in his own way therefore to contribute to the ultimate victory of the Allied cause – a cause for which he gave his life.

In this extensively researched and very welcome new biography, Estel Eforgan does full justice to Leslie's career as actor, director, writer, producer and propagandist. She also throws light on many less well-known but equally fascinating aspects of his life: his Hungarian Jewish family background, the persistent rumours of his involvement in British espionage activities and the still-debated mystery surrounding the doomed KLM flight 777 on which he perished.

Jeffrey Richards
Lancaster University

Preface to the Second Edition

Since the hardback edition of the book was published, I am pleased to say that Leslie has at last received some public recognition. At his Surrey house, 'Stowe Maries', where he lived and worked for many years with his family, a blue plaque was unveiled on 9 September 2011, to commemorate his work as an actor and producer.

Figure P1. The blue plaque at Leslie's Surrey home, Stowe Maries. Standing underneath is Mr Derek Partridge, who as a small child in 1943 was turned away from the doomed Lisbon Flight 777. (Photograph kindly supplied by the present owner of Stowe Maries, Mr Terry Pentony.)

A LA MEMORIA DEL ACTOR LESLIE HOWARD
(1893 - 1943)
IN MEMORY OF LESLIE HOWARD (1893 - 1943)

que frente a esta costa encontró la muerte el día 1 de junio de 1943 al ser derribado
su avión IBIS por aviones alemanes de la Luftwaffe.
who was killed off this coast on the day 1ª June 1943 when his plane IBIS
was shot down by the Luftwaffe.

Y a sus compañeros / and in memory of his companions:

QUIRINUS TEPAS, O.B.E.	Captain
DIRK de KONING	First Officer
CORNELIUS VAN BRUGGE	Wireless Operator
ENGBERTUS ROSEVINK	Flight Engineer

IVAN JAMES SHARP
ALFRED TREGEAR CHENHALLS
FRANCIS GERMAN COWLRICK
ROTHA VIOLET LETTIE HUTCHEON
PETRA HUTCHEON (11 años)
CAROLINA HUTCHEON (18 meses)
WILFRID JACOB BERTHOLD ISRAEL
GORDON THOMPSON MACLEAN
CECILIA AMELIA FALLA PATON
TYRRELL MIDMAY SHEPVINGTON
KENNETH STONEHOUSE
EVELYN PEGGY STONEHOUSE

A la tripulación del avión perteneciente al 58º Escuadrón de la
ROYAL AIR FORCE, derribado en este lugar el 12 de noviembre 1942.
In memory of the crew of the plane belonging to the 58ª
ROYAL AIR FORCE squadron, shot down here on 12ª November 1942

KENNETH BRIAN WILLSON (1922 - 1942)
LESLIE CHARLES FROUD (1921 - 1942)
ALEXANDER SEATON LORIMER (1909 - 1942)
DOUGLAS ARTHUR HARSUM
HERBERT KITCHENER BROMAGE (1915 - 1942)
STANLEY BRIMER (1919 -1942)

Caídos por la libertad de Europa 1939-1945, su recuerdo permanece entre nosotros.
They fell fighting for the freedom of Europe 1939-1945, their memory remains among us.

Non omnis moriar

EMBAJADA DE S.M. BRITÁNICA EN ESPAÑA.
EMBAJADA DE HOLANDA EN ESPAÑA
CONCELLO DE CEDEIRA.

Patrocina / Sponsored by:
ASOCIACIÓN HISTÓRICO CULTURAL
" THE ROYAL GREEN JACKETS " DE A CORUÑA.

Figure P2. The plaque on the Cedeira Monument. By courtesy of Snr José Rey Ximena.

A more serious ceremony took place in July 2009, near Cedeira in Spain, when a monument to all those shot down in Flight 777 (the *Ibis*) was unveiled. This was thanks to the efforts of The Royal Green Jackets Association, and Senor José Rey Ximena, whose book, *El Vuelo de Ibis*, describes how Leslie visited Spain in 1943 in an effort to dissuade Franco from joining the Axis powers. The sculpture represents a DC-3 propeller similar to that on Leslie's plane, and carries a plaque with the names of the victims. The monument is sited on the land nearest to where the *Ibis* was shot down.

In 2009 Ivan Sharp, the grandson of one of the passengers on Flight 777, who has the same name as his grandfather, arranged for a memorial plaque for the crew and passengers of BOAC Flight 777 to be dedicated at Lisbon Airport. On 1 June 2010, a similar plaque, paid for by Mr Sharp, was unveiled at Whitchurch Airport in Bristol and a brief memorial was held by the friends and family of the those killed on the flight. At the time of writing, the possibility of a blue plaque in London commemorating Leslie is being considered by English Heritage. However, the difficulty is to find an address at which the plaque can be displayed, where Leslie lived and which is still in existence. One possibility is 54 Comeragh Road, Fulham, the address from which Leslie launched an assault on Britain's silent film industry. No decision has yet been made.

Research sites on the Internet continue to contribute worthwhile stories on Leslie. The Multiply website (now at Lesliehowardsociety.org) has run for over ten years, thanks to the efforts of Margaret King and supported by the brilliant researcher James Oglethorpe. Many old legends have been explored, and many new ones reported. There is also a faster moving Leslie Howard fansite on Facebook, which has occasional updates from those still involved in Leslie's story.

An informative website is hosted by Mrs Jan Pick, a long-time Howard family researcher and fan. This is part of her Howard family tribute, at http://www.alanhoward.org.uk/howard.htm, and includes photos and documents that could not be used in this book due to copyright reasons. A section on Leslie's early years shows photographs of Upper Norwood, where Leslie grew up, his school, and school reports, and a letter from his father to the West London Synagogue in 1891, arranging his marriage to Lilian Blumberg. There is also a photograph of his mother Lilian Blumberg and a cutting from *The Stage*, 1913, showing a review of the Anomalies Dramatic Club's production of *His House in Order*, with Lilian in the cast.

A section on Leslie's youthful efforts shows his story from *The Penny Magazine* of 1913, photographs from the production of *The Title*,

Leslie's earliest stage success in 1918, and photos from the infamous film *The Lackey and The Lady*, which led to a well-known court case. There are also letters from Leslie to Adrian Brunel, the early British film producer, in 1920 and 1921, boasting of Leslie's various successes on Broadway.[1] A 1926 letter to Gilbert Miller, Leslie's agent, mentions the production of *Her Cardboard Lover*, and Leslie's gambling on the US stock market.[2]

The last section, on Leslie's later life, shows a 1935 picture of Leslie in vivid colour, enthusiastically advertising cigarettes. Final pictures of Leslie show his last trip to Portugal and Spain, waving a sad farewell to musician Philip Newman, and most poignantly with Conchita Montenegro, long-time friend and lover.

*   *   *   *   *

POSTSCRIPT 2012

Some stories I covered in the book can now be updated, partly thanks to the long-running Leslie Howard research group, run by Margaret King and James Oglethorpe. These stories fall under three main headings – that of Josette Ronserail, Leslie's last companion; the sculptor Oscar Nemon and the mystery of the missing busts of Leslie and Violette; and one last story of a possible origin for the character of the classical archaeologist in Leslie's 1941 film, *Pimpernel Smith*.

Josette Ronserail

The story of Josette Renee Paule Ronserail, Leslie's last companion, received an unexpected rejuvenation when her family in Australia was contacted by Ivan Sharp, the grandson of one of the victims on Flight 777, and a member of Margaret King's chat group. It was found that Josette's story had been told by Toreska Torres, published as a *roman-à-clef* under the title *Women's Barracks*.[3] Torres, like Josette, was a member of the Free French and the British Special Operations Executive, the wartime sabotage operation started by Churchill himself. Torres' novelization of this experience includes the story of Josette and Leslie – a wartime romance, albeit with some rather cynical overtones by the author.

Unlike my speculations about Josette as a hardened character, perhaps set to spy on Leslie, she emerges as rather vulnerable, much in need of emotional support. As Torres tells it, Josette had fallen in love with a handsome and idealistic member of the Free French, now thought to be Claude Burin des Roziers, a naval officer in De Gaulle's confidence. Des Roziers came from an intensely patriotic family of French aristocrats, who escaped to England, leaving his wife and small son behind, to fight alongside De Gaulle. His brother, Etienne Burin des Roziers, worked at the French Embassy in Washington, and resigned from it when the US recognized the Vichy regime (which cooperated with the Nazis) in 1942. Etienne also went on to join the Free French.[4]

The brief love affair of Claude and Josette produced a child – a complication neither had bargained for. Claude left for the theatre of war in Africa, leaving Josette and the child behind forever, with only the classic fading photo for a memory. It is possible he never knew of the child. But it meant that Josette had to resign from the SOE. Somehow, she met Leslie, who was very close to the Free French after the death of Violette, his much loved mistress. Leslie, moved by her plight, and perhaps by her great beauty and vulnerability, undertook to look after her and the child. Another signed photo exists, this time by Leslie to Josette's son, also named Claude. Both photos, all that was soon left of her lovers, were bequeathed to her children.

Oscar Nemon
In 1939, the artist and sculptor Oscar Nemon, recently escaped from Yugoslavia, was in hiding from possible internment at the gently rural shelter of the Abinger Hatch Hotel, near Dorking, Surrey. He knew little English, but had managed to engage the sympathy of the hotel

Figure P3. Nemon's heavily stylized art deco busts of Leslie and Violette, now vanished. Photos kindly provided by Lady Aurelia Young, Nemon's daughter.

staff, who helped him find tuition from a celebrity who lived nearby, Sir Max Beerbohm. Leslie's family home was also near.

Into the Inn one day came a beautiful young woman – Violette Cunnington, Leslie's mistress at the beginning of the war. Mr Nemon made her acquaintance, and eventually, after learning who she was, asked both her and Leslie to sit for portrait busts. The work was a long time in hand, as both Nemon and Leslie had many calls on their time. Nemon kept in touch with Leslie over the next few years, and Leslie came to Nemon's studio a number of times, and met other well-known sitters for Nemon, as well as other Jewish refugees. By 1942, Nemon had made several portrait heads of Leslie and Violette. Violette's sudden death came in November of that year. Leslie's grief and feelings of loss were not soon abated, and by April 1943, Leslie had asked Nemon to provide figures for a memorial garden to Violette, that he wished to site near Denham.[5] Then came Leslie's own death. Nemon was left uncertain about where to send the portraits, until he received a

Figure P4. A later model of Leslie by Nemon. Leslie was sitting for this just before he left for Spain. Nemon hoped it would be a study for a full-length statue.

solicitor's letter, representing the Howard estate, dated 1st September 1944. Part of it stated:

> A cheque has been signed by both the executors for £175 and we shall be glad to know what arrangements can be made as to the collection of the busts; it being understood that the £175 is paid on terms that the busts are handed over and that no photographs or any other representations of the busts or of the sitters shall in any way be used by you.

An additional paragraph emphasizes the conditions attached to the payment. From the letter, it seems that the busts were to be collected from his studio by the solicitor. The busts have never been seen since. In 2012 Nemon's daughter, Lady Aurelia Young, who is writing the biography of her father, tried to trace the busts. They could not be found; and the mystery remains.

Pimpernel Smith

I have been shown evidence that Leslie met Ernst Chain through Oscar Nemon.[6] As described in the book, Leslie used Chain as the first character Pimpernel Smith rescues. Leslie also referred to other real life characters and institutions in this film, which leads to another story which I have not quite managed to pin down.

Paul Jacobsthal was a Jewish professor of archaeology at the University of Marburg, Germany. He specialized in prehistoric Celtic art. After the Nazis came to power in 1933, his views were increasingly regarded as subversive. The entire study of archaeology became politicized and Jacobsthal's research, providing evidence of the pan-European origins of Celtic art, did not fit with Nazi ideas of an early Aryan 'master race'. Jacobsthal was forbidden to carry on his work, and dismissed from his post. He escaped to Oxford in 1936, was sheltered at the University, and elected to the British Academy. His great work, *Early Celtic Art*,[7] was published in 1944.

The film's hero, Professor Smith, is a professor of classical archaeology, as Jacobsthal was. Smith visits Germany on the eve of the Second World War, with the supposed purpose of finding evidence of the Aryan master race. At the end of the film, Smith tells the Nazi Reich Chancellor that the art and relics he has found, 'prove the complete non-existence of an early Aryan civilisation'.

If Smith was not modelled on Jacobsthal, all that can be said is that this was a tremendous coincidence.[8]

* * * * *

Research on Leslie continues, especially in the area of the plane crash, and Leslie's now submerged links with British secret service. As I and other researchers have found, the more we explore the background, the more mystery emerges. Leslie keeps his secrets still.

E. Eforgan
September 2012

Figure P5. The Cedeira monument to Flight 777, showing the name plaque. By courtesy of Snr José Rey Ximena.

NOTES

1. The letters are held by the British Film Institute.
2. Kindly shown to the author by the collector Elizabeth Adams.
3. Toreska Torres, *Women's Barracks* (London: W.H. Allen, 1953).
4. *The Times*, 24 April 1942.
5. Extracts from Nemon's unpublished memoirs include the following comments: 'he [Leslie] was inconsolable and wrote her a 10,000 word letter which finished "Violette, I shall be with you soon"'; and, 'He commissioned me to make a memorial for the two of them for the Garden of Remembrance, and I got the maquette under way. But it was the beginning of the war. Howard went off to Spain, on a mission, intending to finalise arrangements about the memorial on his return.'
6. By Lady Aurelia Young, Oscar Nemon's daughter.
7. Paul Jacobsthal, *Early Celtic Art* (Oxford: The Clarendon Press, 1944).
8. Information provided by Sally Crawford and Katharina Ulmschneider, Institute of Archaeology, Oxford University. Sally and Katharina are determined to find out why Jacobsthal's file at the Home Office has been 'redacted' (censored).

CHAPTER ONE

1893–1914: An Englishman

Lisbon 1943: Leslie Howard, well-known film star, had risked an Atlantic flight to Lisbon to promote the Allied cause. His host at an evening film screening introduced him, to no one's surprise, as the very model of an idealised Englishman.[1] But somehow, at that time and place, Leslie was in no mood for convenient half-truths. 'I started as Hungarian', was his amused, and most unexpected, reply. The surrounding journalists were astonished. Some would not believe it until they had confirmed it from other sources. The most famous Englishman on film had just revoked his image.

Leslie's real family history had, in the fashion of the time, suffered the rearrangement of publicity agents. In fact it had followed that of many ambitious and talented contemporaries. Leslie's father, Ferdinand Raphael Steiner, had been born in Hungary, in Szigetvár, an ancient walled town in a rural area.[2] But there were not many prospects there for his family, and they joined the large number of Austro-Hungarian Jews who filtered into Vienna, the Empire's capital, in the late 1800s. They were in search of a secular education and even a new mode of life. Vienna offered unique opportunities for the exploration and exchange of artistic and philosophical ideas, and was approaching the most notable period of its history.

Ferdinand's father made his living as a commission agent, and was sufficiently successful to provide his son with an excellent formal education, and classical music training as a pianist. However, although Ferdinand had considerable talent and commitment, he never quite managed a public career, or to reach the highest levels of achievement, the opportunities to do so perhaps not being open to him. He finally resigned himself to follow his father in earning a living as a financial agent and stockbroker. Trade and travel in Europe were more fluid then, and in 1886, when he was 24, he came to England to work on the stock exchange and make use of his facility for languages and knowledge of foreign markets.

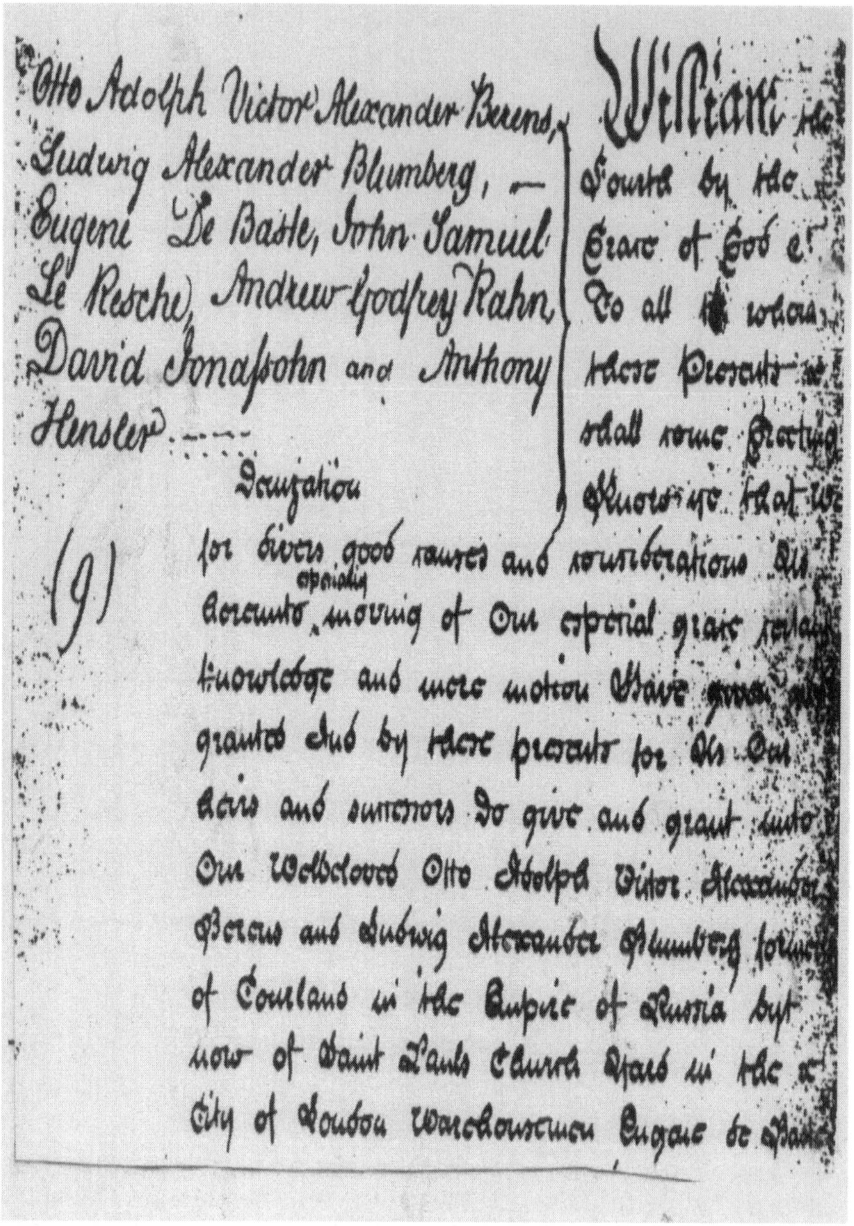
Otto Adolph Victor Alexander Berens, Ludwig Alexander Blumberg, — Eugene De Batle, John Samuel Le Resche, Andrew Godfrey Rahn, David Jonasohn and Anthony Hensler ----

Denization

William the Fourth by the Grace of God &c. To all to whom these Presents shall come Greeting Know ye that we

(9)

for divers good causes and considerations Us thereunto especially moving of Our especial grace certain knowledge and mere motion Have given and granted And by these presents for Us Our heirs and successors Do give and grant unto Our Wellbeloved Otto Adolph Victor Alexander Berens and Ludwig Alexander Blumberg formerly of Courland in the Empire of Russia but now of Saint Pauls Church Yard in the City of London Warehousemen Eugene de Batle

Figure 1. Denization papers of Ludwig Alexander Blumberg and others, 1834. 'William the Fourth, by the Grace of God ... we for divers good causes and considerations do give and grant unto Our Wellbeloved ... Ludwig Alexander Blumberg ... so that he shall be a free denizen and all his heirs and successors ... and that in all things shall be treated, reputed, held and governed as Our faithful liege subjects within Our United Kingdom of Great Britain.'

It was then a time of great migration and upheaval for European Jews. Between 1881 and 1914, approximately two and a half million moved permanently out of central and Eastern Europe, out of a total world population of nine million. The great majority of these travelled to North America; about one hundred thousand came to Great Britain. At the same time amongst these communities, ancient ideas and traditions were being increasingly challenged, and there was a movement known as the 'enlightenment', away from strict religious orthodoxy and towards the knowledge and civilization of Western Europe. For many middle-class Jews, their religion had come to seem beside the point.[3]

Despite the willingness of these emigrants to assimilate in the countries which accepted them, such a large movement of peoples was bound to cause concern. In England their arrival was greeted with some dismay, both from the population at large, but also from more established Jews. This older community feared that attention would be drawn to themselves, and that hostile feeling would be stimulated, and in this they were correct.

Leslie's mother, Lilian Blumberg, came from a family with English middle-class connections over several generations. Their first ancestor in England was Lilian's grandfather, Ludwig Alexander Blumberg, a wealthy merchant of Jewish origin, who had arrived in 1834 from Courland in Russia, and originally from East Prussia. The family's language and culture were Germanic. They had been distillers and brewers, a common Jewish occupation, and some members of the family carried on the trade in London.[4]

The welcome given to immigrants at that earlier time was a little less uneasy than in later years. Ludwig's papers of denization include a noble greeting from His Majesty and a bland acceptance from what was then the richest, most powerful and most religiously tolerant empire in the world.

Ludwig (later Louis) Blumberg set up his warehouse importing luxury French and German goods in St Paul's Churchyard, in the looming shadow of the great cathedral. His company, Blumberg and Berens, prospered and he brought over his brothers and sister and their families. In 1835 he married Jane Wetherill, a gentleman's daughter of Brockham in Surrey, a union which produced six children. He made enough money to consolidate his business, and acquired a number of imposing houses in west London. He was the first occupant of a newly built prestigious mansion at 20 Kensington Palace Gardens, so grand that it was

Figure 2. General Sir Herbert Edward Blumberg, RMLI, Leslie's cousin. (Taken from his book, *Britain's Sea Soldiers* [Liverpool: The Lyceum Press, 1924]).

later to be owned by the Sultan of Brunei. He was eventually to leave an inheritance that would last until his grandchildren's time. A sight of his will gives some of the slightly Pickwickian atmosphere of that time for a benevolent and wealthy employer, with its numbers of bequests to employees and friends as well as family.

Louis Blumberg's children had been gifted with sufficient talent and handsome looks to make their mark in the next generation. The two younger sons were sent to Cambridge, Leslie's grandfather Charles to Trinity College and Charles's brother Frederick to Gonville and Caius College. It was necessary there to take an oath as members of the Church of England before being admitted to the university. There was little difficulty about this, as their father had married in church into a solidly respectable English family; as indeed did all his children.

Charles Blumberg prepared for a career as a barrister, and was admitted at the Inner Temple in 1860. He was called to the Bar in 1863 and practised on the western circuit, so far as he practised at all, after inheriting considerable private means, until his death in 1911. The profession seemed to have suited family abilities, and Leslie's cousin Alfred Blumberg also practised as a barrister from 1882, after attending St John's College, Cambridge.[5]

The elegant appearance and well-modulated voice helpful to a barrister (and which later perhaps became evident in the theatrical strain in the family) might also have expressed themselves in Frederick's choice of career. In 1859 Frederick Blumberg, aiming at the highest reaches of English society, entered the fashionable and prestigious regiment of the Seventeenth Lancers. This was known for its elaborate uniform, its dashing style and its participation in the Charge of the Light Brigade, which had occurred five years previously. Entry to the officer class generally meant the purchase of a commission at this time and whether by ability, financial backing, or both, Frederick rose to the rank of captain by 1864.

As it turned out, the regiment saw no active service during this time, serving mostly in India after the Mutiny had been quelled, but a soldier's life held other hazards. Frederick's regiment had then a poor name for the care of its men. By the time he had become captain, Frederick had spent five years with the Lancers living in cantonments in Secundarabad, amongst a poverty-stricken native population eager to provide every service for the officers. His lack of military background and experience may have lead to the tragedy which followed, as on his return home in 1865 he succumbed to syphilis, the great hidden plague of the nineteenth century. After a long illness, he died in 1882 in a private asylum in Staffordshire.[6]

He left behind two children. His eldest son Herbert, brought up amongst the soldiers and barracks in Portsmouth, rose to the highest military rank as General Sir Herbert Blumberg of the Royal Marines. His obituary in *The Times* called him, 'one of the ablest Marine Officers of his generation' and added that 'his work during the [First World War] and after was invaluable'.[7]

However, a lifetime of public service left Sir Herbert with little to show besides his title. His father Frederick had left an estate of over £20,000 in 1882: his own, on his death in 1934, was £2,000.[8] Grandfather Ludwig had died in 1857, and although some business interests remained, much of it had been converted to solid investments, and the family took up the occupations of a more leisured class.

In 1868 Charles Blumberg married Mary Elizabeth Roworth, the sister of a Cambridge friend. Mary Roworth's family were respectable and successful tradesmen, although her father had by then sold his share of the family printing business, and assumed the style of a Victorian gentleman. At one point in the eighteenth century a branch of her family ran a printing business near the Strand, which was responsible for printing the first editions of Jane Austen's *Sense and Sensibility* and *Pride and Prejudice*. Mr Roworth the printer is mentioned in Jane Austen's letters.[9]

By 1890 Charles Blumberg and his wife Elizabeth were well established in Upper Norwood, a quiet, respectable suburb with dramatic and musical associations. It was at one of their 'at homes' that their daughter Lilian met Ferdinand Steiner, where he had been introduced as a piano accompanist for her singing. Ferdinand was 28 years old, serious, accomplished, assured. Lilian was much struck by him, but her parents were far from approving. Mr Steiner was part of the unpopular wave of immigrants at that time, a foreigner with little standing in English society. But love overcame all protests: Ferdinand was able to provide for a wife, and in 1891 he took out naturalization papers, and hurriedly arranged a runaway match. Lilian's parents greatly disapproved, and relations between the young couple and the bride's parents were difficult for a number of years, although a closeness with her brothers and sisters remained.

Ferdinand married Lilian in the West London Synagogue, which had been established by reforming and liberal-minded members as an alternative to the strictly orthodox religious leadership of the day.

(Ferdinand Steiner's letter, written in elegant English, still exists in the archives of the West London Synagogue, held at Southampton University.) Even so, the marriage was irregular to say the least. The Blumberg family had ceased to be Jewish at least since Ludwig's marriage in 1835, and possibly even before this. The ceremony itself, with its picturesque traditions must have seemed immensely strange to Lilian, and to her brother, who accompanied the couple as a witness. Most significantly, Jewish descent is through the maternal line, and Lilian Blumberg could not properly be married in any synagogue, although the marriage was valid in English law. Nor could any of her children, including Leslie, be counted as Jewish.[10]

The reason for Ferdinand's decision to marry in synagogue might simply have been tradition. It is possible that travel abroad was in mind, and Lilian would then have needed to be respectably and suitably married. In any case, Ferdinand's membership of this synagogue was allowed to lapse immediately, which in a way was a pity, as the small, select membership contained some of the most prominent and wealthy Jewish families in England. As events turned out, all connections here were severed, and influences which might have been of some importance to Leslie in the later part of his life were never rediscovered.

On 3 April 1893 Ferdinand and Lilian's eldest child, Leslie Howard Steiner, was born at the family home at 31 Westbourne Road, Forest Hill. He was reportedly a most beautiful child, though short-sighted, with deep blue eyes and curly blonde hair, and even with his father's sterner influence did not entirely escape some maternal cosseting and spoiling.[11]

When Leslie was 5 years old, Ferdinand took his family back to Vienna and they remained there for about five years, which had a strong early influence in the boy's childhood. Fin de siècle Vienna was at the height of its brilliance, with an explosion of cultural innovation at this time. For half a century there had been a movement into the city, from all parts of the Austro-Hungarian Empire, of those Jews most able to make their mark by a participation in western culture. It has even been argued that much of this cultural phenomenon was Jewish in its essence. A large proportion of the most prominent names, such as Freud, Schoenberg, Mahler, Schnitzler, Wittgenstein, whose influence is still felt, were of Jewish descent. Hugo Bettauer, a contemporary social commentator, described how Jews ran the banking system, showed the way in literature, politics, medicine, philosophy and journalism, patronised the arts, supplied the most famous actors and singers, filled the coffee houses with intellectual debate, and even led the fashion in clothes, leisure and lifestyle.[12]

Ferdinand had been a part of this as a young man when he had studied music, a field where Jews were very much to the fore, especially in the modern movement. Now he introduced his wife and family to Vienna, and there is no doubt that they much enjoyed it. Some of Leslie's (and his mother's) memories remain in a story that was published after the family moved back to England, in the *Penny Magazine* of November 1913.

> In striking contrast to an English Sunday night is that of Vienna ... in the cafes there is not a seat to be had ... The tables on the pavement, surrounded by little orange trees in green tubs, are more in demand than those inside. The scene was so typically Viennese. It was brilliantly lighted, officers in striking uniforms smoked cigarettes or sprawled across the tables to talk to pretty women, who chattered incessantly, shrugging expressive shoulders ... The orchestra, barely audible above the hum of conversation and laughter, mingled with the noise of trams passing up and down the Ringstrasse, accompanied by much clanging of their bells.[13]

Unfortunately, at the same time as assimilated Jews were making their mark in Vienna, the conventions of this society laid on them suffocating restrictions. Such was the anti-Semitism and intense race consciousness that it was impossible to live in Vienna without a clear identity. It was not a matter of religious practice, but everyone in the city, from aristocrats to servants, could judge the origins of any family and treat them accordingly. The Steiners would have been part of a community that was increasingly secular, but inescapably Jewish. Leslie and his family were afterwards remembered by some of the artists and writers who, expelled from Austria, found their way to America and Hollywood, where their cultural contributions were added to the mix. One irony was that those who had known him there, not realizing his later upbringing, regarded his 'English gentleman' persona in the film world as an amusing imposture.

It may be that an education in these brilliant surroundings was intended for Leslie, his new brother Alfred and sister Doris (later Dorice). However, in the face of limiting anti-Semitism, and with other uncertainties of that time and place, in 1903, when Leslie was 10 years old, the Steiners made the decision to return to England. Luckily, a reconciliation was awaiting with Lilian's parents, especially in view of

Figure 3. Leslie's High Street, circa 1890, showing the Crystal Palace.

another coming birth, and the family were welcomed back into the fold. They were helped to buy the house next door to the Blumbergs in Jasper Road, Upper Norwood.

Along with this help came the considerable weight of the Blumberg family traditions and expectations. The new Steiner family had to fit in to the respectable English society which surrounded them. Foreign words, accents and manners needed to be eradicated. The family surname was pronounced and later written as Stainer, and Ferdinand became Frank. Leslie and the other children were prepared for an English middle-class schooling and any Germanic traces were punished by Leslie's new relatives. Disapprobation for these things was sharp, and Leslie remembered his grandmother cancelling treats and his otherwise kindly Uncle Wilfred forcing him to eat a piece of toast spread with mustard when he spoke in German.[14]

These disjunctions must have been bewildering for the young Leslie, and he remembered becoming shy and withdrawn at this age. These were elements of his personality which long remained with him – one side of his heritage had been displaced, in accordance with the values of the day, and full confidence in his new one would take some time to develop.

But there were consolations. The place where they had come to live was as pleasant a suburb of London as then existed. In fact Upper

Norwood was an area inhabited by many quietly assimilated, comfortably off Jewish families. One incident in 1899 had seen Emile Zola, on the run from the French authorities and the intense anti-Semitic feeling in his own country during the Dreyfus affair, staying quietly in Upper Norwood, sheltered in the Jewish-owned Queens Hotel in Church Road. The French artist Camille Pissarro and his family, a friend of Zola's, also Jewish, lived nearby and may have made some arrangements for him. No one discovered Zola's whereabouts at the time, although the British press made many efforts to find him. Ernest Vizetelly, Zola's publisher in England, later wrote a red-herring book, hiding his Jewish associations and suggesting that Zola had no contacts at all in England.[15]

No oppression operated in wider English society, and life was safe and ordered. The Steiner's large new house was comfortable, supplied with servants, and had five storeys looking down on a sloping garden and a spectacular view over the whole of London. To add interest, just around the corner was the Crystal Palace, so huge and futuristic as to seem surreal in the surrounding cobbled streets. This was an endless source of fun, as its attractions were very varied, including a picture gallery, concerts, military displays, fairground rides, balloon ascents – all a child could wish for.

In 1904 Leslie started at a local prep school, Belvedere House, run by a Mr Bolland on enlightened lines. Leslie enjoyed his time at the school, and even showed an early interest in writing plays and stories, authoring a Christmas play in Latin for an audience of parents. If this sounds perhaps a little over-impressive, it is lent some credibility by Leslie's acknowledged talent for languages.

Leslie's next school, however, was rather less sheltered and pleasant, and not such a happy experience. In September 1907, when he was already 14, he was admitted as a day pupil to Alleyn's School in Dulwich. The school had been founded as Dulwich College in 1619 by Edward Alleyn, a celebrated actor and theatre manager. It was re-organized in 1882, so that Alleyn's School and Dulwich College were separated, with older boys continuing their education at the College. Alleyn's had no elite pretensions, aiming at the sons of local businessmen and middling professionals, the fees then being four guineas per term. It provided an excellent, up-to-date education in spacious modern buildings, teaching the classics, mathematics, science, English and modern languages. There was a library full of books about exciting parts of the Empire, a photographic laboratory, a recently built gymnasium, tennis and cricket grounds and a pavilion.[16]

A view of Leslie's school reports does little to suggest that he entered wholeheartedly into all these activities. Leslie's short-sightedness and shyness may have contributed to his difficulties at Alleyn's. The style of the reports was far more blunt than would be allowed today, but even so it is hard to imagine the circumstances that prompted the penultimate comment – 'a shuffler, little power, little energy, no morals' – an insight into a personality or a moment of irritation? One explanation may be Leslie's German name and accent – deeply unpopular at that time. (A trace of Leslie's German still remained years later, and can be heard at the end of his 1932 film, *The Animal Kingdom*.) Leslie was nearly 17 years old when this comment was made. The final summary of his years there consists of the word 'unsatisfactory'. An unhappy experience all round, with no very apparent explanation.

Leslie did at least manage to excel at modern languages; he had his father's facility and his own youthful knowledge, and he spoke German and French well. He perhaps made use of the photographic society provided at the school at that time – photography and the early cinema were strong interests. He also enjoyed the sporting life of the school to the extent of becoming a good tennis player, but was never apparently to be found attempting cricket or rugby.

There remain a few hints of the type of life and atmosphere of the school. One of them is the school stories of P.G. Wodehouse who had attended Dulwich College from 1894 to 1900. (Wodehouse possibly borrowed the name of one of Leslie's classmates at this time, a young Mr Wooster, who appears on the report register as a 'most gentlemanly student'.) *Mike and Psmith* and *Mike at Wrykyn* give an enjoyable picture of an idyllic English public school where a preoccupation with cricket and adherence to rigid schoolboy morals are far more important than any lessons. The feeling is of a complacent but very amiable belief in the timelessness and superiority of the English nation, and a cheerful indifference to social and political questions. An examination of the contemporary issues of Alleyn's School magazine goes some way to support the picture. A visit to the school today leaves the impression that, apart from the emphasis on schoolboy sport, not all of this has entirely evaporated.[17]

Despite his poor reports, and the fact that Leslie never remembered his schooldays with nostalgia, the values that influenced Leslie at Alleyn's, similar to those of his prep school, remained with him for the rest of his life. Many later commented on his appearance and behaviour as a quintessential English gentleman, and Leslie took in the standards of liberal outlook, honourable behaviour and the unquestioning patriotism of the time.

Leslie left the school at the age of 17. His leaving certificate shows that his occupation was to be, 'Junior Clerk, Purser's Office, (Steamboat)', on the nearby River Thames. But whether this post continued for very long, or even was taken up at all, is now lost in the mists. It certainly was not retained as part of the family history because Leslie is next heard of as a clerk in Cox and Co.'s bank, army financiers, a place which his father had found for him and in which he had to remain for some time.

Leslie's interest in writing and drama may not have been in evidence at Alleyn's, but they were much encouraged at home. The whole family had musical and theatrical leanings. Uncle Wilfred Noy Blumberg had dropped his surname to begin a stage career. Another uncle, Arthur Howard Blumberg, (possibly the originator of the Howard acting name) had also gone on the stage, appearing professionally with the Compton Comedy Company, until his sad early death in his thirties. Their sister Lilian, Leslie's mother, with similar interests, could not go so far, but she did appear on stage in minor parts with some well-known amateur dramatic companies.[18]

There were also plenty of trips with the children to the West End, where stars such as Gerald du Maurier – a matinee idol with his own casual style of acting – could provide role models and leave a lasting impression. Lilian conspired with her oldest son, wrote plays and stories with him, and eventually they formed a local amateur dramatic club with the family house as headquarters. They organized several public performances at the nearby Stanley Halls in South Norwood.

In 1912, *The True Artist*, written by Leslie, and *Ours*, starring Leslie and his mother, were performed. In 1913 the company presented *Deceptions*, a one-act play written and starring Leslie, and *The Perplexed Husband*, written by Alfred Sutro and performed by Leslie, his mother and his sister Doris. The entertainment seems to have been mainly attended by friends, but was quite professionally directed. Alfred Sutro was a very well known playwright and this work had been written by him only a year or so earlier. It is possible that the Blumberg and Steiner families might have known Sutro, with their theatrical contacts and Sutro's connection with the area – his wife was Sir Rufus Isaacs' sister, and their family lived around the corner in Upper Norwood. Leslie's mother Lilian was much involved in the amateur theatrical world, later taking Leslie's stage name herself, although she did

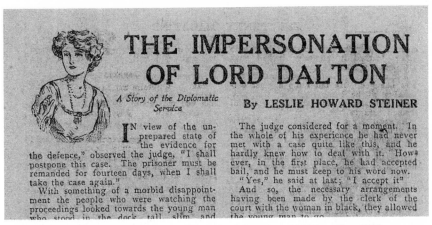

THE IMPERSONATION OF LORD DALTON

A Story of the Diplomatic Service

By LESLIE HOWARD STEINER

IN view of the un-prepared state of the evidence for the defence," observed the judge, "I shall postpone this case. The prisoner must be remanded for fourteen days, when I shall take the case again."

With something of a morbid disappointment the people who were watching the proceedings looked towards the young man who stood in the dock, tall, slim, and

The judge considered for a moment. In the whole of his experience he had never met with a case quite like this, and he hardly knew how to deal with it. However, in the first place, he had accepted bail, and he must keep to his word now.

"Yes," he said at last; "I accept it"

And so, the necessary arrangements having been made by the clerk of the court with the woman in black, they allowed the young man to go.

Figure 4. Leslie's first published story, in *The Penny Magazine* of 15 November 1913.

not achieve significant success. As James Agate, the celebrated theatre critic of the day noted, there appeared to be one amateur dramatic club for every hundred members of the population at this time.[19]

A contemporary actress, Mabel Constanduros, remembers Leslie as a confident leading light of the amateur stage:

> I remember Leslie Howard joining our dramatic club [Sutton]. He was a nice, fresh-faced boy with a charming smile, but none of us saw then the promise of stardom in his acting. He asked me to play for him in *The Eldest Son*, which he was producing, and in which he was playing the lead. The performance was quite chaotic – except for Leslie himself.[20]

Leslie's authority at such an early age seems to have gone unquestioned by those around him. Perhaps it was due to his family position as the favoured eldest son, or the natural confidence which comes with good looks. Whatever the reason, it seems to have been an essential part of him throughout his life.

At this time, just at the end of the Edwardian era, Leslie had grown into a slim, elegant young man, reserved with strangers but confident and companionable amongst friends. The family had been completed with the birth of his brother Arthur in 1910, and the house, with its lively atmosphere, domestic servants and strict paterfamilias, could itself have been a setting for the theatre of the day. It was a formal household, and the children were expected to take themselves and their responsibilities seriously.

Despite his successes on the amateur stage, Leslie continued to work at the bank in Whitehall. Ferdinand Steiner, drawing on his own disappointing and frustrating experiences as an artist, could not believe that his son's talent was enough to make a living. In fact it would have been possible for Leslie to train formally as an actor – the Academy of Dramatic Art at Gower Street had opened in 1905 and was a perfectly respectable establishment. His father's disapproval could surely not have stood out against a combined family onslaught. The opportunity however was not taken, perhaps due to Leslie concentrating on his writing, as it was in this area that he hoped to make his mark. Leslie's mother had always encouraged his gift for storytelling and writing. Now, with her help, he began to prepare pieces for publication in the popular magazines of the day.

The Penny Magazine was an enormously popular weekly in its time, aiming at the middle-brow reader and containing something for everyone. There were stories, non-fiction articles, advice, jokes and photographs but perhaps best of all were the backstage articles on the reality of the theatre, and especially on the new cinema world. The stories were of a simple adventure and romance genre, which we now read with a satirical eye, and of course Leslie's followed the pattern. His very youthful hero is recognisable, 'tall, slim and refined looking, with a frankness of expression that was pleasing to the eye'. This protagonist manages to triumph over all while engaging in an ardent romance with an older, beautiful and sophisticated woman of mystery. It is not surprising that Leslie later described to his children his long hours daydreaming in the high attic room that overlooked all of London. The habit was to be lifelong, his romantic fantasy life leading him into trouble on several occasions.

Ronald Howard, Leslie's son, was convinced that his father had sold some stories to *The Strand Magazine* at this time. Unfortunately, an examination of contemporary issues shows that this was not the case. However, they do indicate why Leslie was so inspired to try his hand at short-story writing. This magazine contained the foremost popular writers of the century, then producing some of their best work: Arthur Conan Doyle's Sherlock Holmes stories were still appearing, P.G. Wodehouse was at his best, and there was Edgar Wallace, Somerville and Ross, O. Henry, 'Sapper', Arnold Bennett, Jerome K. Jerome, W.W. Jacobs, H.G. Wells, Phillips Oppenheim and many others. Leslie's youthful efforts could not compete, but the immersion in this idealized world, with its simple romance and straightforward morality, left a strong impression.Periodicals such as these have great value for what they reveal of the day's attitudes and interests. While reading about the home life of favourite stage stars, or looking at photographs of film sets, Leslie and his family would also take in many articles, cartoons and stories reflecting the racial and social attitudes, deeply ingrained, of that time.

WHICH IS THE FINEST RACE?

A Symposium of Artists, Scientists, Athletes, and Travellers.

THE VENUS DE MILO.
The Greek type of beauty.

LADY BEATRICE POLE-CAREW.
The Greek type in English beauty.
Photo. Lallie Charles.

IN these days, when the science of human breeding is attracting widespread attention, is it not important that we should have some standard of physical perfection set before us ?

superiority even to Englishwomen ? There is Professor Otto Bergmann, of Munich, whose dictum is as follows :—

" The English frequently arrogate to themselves a physical perfection as a race which they are far from having attained. While it is true that amongst their upper classes height

Figure 5. From *The Strand Magazine*, February 1912.

The effect of items such as these on Leslie is difficult to assess. His early foreign experiences had been overlaid by his later education and training and were to be submerged for much of his life. But they were never entirely erased, and these forgotten loyalties were ultimately to resurface, with dangerous consequences.

But for now Leslie was young, healthy and surrounded by a large sociable family and plenty of friends. There was sufficient money for an untroubled existence and Leslie endured his job at the bank, enjoyed his leisure time and dreamt of an artistic career. As the summer of 1914 arrived, he was just 21 years old.

NOTES

1. Ronald Howard, *In Search of My Father: A Portrait of Leslie Howard* (London: W. Kimber, 1981).
2. Ferdinand Steiner: information from his naturalization papers in the National Archives, Kew, and from his birth certificate and other records of births, deaths and marriages in Szigetvár

and Hungary. Research in Hungary carried out by *Családfa Genealogical and Probate Research*, Budapest, Hungary.

3. For example, the director of the Israelitische Kultusgemeinde of Vienna, Heidrun Weiss, states, 'Your reflection about the Viennese Jewish situation between 1870–1925 is absolutely correct. They renounced from their religion vehemently, but not of religious causes, there was a pragmatic background.' Email to author 13 September 2002.

4. Ludwig Alexander Blumberg and his family: information from his will and from his papers of Denization at the National Archives, Public Records Office. Also from birth, death and marriage certificates of the family at the Family Records Centre, census records, Kelly's directories and contemporary London business directories. Guidance from Alexander Beider, *A Dictionary of Jewish Surnames from the Russian Empire* (Teaneck, NJ: Avotaynu, 1993). Blumberg family as distillers, see Court of Common Pleas, *The Times*, 1 July 1857. Louis Blumberg's house in 1852 from C.R. Ashbee *et al.* (eds), *The Survey of London*, vol. 37, 'Northern Kensington' (London: the Greater London Council and Athlone Press, University of London, 1973), and the Post Office Directory for 1852. 'Sultan of Brunei's house', local information.

5. The records of Charles, Frederick and Alfred from Venn's *Alumni Cantabrigiensis*, University of Cambridge (Bristol: Thoemmes Press, 2001), and Joseph Foster, *Foster's Hand-List of Men-at-the-Bar* (1885).

6. Frederick Blumberg's story from his regimental records at the PRO, the regimental history of the Seventeenth Lancers and their archives, and his death certificate.

7. Sir Herbert Blumberg's picture from his book, *Britain's Sea Soldiers: A Record of the Royal Marines During the War 1914–1919* (Devonport: Swiss, 1927). His obituary from *The Times*, 18 August 1934.

8. General Blumberg's legacy from *The Times*, 15 September 1934. Frederick Blumberg's legacy from his will.

9. The Roworth printing business continued in the same name until the 1970s. Information from Mr Michael Roworth, family genealogist, who estimates that he is 'second cousin once removed to Leslie'. Email to author, March 2006.

10. Ferdinand and Lilian Steiner's marriage details from the marriage certificate at the Family Records Centre, and from the Archives of the West London Synagogue, held at the Hartley Library, University of Southampton, including Ferdinand's letter to the synagogue (MS 140 AJ 59/16/6) and his lapsed membership.

11. Details of Leslie's early years from his own children's memoirs – Leslie Ruth Howard, *A Quite Remarkable Father* (London: Longmans, 1960) and Ronald Howard, *In Search of My Father*.

12. Description of Viennese culture and social conditions from Stephen Beller, *Vienna and the Jews 1867–1939: A Cultural History* (Cambridge: Cambridge University Press, 1989) and Robert Wistrich, *The Jews of Vienna in the Age of Franz Joseph* (Oxford and New York: Published for the Littman Library by Oxford University Press, 1990).

13. Leslie Howard Steiner, 'The Impersonation of Lord Dalton', *The Penny Magazine* (November 1913).

14. Howard, *A Quite Remarkable Father*.

15. Zola's visit: Nicholas Reed, *Camille Pissarro at the Crystal Palace* (London: London Reference Books, 1987), Frederick Brown, *Zola: A Life* (London: Macmillan, 1996) pp.764–5, Anne Thorold, (ed.) *The Letters of Lucien to Camille Pissarro, 1883–1903* (Cambridge: Cambridge University Press, 1993), p.587, Ernest Alfred Vizetelly, *With Zola in England: A Story of Exile* (Leipzig: B. Tauchnitz, 1899).

16. All details of Alleyn's School and Leslie's school records courtesy of the school archivist, Mr A.R. Chandler, and the headmaster, Dr. C.H.R. Niven. Also from A.R. Chandler, *Alleyn's: The Coeducational School* (Henley-on-Thames: Gresham Books in partnership with Alleyn's School, 1998) and copies of the school magazine 1907–1910.

17. In 1997.

18. For example, *The Stage*, December 1913 notes Leslie's mother appearing in a small part with the Anomalies Dramatic Club as a French governess in Arthur Wing Pinero's play, *His House in Order*, under the name of Mrs Lilian Steiner. The Anomalies Dramatic Club of Streatham was quite well known – Mrs Patrick Campbell, Bernard Shaw's muse, was a member before she became a professional actor.

19. James Agate, *A Short View of the English Stage, 1900–1926* (London: H. Jenkins, 1926).

20. Mabel Constanduros, *Shreds and Patches* (London: Lawson and Dunn, 1946), p.37.

CHAPTER TWO

1914–1916: A Small Adventure

The Great War when it first came was viewed as a grand source of excitement. Leslie was stirred by the intensely romantic spirit of the day and gave up his job as a bank clerk without regret. He joined the army soon after the war's beginning. The coming battle was being widely spoken of in the press as 'The Great Adventure', and poet Rupert Brooke had expressed the feelings of 1914: 'Now God be thanked Who has matched us with this hour'[1] and urging 'Leave the sick hearts that honour could not move'. But public opinion was undisturbed at first – the mighty British Empire would surely not be too troubled.

Leslie's family thought it best for him to try to join the militia, rather than the regulars. Possibly encouraged by seniors at Cox's bank, Leslie applied to the Inns of Court Regiment, which operated as the officer-training school for this 'elite' section of the military. As this regiment was traditionally connected with the legal profession, Leslie's barrister grandfather and cousin might also have helped his application. Leslie had in his family background a member of a distinguished regiment who had served with some of the country's most famous soldiers, and a general who had been knighted for his services. Living up to all this would have been too overwhelming to think about.[2]

In command of the regiment to which Leslie applied was Colonel Henry Francis Launcelot Errington. The qualities he was looking for in his new recruits could be simply expressed, and they are summarised on a contemporary poster. The ideas behind them retained an element of the old obligations of a gentleman; the attitudes of selfless service and cheerful leadership would naturally belong to an upbringing with the correct manners and etiquette. The Inns of Court Regiment was therefore particular about its recruits, accepting only one in ten applications, and insisting on only those from 'the greater public schools'. But after some complaints about exclusions, the colonel was forced to ask the War Office for a definition of the 'suitable' public schools. The answer, rather quellingly, was that 'a public school is a school open to the public'.[3]

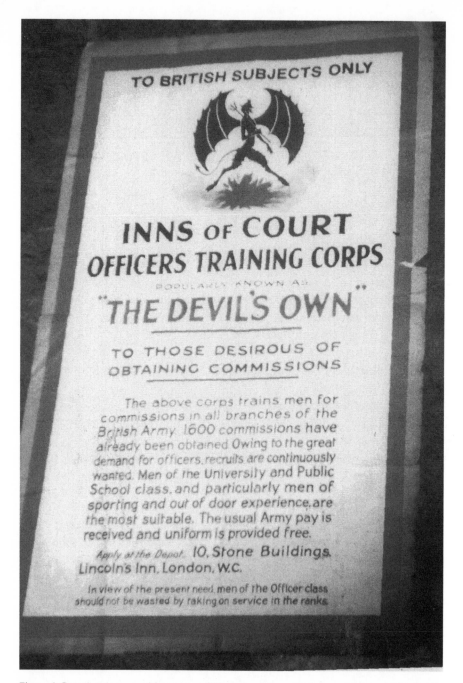

Figure 6. Contemporary recruiting poster of The Inns of Court Regiment, nicknamed 'The Devil's Own'. Taken from Colonel F.H.L. Errington, *The Inns of Court Regimental History of the First World War* (1924).

THE COMPANY.

Programmes of lectures were drawn up, but, like most programmes, they were better on paper than in practi
he orderly sequence would be broken up by the sudden intervention of a C.O.'s lecture; or a wet day would invo
pending the greater part of the time in-doors, when the stock of lectures would be drawn on. Companies mana
heir lectures in their own way, but the following list will give some idea of the staple subjects :

Qualities needed for an officer or soldier (given normally when a new batch of recruits joined the Compan
Discipline.
Sanitation.
Musketry.
March Discipline.
Entrenchment.
Tactical principles.
Advance Guards (also Rear Guards and Flank Guards).
Outposts.
Attack.
Defence.
Trench Warfare.
Map-reading.
Scouting and Reconnaissance.
Night Operations.
Village and Wood Fighting.
Messages.
Wire Entanglements.
Military Law.
Principles of Strategy and Tactics, historically illustrated.
History of the war (especially from Mons to the Marne).

Figure 7. List of training subjects for officers. Taken from Colonel F.H.L. Errington, *The Inns of Court Regimental History of the First World War* (1924).

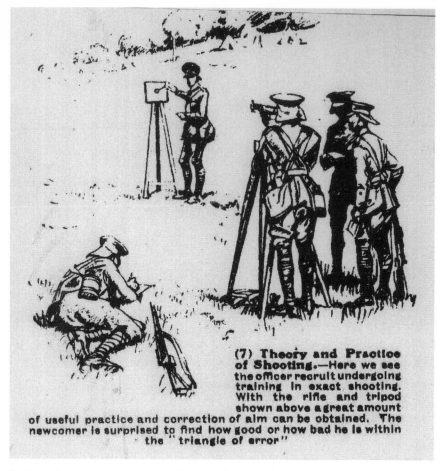

(7) Theory and Practice of Shooting.—Here we see the officer recruit undergoing training in exact shooting. With the rifle and tripod shown above a great amount of useful practice and correction of aim can be obtained. The newcomer is surprised to find how good or how bad he is within the "triangle of error"

Figure 8. Shooting practice at the Berkhamstead camp. Taken from Colonel F.H.L. Errington, *The Inns of Court Regimental History of the First World War* (1924).

Whatever the perceived status of Alleyn's, Leslie's background and appearance were enough to be acceptable to the selectors. He attended a formal interview at 10 Stone Buildings, Lincoln's Inn, then a solemn attestation ceremony. After acquiring considerable quantities of uniform and accoutrements, he was sent to Berkhamstead camp to train under canvas in October 1914.

Training, besides etiquette and behaviour proper to an officer, included drill, field work and musketry, and there were night manoeuvres and long marches through countryside and villages, with admiring onlookers providing some encouragement. In addition to the physical work, this page from the *Regimental History* gives a list of subjects covered.

Nothing concerning either bombs or gas was taught here at this time (although they were introduced later). The trainees were therefore unprepared for the reality of the war to come – the shattering bombardments and clinging phosgene and mustard gas that many of them would encounter within a few months. Nor were the young men in their

Figure 9. The Proud Cavalry Officer: The uniform worn by Leslie in 1914.

pristine uniforms, given the slightest idea of all that was in store for them – the wreckages of rural villages blown inside-out, the filth and lice in the billets, the jumble of mud, blood, bones and barbed wire in the unforeseen static trench warfare of the next four years.

Leslie spent about five months at the camp being trained, and gained some muscle, some experience and much suitable knowledge. He returned home to his family on leave looking very smart in his uniform. Leslie's appearance and physical fitness must have been impressive. There is some evidence that the family maid had to leave the household to care for a son at about this time; the suggestion was that Leslie was the father. The presence of obsequious servants living in a suburban home is one practice of that time almost unimaginable now. The affair must have been short-lived, but was likely to have further estranged Leslie from his father, who was making understandable efforts to get his son safely married off.[4]

Immediately after his training at the officer school, in March 1915, Leslie was accepted as a second lieutenant in the Northamptonshire Imperial Yeomanry, (NIY) a mounted territorial regiment. This selection was helped by the fact that the commanding officer, Colonel Cazenove, was a director at Leslie's bank. As it happened, the choice was both lucky and disastrous. Disastrous because cavalry regiments were almost immediately outmoded by trench warfare and were to be diverted for a long time to the dreariest possible battlefield chores. Lucky in a way, because most of the chores were behind the lines and there was less immediate danger of injury and death.

Leslie was initially assigned to the second and later the third regiment, both intended to provide reinforcements for the first, which had gone straight out to France in 1914. This first regiment had more experienced men, and eventually fought at the Battle of Neuve Chappelle in 1915. They and the Northumberland Yeomanry were the first such regiments to be sent out.[5] Leslie and the second-line troops undertook another ten months training before they were sent into battle. This was perhaps because the majority of them were raw recruits, and had to start from the basics of learning to ride, but also because no one by now was quite sure what to do with the yeomanry cavalry.

The only remaining witness to Leslie's time in the Yeomanry is Arch Whitehouse, a trooper who happened to have Leslie as his officer. Mr Whitehouse wrote *The Fledgling*, a book of his wartime exploits in which the author, fresh from a glamorous trip to New York and depressed to be back home in a funereal England, describes the NIY and everything

That Sword.

How he thought he was going to use it——

——and how he did use it.

Figure 10. The disillusioned reality, two years later. Cartoons of Bruce Bairnsfather. First published in *The Bystander*, 25 August 1915.

connected with it in the gloomiest possible terms.[6] The officers, local gentlemen and farmers from the Northampton hunting country, were characterized as amateur and snobbish incompetents. Leslie, aged 22, is pictured as the one pleasant and intelligent exception, but out of place in every way; he 'was a very young, naive, slim, rather fragile looking officer. He in no way represented our hunt-country product of the dashing cavalry officer ... He spoke with a slight lisp, and his speech bore a hint of continental accent.' Whitehouse adds that unfortunately, 'I was the only man in the regiment who had a kind word for him', and that, 'few troopers had much respect for him'.

Meanwhile the regiment endlessly trained, first at Towcester, later at Colchester and elsewhere. They learned to drill, ride and care for their mounts, and covered large areas of countryside, on bicycles where they were not yet trusted with horses. The mounted training at least must have felt heroic – such regiments were still learning to use the sabre to cut a man's head off at the gallop. Most of Leslie's regiment finally left for France in December 1915. Leslie however, remained. Part of the reason why is found in the proceedings of a medical board attended by Leslie in January 1916 at Colchester Military Hospital, although even this does not shed much light.

The assessment reads:

> The board having assembled pursuant to order, and having read the instructions on the back of the form, proceed to examine the above-named officer and find that; he states that he suffers on and off with headaches and a feeling of faintness. This in proportion to the amount of physical work he has to do. Says he has had pyorrhoea, for which he has been treated but at present there are no evidences of this trouble.
>
> Present condition. He looks well – his manner shy and nervous. Suffers from frequent nocturnal emissions. Heart is sound. No evidence of any organic trouble. The board is of opinion that plenty of work would be best in his case.[7]

Leslie's disability is described as 'neurasthenia'. The file was released in 1996, together with most other officers' records. A note in the file states that it has been 'weeded' – that is, unnamed papers have been removed.

Leslie stayed at Colchester with the remains of the NIY reserve. He was now living in lodgings at Crouch Street, around the corner from the old church of St Mary at the Walls. It was at this church that he

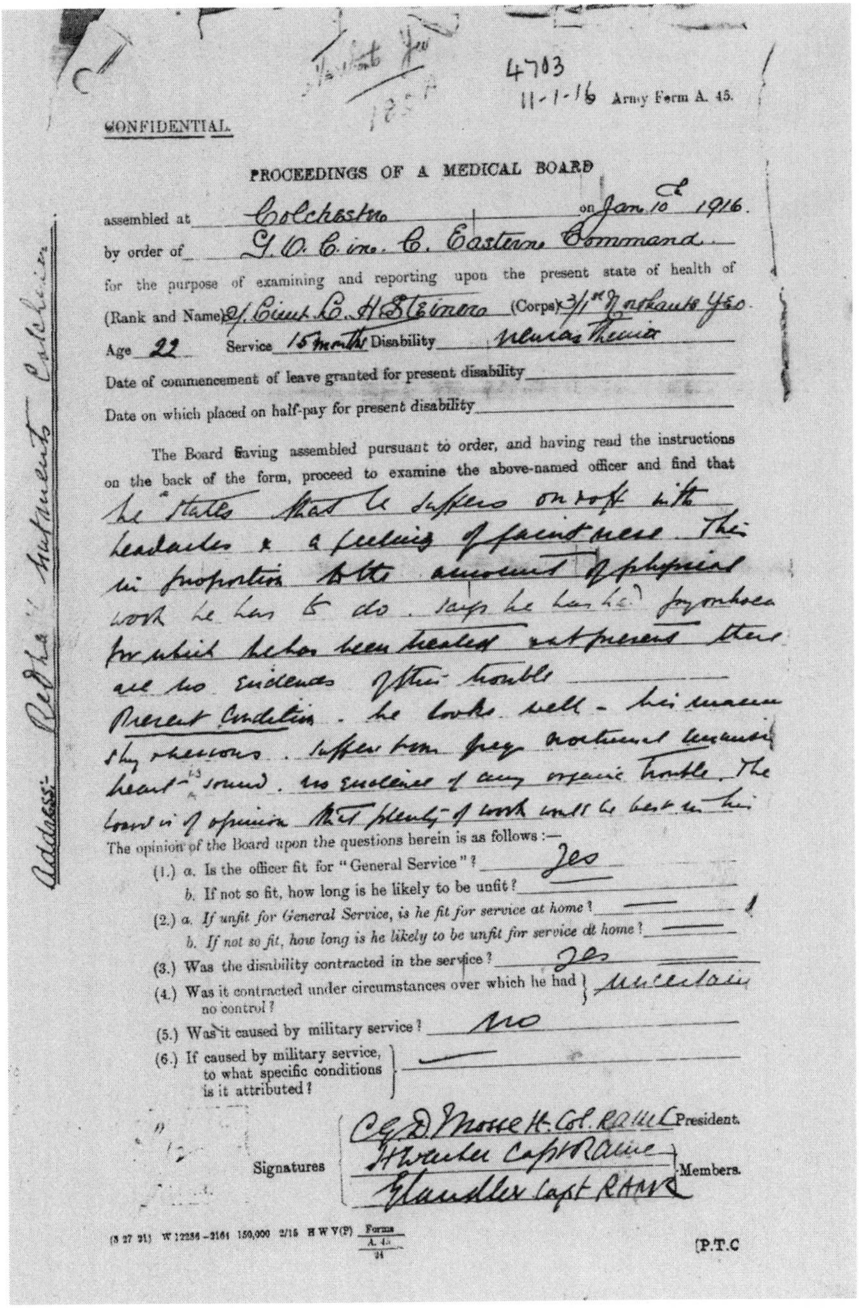

4703
11-1-16   Army Form A. 45.

CONFIDENTIAL.

PROCEEDINGS OF A MEDICAL BOARD

assembled at _Colchester_ on _Jan. 10_ 1916.

by order of _G. O. C. in. C. Eastern Command_

for the purpose of examining and reporting upon the present state of health of

(Rank and Name) _2/ Lieut. L. A. Steinero_ (Corps) _3/1st Northants Yeo._

Age _22_ Service _15 months_ Disability _neuras theuia_

Date of commencement of leave granted for present disability _____

Date on which placed on half-pay for present disability _____

The Board having assembled pursuant to order, and having read the instructions on the back of the form, proceed to examine the above-named officer and find that

[handwritten] he states that he suffers on & off with headaches & a feeling of faintness. This in proportion to the amount of physical work he has to do. ... for which he has been treated at present there are no evidences of the trouble. Present Condition. he looks well — his ... they ... heart sounds. no evidence of any organic trouble. The Board is of opinion that plenty of work will be best in his ...

The opinion of the Board upon the questions herein is as follows :—

(1.) *a.* Is the officer fit for "General Service" ? _Yes_

    b. If not so fit, how long is he likely to be unfit? _____

(2.) *a.* If unfit for General Service, is he fit for service at home ? _____

    b. If not so fit, how long is he likely to be unfit for service at home ? _____

(3.) Was the disability contracted in the service ? _Yes_

(4.) Was it contracted under circumstances over which he had no control ? _uncertain_

(5.) Was it caused by military service ? _no_

(6.) If caused by military service, to what specific conditions is it attributed ?

Signatures _C. G. D. Moore H. Col. RAMC_ President.
H. Wauler Capt RAMC } Members.
Chandler Capt RAMC

(3 27 21) W 12236—2161 150,000 2/15 H W V(P) Forms A. 45   [P.T.C

Figure 11. Leslie's medical assessment, January 1916. Taken from Leslie's military records, National Archives.

married three months later, in March 1916. His bride was a local girl, Ruth Evelyn Martin, aged 21, daughter of a laundry manager, a tall, fair, conventional English girl.[8] The courtship had been brief, but the wartime atmosphere accelerated matters. Ruth Martin, herself rather uncomfortable with a new stepmother at home, had reason to look for her own establishment. Leslie's needs and loneliness at this time are evident.

Neither set of parents seems to have been consulted. Leslie's father came down to visit him and express disapproval, but the young couple were set on their venture and there was little he could do. Leslie was soon to be discharged from the Yeomanry and from any further military service. Family history has it, and it is quite possible, that Leslie was posted to France twice during the brief period between his marriage in March 1916 and his discharge in May of the same year. During the few weeks when Leslie might have joined them, the NIY was split up, one squadron in billets at Harponville, some near Ypres and Arras. From the few records that are left, April and May 1916 were relatively quiet times, with the men preparing for the next battle, digging trenches, felling trees and employed as guides, but by no means entirely out of the bombardments and danger. The regiment went on to fight valiantly, earning battle honours in Arras, Scarpe and in the Italian campaign.

Little evidence remains to judge the events of this time. The remaining papers of the NIY are kept at the Northampton Record Office and the National Archives at Kew. These include photographs of the officer complement, which was small and changed little throughout the war, and various diaries, articles and despatches from the men of the regiment. No sign of Leslie can be found in any of these. Additional evidence can be seen in the Inns of Court Regiment's post-war collection of records for all the officer candidates who passed through their hands at this time.

The documents from the Inns of Court officers' records show that the letter denoting service in France or Flanders does not appear after Leslie's name; according to these lists Leslie never fought in France or saw conflict of any kind.

It is likely that his service was too brief to be recorded. However short his experience, he would have had the opportunity to encounter all the horrors of that place and time, for which he clearly had so few defences. There is some later evidence that Leslie spent time in France, and that he went through some ordeal. One piece of the puzzle is a letter from Leslie to the *New York Times* in 1922, explaining in detail the

Figure 12. Inns of Court Regiment Records. Taken from Colonel F.H.L. Errington, *The Inns of Court Regimental History of the First World War* (1924).

Figure 13. Inns of Court Regiment Records. Key to notes. Taken from Colonel F.H.L. Errington, *The Inns of Court Regimental History of the First World War* (1924).

traffic laws of France, which argues some familiarity with the country.[9] Another is his daughter's memory that Leslie had difficulty travelling alone in sleeping compartments in trains as they often gave him nightmares. He would then emerge into the corridor shouting and banging, disturbing the other passengers.[10] These apparent symptoms of shell shock are too circumstantial to ignore. There are also Leslie's own words, and he is quoted in newspaper interviews on several occasions as saying he had 'been to France' or 'been to the Front'.[11] He never claimed to have done any fighting.

On 18 May 1916 a brief note in his file announced '2nd Lieutenant Steiner to relinquish his commission'. There is nothing further. He had been quietly dropped from the strength – so quietly that hardly anybody in the regiment knew what had become of him. His former friend Archie Whitehouse even confabulated a theory that Leslie had been sent on a secret spying mission because of his knowledge of the German language.[12] (Whitehouse went on to write a number of books on military history and espionage and seems to have been preoccupied with the subject of spying. He was later criticized by author Nigel West for adding more false circumstance to the murky legend of Mata Hari, a German agent of the First World War.[13]) The reality was that, simply for the honour of the regiment, his discharge was handled as discreetly as possible. It was unthinkable to make public the failure of an officer and gentleman belonging to the Yeomanry; nor would the troopers have been given the dispiriting knowledge that one of the officer class had been found unfit for service.

Leslie had missed the war, the defining experience of his generation. It would have been enough to alienate him to a great extent from those contemporaries who managed to endure the nightmare. Those who fought through the battle and saw the huge waste of life and the shambles of command were left with a cynicism that dispelled traditional values. Leslie remained a romantic, never quite leaving the Edwardian idyll of his impressionable youth.

His failure contributed to a sense of dislocation for Leslie, in the aftermath of it all, and it is possible that other scars persisted. He had started with a mind full of heroes and their noble actions and had not managed to live up to these ideals. He remained for the rest of his life something of a hypochondriac, convinced without much evidence that he suffered from chronic heart trouble. It was a characteristic which his family tended to mock, until Leslie's reactions showed that this belief was not to be too deeply questioned. Leslie returned home to

Norwood with his new wife who, if she could not quite boast of a shattered war hero, at least possessed a living and intact husband, a blessing not bestowed on hundreds of thousands of others.

NOTES

1. Rupert Brooke, 'Peace' (1914), in *1914 and Other Poems* (London: Sidgewick and Jackson, 1915).
2. Family details from Leslie Ruth Howard, *A Quite Remarkable Father* (London: Longmans, 1960) and from family genealogical records.
3. Details of Leslie's military history from *The Army List*. His First World War record file in the Public Record Office, Kew, (WO 374/65069) and from Col. F.H.L. Errington, *The Inns of Court Officers Training Corps During the Great War* (London: Printing Craft Ltd, 1922). Guidance from The Honourable Curator of the Inns of Court and City Yeomanry Museum, Mr Dennis Durkin.
4. Personal anecdote from Upper Norwood Library local studies librarian, Mr Savage, who met Leslie's putative son in 1985. This man was then aged 70 and was the child of the family maid at Allandale, Leslie's house in Jasper Rd, Upper Norwood. He had been told by his mother and was convinced, whether mistakenly or not, that Leslie Howard was his father. Mr Durkin, curator of the Inns of Court Museum adds, 'the incident with the maid is not by any means the only one I have heard of or dealt with, including one from Australia about someone's real grandfather'. Letter to author, 16 April 2009.
5. Details of The Northamptonshire Imperial Yeomanry regimental history from V. Lawrence and P. Hill, *200 Years of Peace and War: A History of the Northamptonshire Yeomanry* (London: Orman, 1994) and H. Cazenove, *Northamptonshire Yeomanry 1794–1964* (Northampton: Belmont Press, 1966). The remaining records of the Northamptonshire Imperial Yeomanry (including pictures of all officers) at the Northamptonshire Record Office, and NIY dispatches from the field at the National Archives. Guidance from Mr W.J. Hornsby and Captain Bellamy, officials of the NIY and Dr C. Swaisland, military historian.
6. Anecdote from Arch (Arthur George) Whitehouse, *The Fledgling* (London: Vane, 1965).
7. The National Archives, First World War records of officers, (WO/374/65079).
8. Details from Leslie's marriage certificate.
9. *New York Times*, 4 June 1922.
10. Howard, *A Quite Remarkable Father*.
11. For example, *New York Times*, 26 March 1922, and *Kinematograph Weekly*, 30 January 1919.
12. Whitehouse, *The Fledgling*.
13. Nigel West, *Unreliable Witness: Espionage Myths of the Second World War* (London: Grafton, 1984).

CHAPTER THREE

1917–1920: Early Film and Theatre

While cinema was still a novelty, Kipling wrote of its first effects on a naive audience – a simple news clip of people hurrying from a train was a spellbinding vision of a moment forever held in time. Some time later Bernard Shaw predicted that the new medium would ultimately supplant live theatre.[1] But there were few cultural voices in Britain who had such aspirations for film – in the early days the atmosphere of the fairground clung to it, and fascinating as it was for some, it was not to be granted artistic significance for decades. For many reasons, the creation of film in this country faltered after the First World War, and there was little understanding of how best to use it as a means of expression. Leslie's own first adventures in the film trade were to be characteristic of the time, and although he eventually achieved some attractive results, he didn't quite manage to break out of the contemporary mould.

Leslie now had the stability of his new marriage, and with a little help from his parents (and grandparents) he abandoned his work at the bank and ventured on a theatrical career. He had good fortune in many ways – his handsome looks, dark blue eyes and fair hair, a beautiful voice (apparently a Howard family inheritance), a charming manner, and his confidence in his own acting talent. There was also the fact that young leading men for the theatre were getting rather thin on the ground in 1916, and he was able to make his mark in the profession in a remarkably short time. However, British theatre had come to the end of one of its most influential eras, while the film industry had very far to go to replace it as the focus of intellectual and artistic interest.

After writing to theatre managers, trying agents, and using such contacts as his family could muster, Leslie was recruited by Ackerman May's agency to fill a leading part in a touring company of *Peg O' My Heart*, a romantic melodrama that had already been popular for some years. Having some qualms about his first professional engagement, Leslie tried a direct approach and went to see A.E. Matthews, a well-known actor who was playing the same part in the West End. Matthews described his half-affronted, half-charmed reaction to Leslie's nervous dressing-room chat in his autobiography.[2] The meeting turned out very well, as Matthews, who had the reputation of being crusty but good-hearted, helped Leslie with the part and also invited him to come horse riding at his house in Bushey. Leslie accepted and spent the time borrowing Matthews's polo pony and knocking a ball round the field. It was the start of a moderate friendship, as they were to work together in the next few years, with mixed success, in both plays and films.

Leslie did well with the tour, absorbing as much as possible of his new trade. When it ended he managed to find another touring part, this time in *Charley's Aunt*, a cross-dressing farce that is still a staple of amateur theatrical companies. The play is jolly enough if played with plenty of energy, but Leslie found the company rather threadbare after touring for years with it in the provinces and the experience depressed him. It was on these tours that Leslie received a white feather, sent anonymously, and that more than once, as was the custom of the day, which would have added further unpleasantness to his memories of the time.[3]

After the tour finished, he managed to obtain an understudy part with Matheson Lang, the well-known actor manager at the Strand Theatre, with work as a stage manager and factotum to the great man, followed by a juvenile lead in Lang's touring production of *Under Cover*. It was with this moderate amount of experience that Leslie finally made his first appearance in the London West End, on 10 June 1917, at the Strand where he had already been working. This was a first performance of the translation of *The Tidings brought to Mary*, (*L'annonce Faite à Marie*) an experimental and spiritual play by the French author Paul Claudel.[4]

It was not Lang's production; the theatre had been leased by another company, the Pioneer Players, the most radical that Leslie ever worked with. This company, which specialised in single performances of new, often pro-feminist and experimental work, was the creation of Edith Craig, daughter of Ellen Terry and sister of Edward Gordon Craig. Edith Craig had herself a considerable reputation for her original stagings, and the company had a run of successful productions until finance overcame art a few years later. The actors worked for very little, hoping that the publicity would get them some notice, and the company became known as the 'shop window' players.

Tidings had an excellent part for Leslie (although perhaps he did not have the ideal background to play it) as a naive but poetical apprentice with quite a lot to say in Act Two. It was one of the Players' most successful productions and highly praised, with some assumption that the success of its scenic artistry was due to Gordon Craig's influence.[5] *The Era* gave an excellent review all round, although Leslie was not specially mentioned.[6]

Leslie had entered a theatre world which was near the summit of its artistic prestige. Theatre-going was a middle and even upper-class pursuit, and extra respectability had been given to the actor managers who ran the West End theatres by a crop of knighthoods in Edwardian times. It was quite usual for eminent persons to attend first nights, and mingle with the actors afterwards. The prime minister, Herbert Asquith, came backstage to congratulate the cast in one of Leslie's productions, *Mr Pim Passes By*.[7] At the same time theatrical dynasties with descendants still on the boards were detailed in *Who's Who in the Theatre*, with names such as Bancroft, Compton, Beerbohm Tree, Boucicault, Irving, Terry, Kemble and others.[8]

In the meantime, Leslie was making use of another asset to help his acting career – his own Uncle Wilfred, who had featured so sternly in his childhood. Wilfred Noy (actually Wilfred Noy Blumberg, but like Leslie his stage name was taken from his first and middle names) had become an early film director after starting on the stage himself. He hadn't managed a London stage appearance, but had been in some good provincial productions, appearing at the Grand Theatre, Southampton in *The Withered Hand* in 1907 and *The Christian* in 1908/09, with Roy Redgrave and Daisy Scudamore, parents of Michael Redgrave.[9] Noy's later reputation was as one of Britain's major silent film directors, and his move to America in 1923 is seen as one of the great losses for the home industry at that time.[10]

Noy had started as a film director with the Clarendon Company in 1909, after ten years on the stage as an actor and director. The company was founded by two associates of Cecil Hepworth, perhaps the best-known early British film-maker. It was sited conveniently for Noy as the studios were at Limes Road, Croydon, quite close to the Upper Norwood family homes. Eventually he was made supervising director for Clarendon, and he seems to have wangled Leslie into a crowd part in the 1914 film *The Heroine of Mons*, before Leslie left to join the army.[11]

Noy also joined up, but was out by 1916, being already 39 years old. Clarendon continued to produce films during the First World War, mainly three- to five-reel films which were usually based on books or plays, and at this time it was one of seven major film companies in Britain. It was later taken over by the Harma Company, which made slightly more expensive films, and Leslie appeared, again briefly, in their first production, *The Happy Warrior* (1917), way down the cast list as 'Rollo'. It was not directed by Noy but presumably he had introduced Leslie to the studio. A review of the film in *Kinematograph Weekly* described it as 'nothing extraordinary, but having one or two notable points of production ... a remarkably stage-managed fist-fight without gloves in a big circus tent, followed by a highly realistic free-fight between rival supporters of the contest ... *The Happy Warrior* is wholesome and clean, the atmosphere robust and pulsating, in short, typically British.'[12] An involved plot concerning the usual lot of aristocratic characters of the day has Leslie as the hero's best friend, nobly giving up an advantageous marriage for love's sake. The film has long been lost, and exists only as reviews and cast-lists in the trade papers.

The film historian Rachael Low rated Clarendon's general output as solid but not particularly inspired, so perhaps not much has been missed. Clarendon Studios closed in the early 1920s, having run (as usual) into financial difficulties, but Noy had already moved to the British Actors Film Company, which had studios at Bushey, Hertfordshire. Noy also worked on the continent, using his knowledge of languages, and it was perhaps this experience which raised him above the average of British film directors working then. Leslie was also living at Bushey at this time, in a cottage on Herkomer Road near the studios, perhaps hoping for a film career to materialize.[13]

With his first substantial London stage part and his appearance in the film, Leslie had quite a successful summer in 1917. He began to consolidate his stage reputation the following year by appearing in a newly produced play, *The Freaks*, at Dion Boucicault's New Theatre in February 1918. Leslie had a major role, and the cast were rehearsed by the author himself, Sir Arthur Wing Pinero. Pinero had a long history of successful plays, but was then falling out of fashion and into stage history, and was not particularly pleased about it. His correspondence of the time shows his fretfulness, his loss of confidence about the theme of the play, and his doubts about the relatively inexperienced cast: 'I am busy rehearsing my new little play. It is indeed a little play in every respect and I have not been able, I grieve to say, to secure a strong cast for it. But with luck it may serve for a while; one can't do more than mark time in these exciting days, I can't anyhow'.[14]

Pinero is sometimes accused of trying to commercialise the radical

criticisms of society made more tellingly by Ibsen, who had a great
reputation by the end of the nineteenth century, and whose influence
was very strong. But the playwright seems incapable of such outright
hypocrisy. He had a gift for making a point with drama, most successfully
an emotional one, with the philosophy behind the effect perhaps a little
vague. *The Freaks* was not one of his best plays, but it was typical in
displaying just these traits.

The play attacks society's hypocrisy: a group of circus freaks come
to visit a wealthy suburban home, in a rather unlikely plot, and the
comparison is made between them and an unattractive visiting society
couple who are relatives of the hostess. The appeal for more acceptance
across social barriers is heavily laboured – Pinero insisted on having
an enormous painted drop scene instead of a stage curtain, depicting a
circus troupe entertaining an audience that was more freakish than the
performers at whom they were jeering. This was copied from a painting by Claude Shepperson, and made a very obvious point to the real
theatre audience, which can't have endeared the play to them. There
was also a fair amount of preaching from the actors, especially the
leader of the circus troupe, as he proclaims dramatically, 'Who is a freak
and who is normal in this world? You who sneer at my poor grotesque
companions, who in spite of infirmities of body, have more true love in
their hearts, than seventy-five per cent of the well-formed and well-en-
dowed'.[15]

Despite all this, Pinero succeeded in fascinating and moving the
audience. Leslie's role as Ronald, the son of the middle-class household,
involves him in a romance with Rosa, a member of the circus troupe. In
some ways his is the most effective character, as his callow love affair
leads to some amusing antics, as described by the cockney Rosa:

> We sat on the public seat under the big elm tree. There was only
> two kids there, with a baby in a pram and Ronald bribed 'em to
> withdraw ... He asked me to be his wife. I said his proposal had
> overwhelmed me with surprise, which he said was a highly proper
> answer to make, and that I required a week to consider me deci-
> sion. Then the kids came back and demanded another tuppence
> and we rose an' left the spot.[16]

But the young love affair is clearly impossible given the mores of the
time, and Ronald is forced to abandon Rosa, who leaves because she does
not wish to 'ruin his chances'. The trouble is that the broken romance
leaves Ronald shattered, and the loss is conveyed most upsettingly to the

audience. Perhaps Ronald was meant by the author to be a less sympathetic figure than he appears, but the emotion is ill-balanced for the play, and the effect is odd. The despairing failure of outsiders to find acceptance in British society might have had a personal significance for the author, whose background was Jewish, although he himself had been honoured and feted for his work. The critics found no such suggestion, and the author seems hardly to have known himself. Leslie's interpretation of the character who loses most by the experience could have been given either a comic or a tragic emphasis, and it is difficult to know now which Leslie chose.

Reviewers were impatient with the play, arguing that Pinero had cheated in having the most sympathetic 'freaks' appear most physically normal, thus losing most of the point of his argument. The actors were commended however, and Leslie got a mention for his sympathetic portrayal of the foolish suburban young man.[17] *The Times* gave a fond review of both author and play, but again thought he had not brought off his theme.[18] *The Freaks* might have continued for a longer run, but was actually disrupted by air-raid bombing twice, which curtailed bookings. It closed for good on 30 March 1918, after fifty-one performances. The play was anachronistic in a sense – a plea for more seriousness seemed otiose in the wider world at a time when men were dying en masse for principles which were becoming less and less certain.

Leslie's next appearance was in another Edith Craig production, *Romanticismo*, a translated Italian play, at a matinee at the Comedy Theatre. *The Freaks* was still playing, but the Pioneer Players put on only a few performances of one production; profits were in aid of the London Italian and other hospitals. There was a respectful review of *Romanticismo*, praising the actors for making the most of the material, including a mention of Leslie; 'Mr Leslie Howard, a very English Italian as the mercurial young Marquis, Mr Pat Kerwan, Mr Geoffrey Guise and Mr William Staveley were all excellent'.[19]

One month later Leslie and Ruth's first child, a son, was born on 7 April 1918. Leslie and his wife named him Ronald Cecil Martin Howard, after Leslie's part in *The Freaks* and Ruth's family name. Ronald afterwards repudiated most of it, especially the Cecil, during his years in America. He also acquired the lifelong nickname of 'Winky'; there was at that time a series of silent comedies featuring 'Winky' and his various adventures, and given Leslie's interest in the film world, this might have been the origin.

The Freaks had ended fairly abruptly, but Leslie had begun to be known in the theatre world. After a very brief outing when he discovered that he could neither sing nor dance (with Iris Hoey in a brief musical opener entitled *Box B*), he was cast in a much more successful play, *The Title* by Arnold Bennett, which ran from July 1918 into the spring of the following year. The play was a startlingly blunt critique of the sale of honours by the Lloyd George coalition government then in power. This was a subject of growing scandal during the war years, and ended in public (and royal) outrage in 1922. Bennett was said to have been given inside details of government practices by the editor of the *Westminster Gazette*, J.A. Spender.[20] The play had 285 performances in London, but was a failure in the provinces and in New York: not really surprisingly, as it was then largely a London in-joke.

The play is set at the home of a senior government minister, who is offered a title but scorns it, considering that he would only be the respectable front-man for others so honoured. These include shady businessmen and war profiteers who are giving thousands of pounds to political party funds in return for their honours, and new press barons who are turning a blind eye to it all in return for theirs. The minister's family includes the bumptious son of the house (played by Leslie), just down from public school with 'revolutionary' modern opinions, and the emancipated daughter, who is a secret journalist. As *The Times* review of the play described it, there was 'Plenty of unpretentious fun, not too recondite, about honours lists, Governments, newspaper-owning families, schoolboys, modern girls, matrimony and other not unfamiliar topics.'[21]

The play benefited from some of the best character actors of the day, including C. Aubrey Smith (as the reluctant recipient of the title), Eva Moore as his wife, and Nigel Playfair as a dodgy newspaper columnist and blackmailer. Leslie had quite a large role as the opinionated 17 year old, and won golden opinions from reviewers: 'The son – one of the most delightfully and admirably acted schoolboys that we remember ... Mr Leslie Howard's schoolboy is a creation of which he can be justly proud.'[22]

The cast must have had good fun with the play, as Leslie struck up some friendships with the older actors which were later important to him. The author, however, suffered the bad luck that might be expected after tangling with the establishment – he was offered a knighthood himself during the production of the play, which he might well have had for his previous literary and government work, and which he had to turn down, as his caustic criticisms would have made him a laughing

MR. LESLIE HOWARD as John Culver,

MR. WILFRED EATON, Permanent Stage Director and Producer of the Play.

MR. C. AUBREY SMITH.

Figure 14. *The Title*: C. Aubrey Smith embodying cragginess. And of course, perfect honour. From *The Play Pictorial*, 23, 193 (1918).

Figure 15. *The Title*: Nigel Playfair as a blackmailer. From *The Play Pictorial*, 23, 193 (1918).

stock if he had accepted. The knighthood was never offered to him again.

Leslie pursued his interest in the film world as much as he could. He was living near the British Actors Studios, which were originally started by Hubert Herkomer, a society portrait painter, who ran an art school at his large estate in Bushey. In 1913 Herkomer turned the small theatre in his grounds into a film studio, and made an early attempt at breaking into the American market. Like many such who were to come, he was badly stung, two American businessmen stealing his films and disappearing. He lost heart, but was nearly at the end of his career.[23] The studios were then bought by A.E. Matthews, who had done very well financially out of *Peg O' My Heart*, and who had acted in some of Herkomer's productions. By 1919 the company had merged with Alliance Films, and had started out on quite a large venture, with many of the most famous actors of the day holding shares in it.[24] For a short time Matthews enjoyed the perks of a film magnate, with grand lunches at the Savoy, expensive hotel accommodation and ambitious plans, for which the financing never quite materialised.[25]

At the beginning of 1919, Matthews thought that his new young friend Leslie would be a good choice for a part in their next film, *The Lackey and the Lady*. The film's director was not Wilfred Noy, luckily for him, but Thomas Bentley, who also had a good reputation as a director, and many years' experience. The result, all the same, was such an infamous disaster that neither Matthews nor Leslie's friend Adrian Brunel, working as a scenario or story editor at the studio, could bring themselves to mention a word of it in their respective autobiographies.[26]

The film told the story of a snobbish nouveau riche man, Mr Dunciman, whose weakly daughter shocks the household by running away with one of the male servants. The servant of course turns out to be a better man than them all, and teaches them a lesson in the meaning of life. *The Kinematograph Weekly*, the major film trade paper of the day, was always very willing to pass on any PR for the industry, and Leslie appears in a February issue with a puff for *The Lackey and the Lady* (together with a moustache that thankfully soon disappeared but helped his character as the shady son of the house).

Kinematograph Weekly reported that, 'something out of the common is promised in the performance of Leslie Howard, who has gained many laurels in *The Title*, as Tony Dunciman, the scapegrace son ... the film is strongly cast all through, and Aubrey Attwood makes Mr Dunciman a decidedly striking British type'.[27] One month later and the film had apparently run into only slight difficulties, 'the frost set in just when the finishing touches had to be given to the film and the Bushey staff had the painful experience of watching its persistence for an altogether unusual length of time', and again one week later,[28] 'the greater part of the work was completed by midday. Shortly afterwards, heavy rain once more set in.'[29]

Just as an observer might conclude that perennial British grey skies were responsible for the gloomy state of the industry, the film was finally presented at the trade show on 13 March. As everyone settled down to see it, Mr Henry Boam, distributor for the company, stepped out and made the announcement that the film was not good enough to be shown. A sensation in court followed as Bentley, the film's director, took action for slander after Boam 'explained' his action with an announcement in the trade press, and the case was heard in a very high-profile manner, a year later at the High Court.

The court hearing revealed much that was wrong in the British industry in general. It might have been an amusing case, as there was plenty for everyone to be sarcastic about, and two of the most able barristers of their generation – Patrick Hastings and Douglas Hogg – were the opposing advocates. But neither was able to display much wit or humour, despite the fact that Bentley made a marvellous straight man, his evidence being dull and humourless. The problem was that the truth was evident to everybody, and no one really denied it, which spoilt the fun. Bentley admitted that 'the film is not the best I ever made'. The film was also described as 'produced in the most adequate way with regard for economy', which said it all. It gradually emerged that the film contained absurd discrepancies, such as showing Mr Dunciman, the wealthy businessman, with fur coat, carriages and a grand house, but hanging his shirt on the bedstead at night in a poorly furnished interior. There was also a 'runaway' horse trotting along in a leisurely manner, and the villains of the piece performing an inappropriate comic turn. The original book, The Lackey and the Lady by Tom Gallon, ought to have taken much of the blame, and it was a classic example of feeble source material leading to a poor film. Anyone responsible for the shambles had cause to be ashamed, including Brunel if he had passed the scenario, although the actors were specifically exonerated by both Boam and Bentley.[30]

Bentley won his case for slander, being awarded £350 and his costs. It may say something for the talent available to the British film world at the time that he continued to direct, without the slightest abilities being evident, right through the silent era and up until his retirement in 1941. His reputation had been built up on filming the works of Dickens, which were so well known to the public that the required scenes and story-telling were already pretty much in place for the director. *The Lackey and the Lady*, unfortunately for Leslie's film career (and Rotten Tomato awarders), was never seen again, being destroyed by Boam on behalf of the distributors.

The case took a year to come to court, but meanwhile Leslie was popular enough to fill his time with stage work. Following *The Title*, he appeared in another great success, *Our Mr Hepplewhite* by Gladys Unger, an American playwright and adaptor, whose speciality was sophisticated light comedy and romance. The play appeared at the Criterion Theatre from April to October 1919. It was a class-ridden tale of a titled young lady's engagement to Mr Hepplewhite, a resourceful store manager. The girl's parents, Lord and Lady Bagley, contrive to show up the suburban manners of Mr Hepplewhite by invit-ing him to the rarefied atmosphere of Bagley Towers, their country home, and succeed in putting off the young Miss Bagley. But the author gives the situation several more twists by having Mr H. aid the impov-erished family in various ways to gain a fortune, and ingratiate himself in all their interests. Finally both the lovers marry other people, more 'suitable' to their station in life, and all ends wittily and happily ever after. Leslie played Lord Bagley, the young lady's brother, described as 'the dissipated young sprig'. For this he earned his first mention in *The Times*, which described him as 'languidly droll'.[31]

After a brief break at the end of the year, Leslie was lucky enough to star in an even more successful play at the start of 1920, *Mr Pim Passes By*, by A.A. Milne. The author sat in on the rehearsals, and must have been extremely pleased with all, as it became quite a money-spinner, going on to a long run in New York (though not with Leslie). The play was yet another society comedy, this time with a tinge of feminism, in so far as an unhappily married wife wins the freedom to choose her own furnishings from her bullying husband. For the rest, the slight plot seems to have depended most on the playing of Dion Boucicault, a very well-loved comedy character. Leslie earned another bouquet in *The Times* for playing yet another son of the house,[32] and a marvellous mention in *Punch* magazine for being 'hardly less good' than Boucicault.[33]

Leslie continued to intersperse London theatre appearances with film roles, and narrowly missed another great success in February with *The Young Person in Pink*. This was a much more substantial showcase for him, and he received enthusiastic reviews for his role in the slight romantic comedy after playing the first night. However, for the main production he lost the part to Donald Calthrop, Dion Boucicault's grandson, possibly because the *Mr Pim* company wouldn't release him. It was a busy year, and Leslie, although a little typecast as the well-bred romantic young man, widened his range as much as possible. There was *Kitty Breaks Loose*, in which a society girl goes on the spree; *The Era* commented, 'Mr Leslie Howard struck out a new line with much success. Dropping his usual gay, insouciant air (it cropped up occasionally) he displayed an earnestness which proves that his scope is wider than he has shown hitherto.'[34] Also *East is West*, a Chinese-American cross-cultural romance (and possibly in the train of *Chu Chin Chow*, by far the most popular play of the post-war years) and even *Rosalind of the Farmyard*, a rural comedy in which Leslie managed to be 'refreshingly boyish,' according to the reviewers, who seemed increasingly familiar with and fond of Leslie's stage-playing.

Life was at its most pleasant and effortless for Leslie; so it might have been predicted that he became a little restless. After the disappointment of *The Lackey and the Lady* court case and the disappearance of what might have been his first major film part, he began to visit the Bushey studios as often as he could, hanging about apparently aimlessly, while hatching a surprisingly ambitious scheme to produce his own films. Adrian Brunel was working as scenario editor at the studios, and like many others was easily charmed by the young Leslie:

> When Leslie was not in the theatre, he was out at Bushey wandering about, thinking, and most days he drifted into the studio. One morning he came up to my office, roaming around sucking his pipe and fidgeting with books and papers ... suddenly he stopped and said to Miss Harper (Brunel's secretary) and me, 'Adrian, we're going to found a film company ... I shall be managing director and will act in our films, and you will be the producer and director' ... He may have misinterpreted my look up at him because he added defensively, 'well I can't think of anyone else – I mean, I honestly do think you are the best in England, and I believe we could revolutionise the film business'. He then began to outline his plan for British Comedy Films Ltd, which was to make short comedy pictures – not the usual slapstick shorts, but miniature features somewhat in the style of the comedies that used to by made by Mr and Mrs Sydney Drew.[35]

Leslie and Adrian Brunel, after one or two tries, managed to start up their own new company, Minerva Films. With youthful confidence, Leslie called in many of the theatrical friendships he had made in the course of the previous few years, and inveigled Aubrey Smith and Nigel Playfair into becoming directors and hopeful stars, and A.A. Milne as early screenwriter. Leslie, Brunel, Richard Powers, and Lionel Phillips (film distributor for British Actors Company) were the other directors. Shareholders included his father, Frank Stainer, with whom he and his family were now living at Comeragh Road, Kensington. Also H.G. Wells and Frank Swinnerton, authors, and various actresses, company directors, stockbrokers and so on, who had been interested in the project and were ready to venture a few hundred pounds or less.[36] Leslie must also have had A.E. Matthews' blessing to borrow his staff and studio facilities. The only person missing from the enterprise was Uncle Wilfred, a more likely candidate than Brunel for 'best director in England', but who doesn't seem to have been associated with it. Possibly his work for the British Actors Company kept him busy, or Leslie preferred to be in charge without the older man's influence.

Milne wrote four light-hearted stories for them, Brunel produced a working script and Aubrey Smith starred in *The Bump* (1920), a tale of a famous African explorer failing to find his way round London (possibly based on a real incident), and some less well-known names, Simeon Stuart and Barbara Macfarlane, in *Twice Two* (1920), a romantic dalliance. For Leslie, Milne wrote two films, *£5 Reward* (1920) and *Bookworms* (1920) – all of course still silent films. Some of these have survived in the archives, the photography pin-sharp after so many years.[37]

£5 Reward seems to have been made first, and suffers a little from the inexperience of the group. Shots of Leslie featuring odd perspectives, his boots taking up far too much of the foreground, or the top of his head out of the frame, can be seen. The characters are not attractive enough to gain the sympathy of the audience, and subtitling Leslie as the 'son of a hundred Earls' makes his laborious pursuit of a local farmer's daughter seem unlikely. *Bookworms*, however, is a small gem, and it is unfortunate that it can only be viewed now by a few film researchers. This tale of a lover attempting to contact an over-protected sweetheart by means of notes in library books ends with all sorts of lonely single-tons, and of course the lovers, finding an accidental happy ending. The film is a twenty-minute 'short', and it may be too much to suggest that it is a lost classic. But it is perfectly done; warm-hearted, amusing, and

most of all projecting a gentleness which is solely due to Leslie's own youthful personality. Leslie's character is shown rising very late each day, eating breakfast in a finicky manner, taking exercise (with Indian clubs, then very fashionable) and doing little else for a day's work besides pursue romance, which shows that Brunel must have got to know Leslie quite well by this time.

Brunel recalled the excitement when the films were shown to distributors:

> At the trade show for all the films at the West End Cinema in Coventry Street, the theatre was packed from floor to ceiling, filled with celebrities of many kinds, including critics, writers, politicians, actors and actresses. Those members of the film trade present looked sour and cynical however. In fact the whole atmosphere seemed somewhat suspicious and I felt that however confident I might have been in regard to the ordinary people's reaction to the brand of humour we were offering, this particular audience would be merciless at the first opening for a laugh in the wrong place.
>
> We started off with *Bookworms*. Very soon the audience was chuckling and before long they were laughing heartily. When it was over the applause was tremendous and went on and on and on – there was real gratitude in it.
>
> Our second, *£5 Reward*, was less uproariously funny, but it kicked off with a lovely introduction of Milne's – about two minutes burlesque of the popular Wild West film, which stopped suddenly and was followed with the sub-title 'Sorry –wrong film'! That put the audience right for the rest of the film, which went over well. We ended with our chef-d'oeuvre, *The Bump*, and in the extravagant language of the showman's trade it was a riot. The applause at the end was only stopped by the orchestra playing 'God Save the King'.[38]

Brunel remembered rave reviews, but it is possible that time improved the recollection. *The Kinematograph Weekly* gave a more moderate judgement. For *Five Pounds Reward*: 'There are good humorous touches that compensate for the thinness of the plot, and sufficient subtlety to recommend it to the superior public to whom the Minervas will chiefly appeal.'[39] And *Bookworms*:

> A great deal of the humour of this film is due to A.A. Milne's scenario and to his effective subtitles. The story is slight enough ... Leslie Howard as the lover is natural and usually amusing, though

he might vary his method a little; the rest of the cast, in travesty parts, play them with the correct spirit of burlesque. It is good, light fare for audiences which appreciate wit as compared with more obvious expressions of humour.[40]

Brunel thought the trade representatives were hostile to British efforts, preferring the more reliable American imports, and that in any case cinemas were forced to 'block book' for months ahead with American films. It may well have been so, but whatever marketing effort was made for the films (Leslie valiantly trying as much PR as possible) they made little impact, and two more comedies, *Too Many Cooks* and *The Temporary Lady*, written by Milne and Brunel and starring Annette Benson and Miles Mander, also disappeared. Brunel finally got Moss Empires cinemas to take the films, at a monetary loss to Minerva. The enterprise went broke, everyone had to lose their money and grit their teeth, and as Aubrey Smith later commented, 'Oh, it was a failure, but although we didn't earn much we learned a lot'.[41] Leslie possessed an unexpected driving force, as Brunel observed, but it hadn't come off this time.

Leslie's next move was just as adventurous – to America, to star in a play produced by the theatrical impresario Gilbert Miller. It might have seemed a good idea to leave the country for a while after losing so many people their money. But Leslie's other experiences had also been mixed – his wartime record was not clear, and the delivery of a white feather was an experience that cut deeper than he (and many others similarly) wanted to remember. Even Aubrey Smith remembered receiving one, although he was 51 years old at the time it happened in 1916, and he had been turned down for the armed forces after trying to volunteer. In his case the exile was permanent, although the major factor in this decision was probably the same as Leslie's – money. The failure of any film-making effort to coalesce in Britain, and the preference for insipid romances about the aristocracy that prevailed on stage may have had something to do with it. For Leslie, the notable stage success he had won with such apparent ease propelled him in the direction of light-hearted theatrical entertainment, and the novel experiences in the New World had to fill in for any chances at his own artistic innovation over the next few years.

NOTES

1. George Bernard Shaw, *Liberty Magazine*, 7 February 1931.
2. A.E. Matthews, *Matty: An Autobiography* (London: Hutchinson, 1952).

3. Leslie Ruth Howard, *A Quite Remarkable Father* (London: Longmans, 1960). It was the misguided custom of the day to send a white feather, to signify cowardice, anonymously to those men of almost any age, condition or health, who were not on the battlefront in France and Belgium.
4. All Leslie's early theatrical career in England from J.P. Wearing, *The London Stage, 1910–1939: A Calendar of Plays and Players*, 3 vols, (Metuchen, NJ and London: Scarecrow, 1990).
5. Katherine Cockin, *Women and Theatre in the Age of Suffrage: The Pioneer Players* (Basingstoke: Macmillan, 2001).
6. *The Era*, 13 June 1917.
7. *The Era*, 13 June 1917.
8. *Who's Who in the Theatre* (London: Pitman, 1912–81).
9. Wilfred Noy's early theatre career from Wearing, *The London Stage*.
10. Kevin Brownlow, *The Parade's Gone By* (London: Secker and Warburg, 1968).
11. Details of Leslie's early film appearances from Dennis Gifford, *The British Film Catalogue*, 3rd edn (London: Fitzroy Dearborn, 2001), with details of film companies from Rachael Low, *The History of the British Film, 1906–1914* (London: Allen and Unwin, 1973).
12 *Kinematograph Weekly*, 30 August 1917.
13. These details of the film world from Low, *The History of the British Film, 1914–1918* and an article about Wilfred Noy in *Moving Picture World*, 14 February 1925, p.725. Leslie's address and movements at this time from the papers of Adrian Brunel, British Film Institute.
14. Pinero's letter to L.E. Shipman, 7 January 1918, quoted in J.P. Wearing (ed.), *The Collected Letters of Sir Arthur Pinero* (Minneapolis, MN: University of Minnesota Press, 1974). See also W.B. Dunkel, *Sir Arthur Pinero: A Critical Biography with Letters* (Chicago, IL: University of Chicago Press, 1941).
15. Sir Arthur Wing Pinero, *The Freaks: An Idyll of Suburbia, In Three Acts* (London: William Heinemann, 1922), p.107.
16. Ibid., p.186.
17. *The Era*, 20 February 1918.
18. *The Times*, 15 February 1918.
19. *The Era*, 27 March 1918.
20. Reginald Pound, *Arnold Bennett: A Biography* (London: Heinemann, 1952).
21. *The Times*, 22 July 1918.
22. *The Era*, 24 July 1918.
23. Michael Pritchard, *Sir Hubert von Herkomer and His Film-Making in Bushey 1912–1914* (Bushey: Museum Trust, 1987).
24. Records of the British Actors Film Company, The National Archives, BT31/22989/141610.
25. Matthews, *Matty: An Autobiography*.
26. Adrian Brunel, *Nice Work: The Story of Thirty Years in British Film Production* (London: Forbes Robertson, 1949).
27. *Kinematograph Weekly*, 30 January 1919.
28. *Kinematograph Weekly*, 20 February 1919.
29. *Kinematograph Weekly*, 27 February 1919.
30. *The Times*, 4 February 1920.
31. *The Times*, 4 April 1919.
32. *The Times*, 6 January 1920.
33. *Punch*, 12 January 1920.
34. *The Era*, 17 February 1920.
35. Brunel, *Nice Work*, p.57.
36. Details from the National Archives, Papers of the Minerva Film Company, 1920, Ref BT 31/25754/165798.
37. Held at the British Film Institute.
38. Brunel, *Nice Work*, p.61.
39. *Kinematograph Weekly*, 14 October 1920.
40. *Kinematograph Weekly*, 28 October 1920.
41. David Rayvern Allen, *Sir Aubrey: A Biography of C. Aubrey Smith, England Cricketer, West End Actor, Hollywood Film Star* (London: Elm Tree Books, 1982), p.102.

CHAPTER FOUR

1921–1931: Broadway

It was while playing in *East is West*, an American cross-cultural romance, which had incidentally upset the censor for its mild naughtiness, that Leslie came to the attention of Gilbert Miller, an influential American stage producer on both sides of the Atlantic.[1] Miller had in mind a play which aimed to exploit the visit of the Prince of Wales to America in 1919. Leslie was offered a 'best friend of the lead' part, one which was possibly quite lucrative, and could make him known in America. It would mean a big upheaval for himself and his family, but was really too good an offer to refuse.

Leslie later recorded his thoughts at this time, hoping to get the anecdotes published and start to establish a writing career, but he apparently never managed to place the articles. They were published many years later by his son, together with most of Leslie's early articles. The piece was called 'American Adventures of an English Actor':

> I walked up St James's Street thinking. I stood on the corner of Piccadilly thinking. I walked down St James's Street thinking.
>
> Then, the result of my thinking being exactly what it would have been if I hadn't thought at all, I thought no more. I walked into the manager's office. 'I will go', I announced, not without a touch of the dramatic.
>
> 'Good', said the manager. 'I will send a cable at once. You sail for New York on Wednesday in the *Balearic*.'[2]

Leslie goes on to describe his ocean voyage (Ruth and Ronald had to stay behind until the success or otherwise of the play became apparent), his first impressions of America on docking, and American hotels, weather, food and customs including prohibition. Leslie was greatly impressed with the Broadway lights, and the hectic crowds of people and cars, which 'made Piccadilly seem like the Black Hole of Calcutta'. Of course the usual grumbles about rehearsing the production emerged, but Leslie soon made friends with leading man Geoffrey Kerr, who was a few years younger than him. Kerr went on to become a successful actor in England and America, and later had several screenplays produced. He too had been brought over for the play by Gilbert Miller, together with his father Frederick Kerr, an impressively aristocratic character actor. Ruth Chatterton, a well-known Broadway actress (and later early 'talkies' film star) had originally been announced to play the romantic young leading lady. However, after reading the part she demurred, saying it did not give her sufficient scope. This might have been true, although she could equally have refused on the grounds of good taste.

The play, entitled *Just Suppose*, describes the visit of a supposedly imaginary Prince of Wales, hiding his identity while on an official visit to America, to the mansion of an old Southern family, and the ensuing romance with the daughter of the house. The Prince, portrayed as a weak, shallow character, is eventually partially redeemed by the love of the noble American girl. After an immense amount of treacly sentiment, he falls in love with her and ends by revealing who he is.

The year before the play was presented, in October 1919, Edward, Prince of Wales, the future King Edward VIII, had made an official visit to America, including Washington and New York, on a goodwill tour. There was great excitement for months before his visit in the American press. The Prince was entertained flirtatiously by young female America at various parties, and unofficially out of hours and out of the control of his stuffy entourage at times. This tour was a wild success, but there had been a great deal of comment in the newspapers about his supposed amorous adventures, and the possibility of his marrying an American girl.

When the play began its out of town tryouts, first in Washington, the local papers remarked that the supposed author, A.E. Thomas, could know little of Southern households or British nobility as he had been born in Providence, Rhode Island, and that all his previously successful plays had been produced by Gilbert Miller. The strong suggestion was that Miller bore most responsibility for the satirical story.[3] This might have been the case. Miller was already an influential figure at this time, known in London as 'the American Theatrical Napoleon', and having bought French plays to New York.[4] Both his parents and his grandmother were well-known actors, and his father Henry Miller was also a producer, owning his own theatre in New York. Gilbert's own background was international, as after his parents' early marriage break-up, his mother had taken him to the continent, and he had been educated in private Roman Catholic schools, according to his mother's religion, in Germany, Spain, England and France. He spoke all these languages, in addition to Italian and Hungarian. At this time he had bought the St James's Theatre and had initiated a number of classical productions with the actor-manager Henry Ainley. He was a member of Bucks club and the Travellers in Paris.[5] He was therefore a much more likely figure to know 'inside' gossip about the Prince of Wales than the author of the play. He and Leslie were eventually to become long-term business partners and co-producers (although Miller's uncertain temperament and ruthlessness over money prevented a close friendship), and this was not the only *succès de scandale* that they both perpetrated.

Having been successful in Washington, Baltimore and Chicago, the play finally had its official opening in New York on 1 November 1920. Leslie portrayed Sir Calverton Shipley, the Prince's friend and protector, with dialogue in 'Bertie Wooster' style. Sir Calverton tries his best to prevent the unofficial visit and ensuing romance, and deals with much petulance from the Prince about the burdens of office. The story was amazingly prescient, as the Prince asks the woman with whom he falls in love to elope with him, and he will give up the throne. But she refuses, saying that the Prince would betray his people and his own honour if he turned his back on his country. The ending is sombre and foreboding, rather odd after all the comic by-play.

For his pains Leslie received a strong mention in the next day's notices – for overplaying. Alexander Woollcott, well-known critic of the *New York Times*, commented, 'There should be a word too, for the amusing and engaging Leslie Howard as the Prince's pal who, however, indulges in the most extraordinary clowning, expressing mild surprise by almost falling down and the slightest embarrassment by something strongly resembling convulsions.'[6] Leslie was always at his worst when he started from the standpoint of the comedian, much better as a romantic lead undermining himself with dry humour and lighter moments. The play received moderately good notices, lasting until January 1921 at the Henry Miller Theatre, after which it went on tour, according to theatrical custom at the time, and much to Leslie's dislike as he grew to hate the loneliness and discomfort of touring.

As far as the British press were concerned, the play was an impertinent outrage. *The Times* commented stiffly that any denial that the Prince of Wales was the character portrayed was 'disingenuous'.[7] But the papers could not say more without encroaching on American free speech. Not surprisingly *Just Suppose* never came to England, and it is difficult to know whether Prince Edward ever heard of it; but in any case the censor would have had good reason to bar it on the grounds that it insultingly portrayed a living person – the son of the monarch, no less.

Leslie was a great letter writer, and during the run of the play enjoyed his new status with letters back home to his friend Adrian Brunel. These were exuberant, not to say boastful and name-dropping, and presumably not for the eyes of his wife Ruth, who joined him in America for the run of the play. He mentions the large American salaries for actors compared with those in Britain, enquires about the progress of the Minerva Company films, and comments on the notables

Figure 16. 'Miss Goss'. Miss Florence Gospel, Leslie's lifelong housekeeper, nanny and friend.

that he was meeting in New York. These included Sidney Drew, a come-dienne whose style Leslie and Adrian Brunel had borrowed for their films, and silent film stars Norma Talmadge, Alice Joyce, Mae Murray and Mabel Normand. Normand is described as being very drunk at a party and insisting in a loud voice that Leslie should go at once with her to California to play in Goldwyn films. Still tongue in cheek, the letter airily dismisses Charlie Chaplin as 'quite a nice little cockney'. Leslie was overdue for getting some of the bounce knocked out of him, but in his case any setback never lasted very long.[8]

Money may have been the original motivating force for Leslie's American career, but New York theatre in the 1920s was one of the great cultural explosions of the century. America was revelling in its newly made peace, the new freedoms of its society, especially those for women, who had finally been given the vote, the ethnic mix, and its technological advances; public radio broadcasts were available, there were all sorts of time-saving domestic inventions, and from architecture to entertainment, the new modernist style was stunningly evident.

American theatre seized the cultural lead from an exhausted Europe. Commercialism fuelled it all, but there was enough energy and interest for attempts at the artistic avant-garde, and for more serious-minded playwrights to have their ideas realized. So that Eugene O'Neill, Elmer Rice and Maxwell Anderson with their serious social commentary, brushed shoulders with *Abie's Irish Rose*, a sentimental rapprochement between the Irish and Jewish immigrant communities of New York which infuriated the critics by becoming the most successful play of the 1920s. In amongst the lively whirl were vaudeville, new-style musicals, revues, follies, opera, burlesque, and theatre productions from all over Europe.

As much as Leslie contributed his talents, he was also lucky to be a part of it all. And despite his accepted persona as a buttoned-up, shy Englishman, he was warmly taken up, from the raciest nightclubs to the Algonquin circle of wits and intellectuals, where he found an occasional but welcome place. Leslie never claimed any particular devotion to art or idealism in the theatre, although he was open to European experimental plays. Neither did he attempt roles much outside his range (with one exception), although this was partly typecasting. When his theatrical career ended sixteen years later, he might have regretted this, but if he did, he never admitted such, but remained defiantly himself. At his worst he was only a matinee idol; at his best he could invoke a magic which transfigured a work. Good material was rare, but when he found it, Leslie made stage history. What he added was unique – it could never be duplicated, and the same play with other actors was often disappointing. In part, Leslie's rapid progress was due to a projection of sensitive masculinity, a very useful quality for playwrights, who are rarely hindered by an actor who imbues extra meaning into their words.

Leslie's daughter later described her father's acting style as professional above all: 'He was a technical actor – one who relied not on emotion but on technique to carry his part. I can never remember him "living" a role at home or for five seconds after he stepped off the stage or away from a camera. He was essentially an unmelodramatic person.'[9]

Perhaps his stage success came too easily, and sometimes he seemed to have more interest in literary achievements. He was a constant letter writer, briefly kept a diary (which was perhaps a little too revealing to be comfortable) and was usually at work on a play. He did manage to get one of his plays produced, with mild success, but it is his articles about his experiences as an actor in the *New York Times*, *The New Yorker* and *Vanity Fair* magazines that are still fresh and sparkling.

Soon after the closing of *Just Suppose*, Leslie, who had been enjoying a success socially as well as dramatically, was considered for a project with a rising young actress, Helen Hayes. Miss Hayes, whose career would span the century, was being mentored at this point by the producer George Tyler. He asked the author and playwright Booth Tarkington to write a play for her. It might have been the case that Leslie was in their minds also, as Tarkington eventually came up with *The Wren*, suitably written for Miss Hayes, but including a male lead described in the play notes as 'Finely handsome, graceful, nervous, temperamental and high-strung'.[10]

Before the play could be produced, Leslie returned to England to enjoy a summer holiday with his wife, parents, and all his family. Helen Hayes was taking a European tour at this time, and Leslie was pleased to show her the town, as she remembered much later in her autobiography: 'Leslie showed me his London from the top of the red double-deckers ... Mother and I felt cozy and at home ... He took us to little theatrical restaurants and wangled free seats for us for many of the West End hits. No wonder that after such an introduction London remains my favourite city.'[11]

The play brought together a prestigious producer, a Pulitzer Prize-winning author and two excellent actors, but they all came up with a disappointing flop a few months later. *The Wren* opened in New York on 10 October 1921 and closed after three weeks. The play had been written around the genuinely sweet personality of Miss Hayes, but was too insipid and spiritless. Miss Hayes collected a nasty review one-liner accusing her of 'suffering from fallen archness'.[12] Leslie did better with critic Alexander Woollcott, who called him a 'singularly engaging English actor' but described the play as 'undernourished'.[13]

Leslie had done sufficient to make himself favourably regarded in the theatre community and from now on offers came to him without too much anxious work on his part. With this confidence, he found a flat for his family at 195 Claremont Avenue in New York and settled in for the longer term. Very luckily, the family also found here Miss Florence Gospel, a most tactful and efficient nanny, general helper and comforter. Leslie's wife Ruth had advertised for a mother's help, and a young Englishwoman living in America had answered. While waiting in the lobby for the interview, Miss Goss, as she came to be known, saw Leslie pass by in a buoyant mood, was immediately struck by him, took on the post and never left the family until Leslie's death. (Leslie ultimately made her an executor of his will, and left her an income for the rest of her life.)

In the dramatic world Leslie had scored a small success, but he was still in no position to pick and choose. The next offer, a play called *Danger*, came from a successful Broadway playwright 'Cosmo Hamilton'. The flamboyant name concealed Mr Henry Charles Gibbs, a rather over-prolific British author of plays and novels of all sorts. He came from a distinguished family, and having had some hits with musical comedies seems to have been accordingly a little high-handed. His recollections of the play are recorded in his memoirs, written in 1924:

> Of the play *Danger*, everything connected with its production brings back memories of quarrels and litigation ... The man who produced the play never for a single instant knew what it was about ... During the most distressing rehearsals he demanded the injection into the play of nearly everything that he had seen in every other play over a period of twenty years, and several things that could not be put into any play without the interference of the police. Finally one of the leading actors became utterly bewildered, as well he might, and after a perfectly natural temperamental outburst, said 'Well, there's something the matter with this bloody act. What is it?' 'The acting', I replied.[14]

The leading man was H.B. Warner, now remembered as an early film

star. The actors actually did their very best with the dreadful material,
but Hamilton probably had a point about the 'man who produced the
play', Carle Carleton, who had experience only of musical comedy,
whereas this play professed to be serious drama. The story was an
indignant moral lesson, supposedly very daring, on the wickedness of
a woman asking for some sexual freedom in marriage. The opening
in New York on 21 December 1921 met with unremittingly hostile
reviews. Alexander Woollcott of the *New York Times* described it as
'flashy' and laboriously written.[15] However, Woollcott added, 'Fortu-
nately for the author, the production has enlisted just such players as
Mr Warner, Kathleen MacDonell (the leading lady) and Leslie Howard,
who have a way of humanizing the most stilted language ever written.'
Miss MacDonell was an early casualty, pleading sickness and disappearing from the cast after a week. She was replaced by Tallulah Bankhead, an
unusual choice, as the part was the passive, conventional heroine of the
piece, rather than the key character, a sparky but scheming feminist. It was
the first time Leslie acted with Tallulah, but the fun didn't last long and
the play closed two weeks later. The play might also have suffered from
being heavily advertised as naughty and 'sexy' only weeks after the grue-
some details of the Arbuckle scandal had horrified America. Hamilton
was so ruffled by the whole experience that the published edition of the
play has no first-night cast list, but a note from the author that the play
was, 'Misproduced in New York in 1922'.[16]

Leslie had a way of keeping his head down through the most
contentious arguments and came out of it all quite well. He almost
immediately started rehearsals for a much more interesting work, this
time by his old acquaintance A.A. Milne (scriptwriter for Minerva) –
The Truth About Blayds. Milne had written three plays at this time,
which hit the peak of his skills as a dramatist: *The Great Broxopp*, *The
Dover Road* and *Blayds*. They were staged one after the other in England
and then America. In January 1922 Milne received a cable from his
New York agent, '*Dover Road* great success artistically and financially
STOP Send *Blayds*'.[17] Leslie's connection to Milne became known and
the *New York Times* asked him to describe the author. His reply was
tactful and humorous, describing Milne as someone Leslie had 'induced'
to write for Minerva Films, but stating by the way that Milne's plays in
America were making far more money than any of his books.[18]

Blayds was already a remarkable theatre phenomenon. The London
opening some months before had been greeted with such enthusiasm
that the whole literary world had focussed on the play. It seemed to be

an instant classic, destined for a place at the head of the canon. *The Times* reviewer compared the play's theme to the work of Ibsen, and said of Milne, 'he is a man of letters. He has impeccable taste, unobtrusive culture and a delicious style ... the play is a work of art.'[19]

Most critics feel that this is still true – for the first act. The remaining two acts so undermine the marvellous first that the whole has now practically been consigned to oblivion, or Christmas performances for amateur companies. For a while the debate continued in influential newspapers and journals as to why this should be so, and whether Milne was a serious talent or had just had a lucky inspiration. Sadly the critics admitted they had been let down. Dorothy Parker summed up the feeling some years later; 'I thought *The Truth About Blayds* was a fine and merciless and honest play. But when Mr Milne went quaint, all was over.'[20]

Leslie wasn't particularly worried at the time, especially as his part has a large showing in the impressive first act, and it is just the sort of material he could bring off perfectly. But the disappointment in the play might have been a factor in confining Leslie to the comedy genre, rather than more experimental or intellectual work. The play opened in New York on 14 March 1922. Leslie made the first entrance, as one of the grandchildren of Oliver Blayds, a poet and Grand Old Man of literature. Leslie's character is lightly satirical and disillusioned, having had his life dictated to him, like the rest of Blayds' family, by the old man's fame and reputation. His character not only immediately lives, as do all the others, but is at once sympathetic and emotionally consistent. The script is elegant and increasingly amusing and the act ends with the revelation that Blayds has stolen all the work that made his fame from a young roommate who had died years before. In the meantime there have been dryly witty references to Browning, Maeterlinck, Meredith and Hardy, amongst other greats of contemporary literature, from sycophantic houseguests praising Blayds. It is all stylishly done, and the overarching theme of a slightly suspect literary eminence, and the hypocrisy that surrounds him and his reputation, was both original and well timed. The audience were dazzled, came back to the next two acts all expectant and were treated to a trivial ending which resolved all difficulties in the most conventional possible way.

The American critics were enthusiastic, and for a while Milne was treated with as much respect and curiosity as his character, Oliver Blayds, in the typically American fashion which Milne had just parodied in his play. The acting was praised, with Leslie singled out as perfectly

cast; 'that whimsical young English comedian who over-played so
shockingly when he first ventured on our stage and who learned better
so quickly, this Leslie Howard should be immediately placed under contract to play nothing but Milne plays as long as they both shall live'.[21]
The Truth About Blayds ran for over a hundred performances, and took
up most of the rest of the season. Luck was in, and Leslie and the family acquired a smart car and leased a summer cottage on Deer Island,
Maine.

Before the summer was over, Leslie had an offer for what seemed to
be a more challenging role in a play called *The Serpent's Tooth*. Unfortunately, the play had reached the stage due to a sort of series of mistakes.
The first mistake was by the New York playwright Arthur Richman, who
thought he could write a serious piece about 'sophisticated' English
people. The second was by John Golden, a prominent Broadway producer, who thought it might possibly do, but only with a brilliant actress.
He proposed Marie Tempest, a marvellous English comedy actress very
popular in America, who was then away on a world tour. Golden thought
that Miss Tempest could never be obtained for the play, so he could let
the author down lightly. But Miss Tempest was ending her world tour,
and seized the chance to work in America. She received great acclaim on
her arrival; but unfortunately the play did not. Leslie had been chosen for
the part because the characters were very English, and he played the
wastrel son of Tempest's charming widow, eventually being sent out to
work on a ranch in the time-honoured manner. The critics scorned the
play, which was the last of Miss Tempest's Broadway career, but Leslie's
work was admired, one critic going so far as to say, 'there is truth in his
playing, sincerity, intelligence, no exhibitionism, no trick technique.'[22]

The play lasted four weeks, but after such encouraging reviews,
Leslie had plenty of offers. If he was perhaps a little indiscriminate in
choosing them there were excuses. He still needed experience, he had
a young family to support, typecasting didn't help, there were hundreds
of plays swirling round Broadway and it was difficult to find excellent
work. But it is a pity, having achieved a place there, that he never managed to appear in a play with an American setting and theme.

There followed a number of negligible pieces; another by Milne,
The Romantic Age, which Leslie could hardly refuse, and *The Lady
Cristilinda*, a Victorian comedy disinterred by its author Monckton
Hoffe, to exploit his recent hit *The Faithful Heart*. Leslie had met
the jovial Irish author in London, and they became good friends. Hoffe
appeared later as a useful scriptwriter in Hollywood, having a gift for

dry and witty dialogue, but this play died instantly. The villain of the piece, 'Ikey-Mo', Victorian slang for a shady Jewish dealer, might not have amused the New York theatre world, which had a strong Jewish component. *Anything Might Happen* and *Aren't We All*, which took Leslie to the end of 1923, were amongst the fag ends of the sophisticated light comedy genre. The latter had a successful run, perhaps because brilliant actors were developing in the modern style in New York, giving some scripts an undeserved sparkle.

Leslie and his family now found a home in Great Neck, Long Island, amongst some well-known theatrical and literary names. A number of people had country places and entertained freely there, including Herbert Swope, editor of the *New York World*, whose guests included notable people from every sphere. Leslie got to know another famous resident, Scott Fitzgerald, charming him into reading his own and his niece's efforts at plays, taking Sunday walks with him and the young Ronald, borrowing a bottle of wine from him for a picnic, and generally adding a surprising domestic note to Fitzgerald's darker story. Leslie commuted happily to New York, and was accepted into the heart of the theatrical and literary world; first nights, cocktails at the Algonquin, night clubbing, parties to welcome visiting actors and more to wave them off, charity dances and impromptu skits on popular plays for one cause or another. Amongst other amusements he suffered the idiosyncratic hospitality of Laurette Taylor, one of the leading ladies of Broadway. So did Noel Coward, and Leslie enjoyed the joke of Coward's play, *Hay Fever*, which appeared two years later. The play was not so much a parody of Miss Taylor's way of entertaining guests, more exact reporting. *Hay Fever* was a huge success in London with Marie Tempest as the parody Laurette, 'Judith Bliss', so giving Miss Tempest a little revenge for her New York pummelling. It was all great fun, never very serious, and Leslie moved effortlessly through it all.

Towards the end of 1923 a play was being developed in England which would realize some of the latent emotion of the time. The author, Sutton Vane, had served in the First World War and had suffered shell shock. Britain was still trying to come to terms with the loss of a generation of young men and hardly a family was untouched by loss. Vane had been an author of mostly failed light farces, and without much conscious intention to deal with psychological dilemmas he created the play *Outward Bound*. It describes a mystical voyage from life to death, the individuals undergoing it finally understanding their lives and accepting their fate. The idea, now perhaps too familiar, was startlingly original at the time. The setting, the saloon and lounge of an ocean liner, was well imagined, the characters known contemporary types, their moral dilemmas the problems of the day. The final ending in which two lovers find redemption and another chance of life now seems too sentimental, but was then irresistibly poignant, releasing floods of emotion in contemporary audiences.

The play started as a low-cost production at the Hampstead Everyman Theatre. Word spread, and it transferred to central London, creating a small sensation. It was eventually revived eight times in England before the end of the decade, but in the meantime a New York production was the next step. The play was the type of format that can work for any time or setting, but the cast needed to be actors of an unforced modern style. Amongst the best in New York were Leslie, Alfred Lunt, Margalo Gillmore and Dudley Digges. Leslie's part was the young lover who ends the play – the author's original description was, 'an ardent young man, about thirty years old. He is good looking, quietly emotional, serious and sincere. He is rather mystic in manner.'[23]

After rehearsals, script discussions and various alterations, the play opened in New York in January 1924 and stunned its audience, even more perhaps than in England where emotions were less openly displayed. There were discussions and letters in the paper, and much speculation about the philosophy behind the action. All the cast were praised, and Leslie and Margalo Gillmore were singled out: 'their episode strikes a chord of tragic suffering and of spiritual exaltation which is as genuine as the little scene between Mr Lunt and Miss (Beryl) Mercer ... these two young actors add a touch of deeply spiritual comprehension'.[24] Some critics even mentioned Dante's Paolo and Francesca. It was the beginning of a time when American plays and films seemed to take over the work of expressing Britain's more constipated emotions, both in theatre and on film. A pity in this case, as Britain had more need of the catharsis.

As a professional actor, Leslie was gleeful about 'reducing the audience to a jelly'. One of Leslie's first published articles appeared in the *New York Times* five months into the run, its dry humour and critical tone presaging that of many others. It was entitled, 'Anyhow They Mean Well':[25]

> *Outward Bound* ... underwent its premiere not so long ago at Atlantic City, having a reception there which was somewhat nerve-shattering. One can understand the annoyance of people who expect a jolly crook play and suddenly discover they have been

inveigled into viewing one man's conception of the judgement day and life in the hereafter. But this doesn't help the actors who had to stand up nightly and receive the slings and arrows and to spend the days being experimented on in rehearsals.

The article goes on to grumble about Leslie's usual troubles – being lionized by fans and bored by touring and rehearsals. Leslie's irritation with long runs didn't lessen over the years. He was 31 by that time, and must have been in a contemplative mood, as he kept a diary from January to August – but never again, as far as is known. His diary records his busy social life with many well-known names, his work and ambitions, and the odd giveaway comment. On Monday 14 January, appears the sentence, 'Feeling immensely pure despite Ruth's doubts'. On 23 March, at a party at Laurette Taylor's, 'made brilliant speech on birth control – or lack of it'. By this time, Ruth had discovered the imminent birth of their second child.

In May the run of *Outward Bound* came to a close, Leslie being already in rehearsal for a new play by Rudolph Lothar, *The Werewolf*, the original German translated by playwright Gladys Unger. It turned out that Lothar was better at opera libretti, and the cynical sexual antics in the play were not appealing to an American audience. In June Leslie was staying in Chicago after a tour of out-of-town tryouts with the play. Ruth had not accompanied him on tour. The hotel was used by other members of the theatrical profession, and one afternoon Leslie caught sight of a striking young woman.

Many, many years later, Claudette Colbert gave a reticent account of that first meeting: 'We met at the Edgewater Beach Hotel in Chicago ... He said to me, 'do you play tennis?' I told him the two things I could do was play tennis and wrestle. When I was a little girl my older brother wouldn't pay any attention to me unless I could.' Leslie's diary entry for 6 June reads only, 'Business improving. Tennis. Wink (Ronald) sends me some flowers from his garden. Bless him.' Miss Colbert continued:

> When Leslie and I became friends, he asked me if I knew anyone in New York who might help me with my career. When I told him no he said he had a friend, Al Woods, who owned the Eltinge theatre and was a big producer. Well, he hired me for a five year contract, and when I appeared in Dynamo five years later, my salary was $900 per week.[26]

Since Miss Colbert (being originally from France) was still playing

French maids and other walk-ons when Leslie met her, Leslie effectively kick-started her career, something she acknowledged with affection.

It was a romance that perhaps took Leslie by surprise, and went deeper than he intended. His affection for his wife and family was undiminished, but he had always been susceptible. With the ensuing guilt, his wife discovered the affair, and relations between them were stormy for a time. Their daughter, Leslie Ruth, was born on the 18 October 1924. On that day it was Ruth who managed to write an entry into Leslie's diary, 'Today I presented my husband with a beautiful daughter, eleven pounds and eleven ounces. Maybe sometime he will write on the subject.' But Leslie made no more entries in the diary.[27]

A year or so after the birth, Ruth was taken seriously ill, and had to undergo an operation. Of that time, her son Ronald later wrote, 'Following the birth of my sister in 1924 there were to be no more children and their relationship appeared to reach a kind of undemanding quiescence, a plateau of acceptance. They shared a home and family responsibilities – but they occupied separate rooms.'[28] Here was a possible origin for Leslie's later reputation with women, and even Ruth's jealousy, both of which became notorious amongst people who knew them. These feelings caused havoc at times, and there was much turbulence ahead for the marriage. That it endured, and remained ultimately a kind and understanding friendship, says a great deal for both sides.

The play that Leslie was rehearsing, *The Werewolf*, quickly received a silver bullet through its heart and Leslie was offered a couple of plays by the Frohman Company, to be presented together. These were, *Isabel*, an extremely light romantic comedy, and J.M. Barrie's *Shall We Join the Ladies? Isabel* had not much interest for Leslie, but he managed to impress the critics. The *New York Times* noted that '[Leslie's] social comedy is no more admirable than of old. But his more serious intervals were played with a freedom and warmth beyond anything I have seen from him; they had remarkable poise and right feeling with technical certainty.'[29]

In 1920 Barrie (author of *Peter Pan*) had started to write a murder mystery to amuse one of his young wards. He was working on the second act a year later when he heard of the boy's death, aged only 21. There was great sympathy for Barrie in the British theatrical world, and the truncated play, *Shall We Join the Ladies?* without any resolution to the mystery it begins, was given a gala performance in aid of charity. Why it was then played in New York is unclear (unless the Frohman

Company had the rights to all his work), but audiences there were duly baffled by it in more than one way.

European plays in America (and vice versa) must always lose something in the cultural translation, and this was true of two sensational plays about to strike New York – Michael Arlen's *The Green Hat* and Noel Coward's *The Vortex*. Leslie was in the less distinguished and more successful play, but the two together turned out to be a little too much Europe at once for the American critics. The author of *The Green Hat*, Michael Arlen, was a young man who followed in the train of society and literary figures in 1920s London. He had high hopes of becoming a famous writer, but had nothing much to say and not a great deal of talent with which to say it. However he did have passion, which he managed to communicate, and the luck to be briefly the lover of one of the most remarkable women of her time, Nancy Cunard. His novel *The Green Hat*, published in 1924, reads as a hyper-emotional love letter to her. Cunard, amongst other things, well-known for her sexual freedoms, was portrayed in it as Iris March, committed to excess in life and love affairs, but able to keep to a code of honour which shamed the supposedly 'decent' people around her. Cunard herself was really much more than this, ultimately striking through every convention not in order to shock, but because she recognised how hypocritical and damaging were the racial and social prejudices of her day. She developed as an author and publisher in the artistic world of Europe, and eventually became a respected social activist, at the same time as her absolute refusal to conform brought her to a degrading end. She seems a heroine fit for the twenty-first century, an opinion not always shared by the literary figures of her own time, many of whom nevertheless used her life to animate their own work.[30]

Arlen's *The Green Hat* was never going to do her justice, but her unique presence, and the passionate emotion and sexual frankness of the book made it an instant best-seller; a great contrast to the sugary romances that were usual for the time. Arlen managed to convert the book into a play through the urgings of impresario Al Woods, but since neither of these works were very coherent, playwright Guthrie McClintic doctored the play with the help of his wife Katharine Cornell, who was to become the leading lady. Great excitement was generated, as everyone waited for the enactment of this controversial tale. And in America the actors, with great skill, did manage to do it justice, giving the play and themselves a great success. (The London production with Tallulah Bankhead in the lead lacked their ability and commitment, and was a failure.) Miss Cornell made her name, Margalo Gillmore was praised as the 'other woman' of a love-triangle, and Leslie also became popular as the male who preoccupied them both. There were outrageously saucy scenes that just passed the censor, swirling emotions to thrill the audience, and ultimately an entertaining but ephemeral work.

The first performance of the play was given at the Garrick Theatre in Detroit on 29 March 1925. The New York opening was on 15 September. Noel Coward's *The Vortex* opened on 25 September, and the critics were shocked by both. The play ran for twenty-nine weeks, and then toured until the summer of 1927, although Leslie left the cast before this. It was a long time to play the same role – that of a weak man at the mercy of events and foil to a strong female protagonist. It prefigured his role as Ashley in *Gone with the Wind*, which might explain why he was so bored at the idea of repeating the role some thirteen years later.

The success of the play raised Leslie's profile and incidentally gave him a chance to show off his writing skills. This was an ambition which went back to childhood, and it was an extra thrill that his first significant published article succeeded wonderfully. Not only that, but it was one of the first to appear in *The New Yorker*, a wittily fashionable magazine that still retains its glamour. Leslie had been introduced to the magazine's creator, Harold Ross, through his friendship with Margalo Gillmore and others of the Algonquin set, from whose general atmosphere the magazine grew. The first issue appeared in February 1925, Ross having laid down for it in his prospectus:

> *The New Yorker* will be a reflection in word and picture of metropolitan life. It will be human. Its general tenor will be one of gaiety, wit and satire, but it will be more than a jester. It will not be what is commonly called radical or highbrow. It will be what is commonly called sophisticated, in that it will assume a reasonable degree of enlightenment on the part of its readers.[31]

Ross did not say that the magazine's politics would be liberal and humanitarian. Perhaps he felt it did not need saying. *The New Yorker* was far too cool to proselytize, but it did much to gently ridicule prejudices that were unquestioned in much of America.

Leslie was perfectly suited. His first article appeared on 31 October 1925, entitled *The Intimate Diary of an Opening Night*, accompanied by a jolly set of caricature illustrations of him. The magazine's future was still uncertain at this point, so perhaps he may take a very small piece of credit for helping it on its way. The article describes Leslie's first-night nerves, the expectation that the play had aroused, and a description of the critical verdicts, some of which were sharp. George Jean Nathan, who had the same opinion of *The Vortex*, a more serious play about the damaging effects of promiscuity, was particularly critical. Nathan seemed to feel that American rather than European decadence should lead the way, and sounded annoyed that there might be a world elsewhere.

Leslie's literary mix of self-deprecating humour and naive amazement at American ways went down very well, and six more of his articles appeared in *The New Yorker* of the 1920s, until Leslie left the New York milieu to join the film world. Their content included his supposed fame and how he coped with it, wry comments on commercialism and some quite cutting attacks on hypocrisy and censorship. Amongst them was one personally revealing paragraph describing a backstage visitor: 'The Insurance Man asks me loudly, "I understand you are a married man Mr Howard?" Most of the dressing-room doors are open, and this remark, for some unknown reason, produces a series of ironic gibes from within the rooms.'[32]

Leslie escaped the stifling summer heat of New York in 1926 by finding a play in London to appear in, with the help of visiting English actor Tom Nesbitt. The play wasn't particularly good, but the whole family could have a long visit home, and Leslie could see his own relatives. The play, *The Way You Look At It*, by titled nonentity Lord Lathom, lasted for a few weeks only. Its daring and decadent characters were becoming too familiar, and the critics were not in favour. Even so, *The Times* noted, 'That the actors all do their best for it the audience recognized, but when [the author's representative] appeared, the gallery made it abundantly clear that the pardon was not general. Much of the trivial stuff was indeed unpardonable.'[33]

Unfortunately Leslie's wife Ruth now became very ill, and had to spend a long time after an operation recuperating in a nursing home. Leslie did his best to comfort her, but had to return to New York for another play, a prestigious production by Gilbert Miller and Al Woods, *The Cardboard Lover*. (This was renamed *Her Cardboard Lover* on the insistence of a later leading lady, Jeanne Eagels.)

Leslie was now in a position to insist on certain provisos in his contract with producer Gilbert Miller. A letter from Leslie to Miller survives, asking for shorter runs, which Miller might reluctantly have allowed.

It also reveals Leslie's wish that a star female name should not be cast opposite him in *Her Cardboard Lover*. He felt that his own presence could sustain the play, and that another star would throw it out of balance. Miller could not be persuaded, and Leslie's fears were to be more than justified.[34]

First in the line of unwelcome leading ladies was Laurette Taylor. Leslie was about to enter into a long spell when the real lives of temperamental women stars would overshadow his talent. Not that he minded much – he was to draw some literary material out of the experiences – but he would rather not perhaps have had such a close-up of personal disasters. This was a time when women were enjoying new freedoms, and this equality existed alongside a more old-fashioned assumption that they had a right to behave like 5-year-olds when they wanted. On the other hand, actors were still treated as serfs by producers, and women especially were manipulated by the competitive males around them. The clash of new and old attitudes resulted in some famous casualties.

The Cardboard Lover had an enormous first-night success, mostly attributed by the critics to Leslie. The theatre manager put up Leslie's picture with other featured stars. Miller tore it down in a fit of temper, but had to agree to its going up again the next night. Leslie knew by this time that there was no actor on Broadway who could match his magical stage presence and his mastery of this genre. He was determined to steal the play whoever the leading actress was and in the event he did, three times over. Even so, it is the three leading ladies who are more remembered.

It is not clear whether Laurette Taylor's problem with alcohol had begun at this point, but it is likely. In any case, *The Cardboard Lover* was not the right vehicle for her. The play was originally French, and the character was a sexually sophisticated and passionate woman behaving outrageously. Leslie played a handsome young man whom the star considers negligible, but who eventually tames her and guides her life into calmer waters.

Rehearsals and a pre-tour started in August 1926, with Gilbert Miller, the author Jacques Deval (speaking doubtful English and described by Leslie as 'an excitable little man'), the translator Valerie Wyngate, the director George Cukor and various others attending. Despite all the efforts and first-class talents urging it on, the play refused to come together, and finally it was evident that Taylor could not sustain the part. She had to leave, but charged breach of contract and was awarded $4,000 in damages. According to her daughter, the

Miss Tallulah Bankhead and Mr. Leslie Howard in another scene.

Figure 17. Leslie looking dishevelled after coping with Tallulah on and off stage. *Her Cardboard Lover*, 1928, Lyric Theatre London.

loss of confidence at this disaster contributed to a breakdown which interrupted her career for many years.[35]

Next was Jeanne Eagels. In this case the potential for tragedy must have been evident, and Gilbert Miller's role in her downfall somehow suggests something unpleasantly vindictive. However, Miller had the idea of asking P.G. Wodehouse to smarten up the dialogue, and while he wrestled with it, Miss Eagels agreed to try the leading role. It was her second star role, her first and most famous having been that of Sadie Thompson, the prostitute main character in Somerset Maugham's *Rain*. She was 36 years old, and had already played many parts on the New York stage. Leslie and the cast's experiences with her in rehearsal of what was now named *Her Cardboard Lover*, were later described, lightly disguised, in one of Leslie's articles for *Vanity Fair*.

Miss Eagels' worst fault perhaps was to take out her own insecurities on minor members of the cast. After the play successfully came out in New York in March 1927, her behaviour was stable for some months, but on tour the pressures were too much for her. It was her misfortune at this time that the play belonged to Leslie – he received great acclaim from both critics and audience for his subtle comedy playing. Her efforts met with critical disapproval, and she could not cope. Her drinking was out of hand, there were incidents when she fell asleep on stage, or stopped the play in full flight to ask for a drink of water. On tour in Chicago, she demanded a red carpet from her dressing room to the street. At last she went absent entirely, and the play closed its American run for good. But Miller was not pleased. Her absence had cost him money – not a great deal, but a few weeks' run. He demanded that Equity, the actor's union, take action against her and eventually it did, handing her an astonishing eighteen months' ban from taking part in any play, anywhere. To so affect an actress's livelihood would be unthinkable now, and Eagels was shattered. Her theatre career ended for good, although she afterwards appeared in vaudeville, and in some early films. A year after the final Equity ban was announced, she died, the inquest reportedly finding an overdose of alcohol, chloral hydrate and heroin.[36]

The final unlucky leading lady for this play was at least something more of a survivor – Tallulah Bankhead. The British production of *Her Cardboard Lover* opened a year later in August 1928. Tallulah had been in London since 1923, amongst other things having played the heroine of *The Green Hat* to moderate reviews. She followed it with a series of fashionably daring parts in which she found reason to appear in her underclothes, which event was breathlessly awaited by her many fans – all women. Her house in Farm Street, near aristocratic Berkeley Square, was notorious for its continual parties.

Tallulah was a one-woman whirlwind, gathering speed. By the time she and Leslie opened in the play, Tallulah was already being anxiously investigated by MI5, Britain's internal secret security service, which hardly knew where to start, so wide-ranging was her wild behaviour.[37]

She had been reported to them on two main counts. The first was for her visits to Eton school during the previous few months, the school's summer term. There she had gathered about her a set of boys, 'numbering five or six, who were convicted of breaking bounds' and who had 'associated' with her. These were named as Lord Rosslyn's grandson, three sons of Sir Mathew Wilson and a boy named Parsons. Two of Sir Mathew Wilson's sons were expelled for the connection. Tallulah was accused of taking the boys out on trips and staying at hotels with them, but the investigation failed to come to any conclusion as both Eton's headmaster and the boys' parents refused to give any information. MI5 were also concerned with the fact that Tallulah's close circle of friends was largely homosexual, that she 'kept' female lovers in both England and America, and that 'the more respectable American actresses' in England were worried that they might be 'tarred with the same brush', in the words of the report. There was much more, all in horrified tones.

The report had no public outcome, and the investigation seemed to be dropped, but Tallulah had overstepped too many limits. More remarkable than all this was the fact that she seems to have created a gay women's circle, which developed so quickly that it was hardly recognised for what it was. The most significant product was Radclyffe Hall's book, *The Well of Loneliness*, which was published in 1928 and at the time of the play was challenging the censor in court. Hall was a great admirer of Tallulah, and had called on her at the theatre a number of times.[38] Tallulah's fans, collectively known as the Gallery Girls, and who cheered for her whenever she went on stage, roaring approvingly when she stripped down to her underclothes, constituted one the century's most public expressions of homosexual feeling. None of which pleased the authorities of course.

Leslie found himself time and again in the middle of someone else's crisis. He liked Tallulah, and was entertained by all the mischief, but generally he locked himself in his dressing room to avoid the frantic adulation which she attracted. Despite all his efforts, her antics on stage overshadowed his acting. The British reviews were almost the same as those in America, all noting that Leslie's acting was remarkable, and that he might as well not have bothered. The *Daily Herald*'s of 22 August 1928 was typical:

> A traffic jam in Shaftesbury Avenue, massed cohorts of women blocking the pavement outside the Lyric Theatre – massed tiers of women cheering and howling inside – an atmosphere of more-than-electric tension – the sort of hungry expectation that must

have preceded a gladiatorial show in ancient Rome – well what would you – it's a Tallulah Bankhead first night! She went at it in true Tallulah style – husky concern, falling inflections, highest-of-high spirits, amazing controlled near-hysteria. After such a scene the play itself comes almost as an anti-climax. It is a light comedy adapted from the French – and not such a bad light comedy ... Leslie Howard made an immense hit as the lover. But peignoir or no peignoir, it was Miss Bankhead's marathon.

Tallulah had one more little surprise for Leslie during the London run of the play. In October 1929 the country received a visit from Aimee Semple McPherson, a well-known American evangelist who had thousands of followers in California for her emotional creed. Her trip to Britain had taken her away from the aftermath of a scandalous court case. In 1926 her attempt to cover a sexual escapade with a tale of kidnapping had resulted in a number of deaths amongst those searching for her. A subsequent trial during which witnesses had disappeared and the truth failed to be established made it clear that millions of dollars rested on her fervent beliefs, her showmanship, and her impulsive and unstable personality. She was left a free woman, the district attorney having made a statement that extramarital sex and a fake story were not criminally liable; but her reputation was hopelessly gone.[39]

Her tour to Britain could never have had much religious point. Her lectures at the Albert Hall, an enormous venue, were attended by curiosity seekers and occasional drunken groups out for a lark. The press, however, followed her closely, and their comments were sceptical. The sexual scandal was not mentioned, but her dubious financial matters were commented on with sarcasm.[40] Her every move was followed. Mrs McPherson, estranged from family and supporters in America, was therefore treated to a rather hostile time far from home, leaving her vulnerable, perhaps, to friendly predators.

Mrs McPherson was the fashionable attraction of the moment in London, and Tallulah, like many other actors and notables there, went to see the show. She booked a box for herself and some theatrical friends, including Beatrice Lillie, a comedienne and actress, and they watched the lecture and singing. Tallulah then sent word backstage that she would like to meet Mrs McPherson, and was accordingly escorted by a member of the entourage and introduced. They shook hands and had a long chat, according to Mrs McPherson's secretary.[41]

Tallulah invited the evangelist back to her home in Farm Street. Perhaps knowing something of its reputation, Mrs McPherson demurred, but invited them for a drink at her own rooms at the select Cecil hotel. They accepted, and Tallullah, accompanied by her actress friends Beatrice Lillie, Audry Carten, Dorothy Dickson and musician Gwen Farrar, visited her there. They took Mrs McPherson with them afterwards to see Beatrice Lillie in her rehearsal for *This Year of Grace*, a revue which was to be presented in New York. This was the last rehearsal in England, and Miss Lillie was due to sail to America the next morning in the liner from Southampton.

Mrs McPherson stayed with the group, finding herself in teasing but friendly company. While Tallulah and Leslie gave the evening performance of *Her Cardboard Lover*, the same group were at a party at Tallulah's house. Tallulah's three-day parties were notorious – she would disappear to the theatre and return afterwards while guests stayed on enjoying her hospitality. What happened when Tallulah and Leslie returned to the house is a little vague. After an indeterminate time spent drinking, amongst other things, Tallulah decided that it would be a jolly jape to take a night drive and see off Beatrice Lillie on her trip back to New York on the liner *Leviathan*. Such night drives were quite the rage amongst the bright young things, whose energy and sleeplessness were often fuelled by cocaine. Mrs McPherson, Audry, Gwen, Tallulah and Leslie were game for the drive from London to Southampton in Tallulah's impressive Bentley.

They arrived, drunk and riotous, at the boat the next morning, and invaded Beatrice Lillie's suite; their hostess duly put up with the nonsense until it was time to sail. In the meantime however, someone had alerted the press. From this point, everybody concerned with the adventure told a different tale to the excited journalists. Tallulah strongly denied that there had been any early morning trip, but other members of the party let out some of the truth. An extraordinary story then developed, as told by Tallulah, that they had started out the previous evening and had got lost in a dense fog which was present from London to Southampton and meant that they had to 'crawl along at a snail's pace' all the way. In addition, the car had broken down and they had had to push it. They then arrived at the boat the next morning.[42]

The story left the journalists unimpressed. The weather that night had been exceptionally fine, as it had all the autumn, with ten hours of sunshine per day and not a drop of rain falling on the south-east coast for weeks.[43] If the Bentley had broken down during the night, how had they arrived at Southampton? There were no all-night garages or emergency services to help them at that time. How had a group of slim and fashionably dressed actresses, in high heels, pushed the car any distance, never mind uphill? Most of all, the journey from London to Southampton took two hours, as Tallulah and all the party very well knew, being show business people who took the New York sailing often. Then why would they set out the previous evening, seven hours before? They would have had a dreary wait of hours at Southampton, not exactly a hot spot, before they could go on the boat. Miss Lillie had travelled separately that same night with her manager from Waterloo Station on the boat train.

The answer to all this is that they had not got lost in a fog, because it had been a clear night. Nor had they broken down. They had set out from London a couple of hours before arriving, having spent the night together at Tallulah's house. Tallulah, Beatrice Lillie and everyone else involved were concerned to protect the reputation of Mrs McPherson. She was the focus of press interest, rather than Tallulah or any of the others. In any case, Tallulah was flagrant about at least some of her own bad behaviour, and a one-night joyride for her was nothing to note.

The one fact they were all concerned to hide was Mrs McPherson's all-night stay with them. They had certainly been drinking at Tallulah's house, but what else they had done during these hours is only suspected. Many years later, in summing up Tallulah's impact on London in those years, socialite columnist Charles Graves said, 'She popularized the words "divine" and "darling" and bacchanalian parties ... Tallulah's gay parties at her house off Berkeley Square became notorious. She allegedly got Evangelist Aimee Semple McPherson tipsy and took pictures.'[44] Tallulah, Audry Carten, Gwen Farrar and Beatrice Lillie are all remembered as predominantly or partly lesbian. Mrs McPherson certainly wasn't. Leslie was, as usual, a wryly amused onlooker.[45]

The story was so scandalous at the time that only hints of it could appear in the press. As usual when dreadful scandal was afoot, Leslie seems to have faded into the woodwork. Whatever frolics he had joined in that night (and it was probably just a hilarious evening) nothing he did ever followed him and he was not questioned about this story. Whenever Leslie was found at the edge of convention, somehow all that emerged was how conventional he was himself. Despite all the schoolboy naughtiness, he rarely drank too much, never took drugs, and always went quietly home to his wife and children.

Tallulah, however, was near the end of her stay in Britain. Press comment was increasingly disapproving, and although no direct accusations were ever made, she was portrayed unsympathetically. She was booed by theatre audiences when the Eton escapade became known. At one point she appeared in a London *Evening Standard* cartoon of theatre characters, holding a 'stripper' doll and looking distinctly the worse for wear, with exaggerated bags under her eyes.[46] The next year she sold her house and returned to America. Her gay fan base had not in the least diminished, but whatever realization had been awakened in them by her and which encouraged open display faded away after she left and never reappeared again in so blatant a manner.

Leslie's experiences with all three leading ladies were rather frankly recorded in articles for *Vanity Fair* magazine between 1927 and 1930. The first, which appeared in the July 1927 issue, commented obliquely on his experience with Jeanne Eagels. It was a description of rehearsals, written in a parody style of Lewis Carroll's *Through the Looking Glass*. Miss Eagels features as the Cheshire Cat, screeching at all the cast, while the producer, as the Mad Hatter, nervously placates her. Another article, three years later in July 1930, was sarcastically entitled 'One Big Happy Family'. This described the difficulty of a large theatrical production with its petty rivalries, clashing egos and potential for misunderstandings. The criticism here is more direct, possibly showing Leslie's exasperation after years of these antics:

> Another way, [of upstaging] for ladies who may be wearing an evening shawl or wrap, is that practised so successfully by the late Jeanne Eagels. Miss Eagels had a great genius for throwing an evening shawl over her shoulder in a variety of ways without stopping – letting the end of it trail down, picking it up, changing its position and shrugging her shoulders. It was extraordinary what Miss Eagels could do with a simple thing like a shawl. When there is no shawl or wrap to use as a magnet for the audience, there is always stamping of the foot or walking round in circles, also a very effective method. Miss Tallulah Bankhead, the American actress who is so famous in London, still finds that when her vis-à-vis is saying his or her best lines, nothing distracts the audience away from the speaker so effectively as a wild rush across the stage, a leap in the air, and landing on a bed or chair. This works wonders and has the effect of causing a laugh from the gallery as well.[47]

Leslie goes on to describe how Tallulah used various techniques for stepping on his lines. In defence he pauses before a comic line, so that the actress has already performed her bit of distracting business, ensuring that this time the line will be heard by the audience.

Leslie describes himself as going to childish lengths in retaliation for such tricks:

> I purchase for ten cents one of those rubber balls, painted with a comic face, from which, upon pressing its sides, a tongue protrudes. I have this handy in my pocket and when the star starts to move up stage I stand deliberately down stage, in front of the footlights, with my back to the audience. Folding my hands behind me, I wait for the critical moment when the star reaches the climax of her speech, and then I disclose the little ball and dexterously pop its tongue out at the audience, causing shrieks of mirth which the star cannot understand at all.[48]

Whatever the hopes, fears and whimsies of his leading ladies, Leslie steadily pursued his own ambition. And that seems to have been simple enough at this time – he wanted to be a matinee idol – *the* matinee idol, the cynosure of all eyes, and especially female ones. Before the end of the decade he had achieved it, both effortlessly and with a great deal of hard work – a lot of it behind the scenes, in negotiating control of finance and material with producers such as Gilbert Miller, gaining the right vehicle roles and getting them staged. From Leslie's descriptions, the acting itself was the easy part. An actor friend later remembered Leslie's comments on acting as 'a silly business for a man to be in ... all that pretending, all that paint and posing and lights, all that buttering up to producers for jobs and the press to help persuade the public to want to see you at work! Ugh!' This was Douglas Fairbanks Jnr, who had been wafted into the film world on the back of his world-famous father's name, and believed that Leslie didn't really mean it. But Leslie had been through enough by this time for his comments to be heartfelt.[49]

Between the New York and London productions of *Her Cardboard Lover*, Leslie gained his first really star part – a wonderful showcase of a play for him, John Galsworthy's *Escape*. In this play, the social class of the characters provided settings for the theme, which examines personal honour in desperate circumstances. Galsworthy wrote the play in America, but being the man he was, completely ignored these surroundings and set his play firmly in England, where it eventually had a very successful London run. All the same he was not above wishing to exploit America's commercial possibilities. His hero had to be English, and Galsworthy suggested in turn Roland Young, Owen Nares, Ivor Novello and John Gielgud. Luckily for him all were busy, as the play was set very much in the present, and needed an actor with a modern, rather than a classical or mannered style. His American producer was Winthrop Ames, a man of long experience in the theatre, who looked about and saw that the part was ideal for Leslie.

The leading character, Matt Denant, has served in the First World War as an officer, and is now at a loose end. Walking in Hyde Park he meets a streetwalker, and falls into a sympathetic conversation with her. They are interrupted by a policeman, who attempts to arrest the girl for soliciting. Denant gallantly defends her, and in the ensuing argument punches the policeman, who falls against a railing and is killed. Denant refuses to run, and the upshot is a five-year sentence for manslaughter to be served in grim Dartmoor prison, then thought to be the harshest prison in England. Two years later, as fog descends on the moor, Denant on a whim makes a break for it from the prison, although there is little chance of escape from the isolated moor without money, clothes, food or any help. In the next few days he meets a succession of people, all of whom immediately recognise him as the escaped prisoner, and all of whom, knowing his story, have a choice of turning him in or keeping him from the authorities.

The author makes good use of the situations to show people of varying backgrounds and their reasons (or unthinking reactions) for helping Denant, with scenes both comic and stirring. Finally Denant plays a long scene in a local village church, in which the parson is willing to help him; but when the parson is confronted by local police who ask him pointedly on his honour whether he has seen the prisoner, he does not know how to answer – and Denant walks out to give himself up, rather than force him to this choice. It doesn't quite convince, although Galsworthy perhaps didn't pursue the theme thoroughly enough to realize why. The play accidentally foreshadowed a later time – the escape of refugees hunted by the Nazis, and the decision of ordinary people in many countries to help them or give them up.

At the time it was an attractive format to highlight the abilities of the leading man to be in turn poignant, witty, ironic and noble. Leslie perfectly obliged, to such effect that the critics delivered the best notices of his career. Brooks Atkinson of the *New York Times* enthused, 'Leslie Howard plays Denant as an extraordinarily engaging young man of excellent sensibilities'. Other comments were similar, or even more lavish.[50]

Encouraged by all this, Leslie was determined to follow his first muse and get his own efforts produced. He had been working whenever he could on one play or another, and according to his own account – 'An

Actor Turns Playwright', *New York Times*, 2 October 1927 – tried out the latest on his own family, who were polite and tactful, and he also imposed the drama on any friend who would stay to listen.

It has to be said that only Leslie's charm and his own success en-sured the production of this play, which went through various titles and eventually appeared briefly in New York as *Murray Hill*, or *Twee-dle Gets Married*, with himself in the lead, and as *Tell Me the Truth (A Bit of Tomfoolery)* in London, without him. Strangely, the London reviews were more tolerant. The play is interesting only for what it inadvertently reveals about Leslie such as the description of himself on his first entrance as 'a tall young man'. His height, at 5' 10", was always a sore point for him, especially with relatively tall leading ladies. The story involves a family living in the old-fashioned New York district of Murray Hill, composed of three old maids and one unawakened, prim young virgin. She and Leslie's character fall madly in love at first sight, and in the only exciting passage, she describes the incident: 'His eyes never left mine for a moment. They seemed to burn right into the depths of my body ... I just collapsed in a dead faint and had to be taken home'.[51]

Leslie, the handsome stranger she has seen, naturally turns out to be witty, wise, charming, worldly and enormously wealthy. After lots of byplay, disguised characters and hopefully amusing misunderstandings, all is resolved and the lovers are happy ever after. Leslie's character still seemed to be dreaming of high romance, and the lack of substance is predictable, but disappointing.

Leslie the playwright in truth had not much new to offer, but the stage actor was approaching the high point of his career. He had been intro-duced to the author of his next play, John Balderston, at the house of Herbert Bayard Swope, editor of the *New York World*. Balderston was head of the *World*'s London bureau. He was also a playwright, whose *Berkeley Square* had already been successfully produced in London in 1926, and who was now looking for a New York version. Swope's wife introduced him to Leslie, saying simply, 'here's your Peter Standish' – the main character of the play.

Berkeley Square was a strange composite effort which had started with Henry James's novel, *A Sense of the Past*, written in James' last years. The novel consisted of some hundreds of pages of diffuse rambling, in which the events of a modern American coming to London to live in a Regency house, and travelling in time to meet some of its former inhab-itants, can just be discerned. Balderston, helped by English journalist and poet J.C. Squire, performed miracles to get the story into shape while retaining a spark of Jamesian spirit. But there were problems. First that James had not been very much interested in a rationale for the plot, so there is no particular reason for Peter Standish's time-travelling or subsequent love affair, which is meant to transcend time and last forever. The love object, Helen Pettigrew, has no particular qualities except passivity, which James seems to have thought marked the ideal woman. Standish falls in love in the eighteenth century, but must return to his own time, forever in search of his lost amour. According to Henry James, Standish is horrified at the morals and manners of those previous days, believing that his own time contains all the 'ripeness, richness and civilisation'.

Balderston, who had gone through the First World War as a correspondent, begged to differ. Instead he added vivid passages to the play which condemned the barbarism of the present. He also added whatever contemporary notions he could throw in, including a reference to Einstein's theory of relativity, and an Egyptian ankh, or symbol of timelessness – he had reported on the opening of the tomb of Tutankhamun in 1922. It is difficult to know what J.C. Squire added, although both he and Balderston were interested in the idea of time travel and clashing cultures. Squire's 'Georgian' poetry rejected American and modernist influences. Perhaps he helped with the mechanics of the plot, which needed to be invented from scratch.

On top of all this, Leslie was determined to add his own thoughts. He worked with Balderston on a second version of the play, which had already enjoyed a successful London premiere, in August 1928 while he was still playing in *Her Cardboard Lover*. It is no surprise to find that what Leslie had done was add to the love story. At least he seems to have improved the leading lady's part as well as his own.

Leslie had many commitments that year. After the long run of *Her Cardboard Lover*, he toured Europe with Gilbert Miller, presumably to see new plays and playwrights. He also agreed to support Gertrude Lawrence in her first straight acting part in the play *Candlelight*. *Berkeley Square* opened in London, for the second time, in March 1929. The London critics, on being presented with the play for a second time, seemed nonplussed. The novelty of the time-travelling idea was now gone. The leading lady in both versions was Jean Forbes-Robertson, and she had gained golden opinions in the first run, and was not worse the second. The critics could see that the theme was confused, and although they praised the playing and the carefully chosen regency staging, they concluded that, 'they [the leading players] hold the audience in lively, breathless expectation of something, some final rapture of the spirit, to which the stage never attains'.[52]

Jean Forbes-Robertson was an elfin, sensitive actress, most famous for playing Peter Pan. She had a quality of other-worldliness which made her perfect for Leslie's lost love in *Berkeley Square*. During the play's run, which ended in April 1929, she and Leslie were said to have had a passionate affair. Some months later she married James (Hamish) Hamilton, the future publisher, at a very grand wedding which Leslie and his wife attended, along with much of the theatre world. The marriage was not successful and was dissolved in 1933. Miss Forbes-Robertson remained on good terms with Leslie, and he was to call on her for help when a tricky problem arose on his production of *Hamlet* in 1935.[53]

After an interval in New York when Leslie managed to escape from Gertrude Lawrence and *Candlelight* (yet another light comedy romance of mistaken identities), *Berkeley Square* opened there in November 1929. This time the play was performed for a fresh audience, and the reaction was far more enthusiastic than Leslie had expected. New York was entranced by the play. His new leading lady was Margalo Gillmore, described as 'luminously beautiful', and she and Leslie made the most of the doomed, mystical romance and tormented protagonists. *Berkeley Square* was later filmed, without many changes to its construction, so that Leslie's performance can still be seen. He is at his most vulnerably heroic, and the play notoriously caused female fans to swoon in the aisles. The critics were as admiring as ever.[54]

In this way, Leslie remained shielded from the Wall Street crash of October 1929. As rehearsals of the play, out-of-town performances and the opening in New York proceeded, it became clear that the romantic and historical piece was an excellent retreat from reality. The extent of the country's financial disaster became slowly apparent. Leslie lost money along with everyone else, but he was protected by the enormous income his performances had generated. He was never known for reckless expenditure, and his gentle manner concealed a sharp businessman, as his letters revealed; he never experienced serious money worries after this date.

A retrospective of Leslie's plays of the 1920s shows him illustrating themes which were current in Britain and Europe to a curious New York audience. His greatest successes explored an old-fashioned England, still confidently in command of civilisation, still exploring such notions as honour and fair play. Leslie loved modern America, he was fascinated by the new inventions, delighted by futuristic buildings and brilliant seascapes, but his own identity as an Edwardian Englishman was never in question, perhaps even emphasised by the comparison. Leslie was an odd mix of seriousness and frivolity, and the 1920s not being a challenging decade, he spent them mostly as an easygoing charmer in pursuit of fun and gratification. He was also a loving family man, an intelligent and hard-working actor, an amusing author, quite astute in business, a traveller in Europe, and a wonderful networker in America and England. They were not qualities that seemed important at the time.

NOTES

1. Paul Marshall, 'The Lord Chamberlain and the Containment of Americanization in the British Theatre of the 1920s', *New Theatre Quarterly* (19) 2003.
2. Ronald Howard (ed.), *Trivial Fond Records* (London: W. Kimber, 1982), p.19.
3. *Washington Post*, 9 May 1920.
4. *Washington Post*, 30 November 1919.
5. Obituary, *New York Times*, 3 January 1969.
6. *New York Times*, 2 November 1920.
7. *The Times*, 9 October 1920.
8. Leslie's letters, dated between December 1920 and May 1921, in the papers of Adrian Brunel, British Film Institute special collections.
9. Leslie Ruth Howard, *A Quite Remarkable Father* (London: Longmans, 1960), p.3.
10. Booth Tarkington, *The Wren: A Comedy in Three Acts* (New York: S. French, 1922).
11. Helen Hayes, *On Reflection: An Autobiography* (London: W.H. Allen, 1969), p.45.
12. Franklin P. Adams, *New York Tribune*, 11 October 1921.
13. Alexander Woollcott, *New York Times*, 11 October 1921.
14. Cosmo Hamilton, *Unwritten History* (London: Hutchinson 1924), p.106.
15. Alexander Woollcott, *New York Times*, 23 December 1921.
16. Cosmo Hamilton, *Four Plays* (London: Hutchinson, 1925). *Danger* was originally titled *The Mother Woman*.
17. Ann Thwaite, *A.A. Milne: His Life* (London: Faber and Faber, 1990), p.109.
18. *New York Times*, 26 March 1922.
19. *The Times*, 21 December 1921.
20. Dorothy Parker, *The New Yorker*, 12 November 1927.
21. Alexander Woollcott, *New York Times*, 15 March 1922.
22. John Golden, *Stagestruck* (New York: S. French, 1930). Criticism from *Theatre Magazine*, August 1923.
23. Sutton Vane, *Outward Bound* (London: S. French, 1924), p.14.
24. *New York Times*, 28 January 1924.
25. *New York Times*, 11 May 1924.
26. Lawrence J. Quirk, *Claudette Colbert: An Illustrated Biography* (New York: Crown, 1985), p.36.
27. Howard, *Trivial Fond Records*, p.48.
28. Ronald Howard, *In Search of My Father* (London: W. Kimber, 1981), p.42.
29. *New York Times*, 14 January 1925.
30. Harry Keyishian, *Michael Arlen* (Boston, MA: Twayne, 1975) and Lois Gordon, *Nancy Cunard: Heiress, Muse, Political Idealist* (New York: Columbia University Press, 2007).
31. Harold Ross, prospectus for *The New Yorker*. Unpublished document, circa 1924, quoted in Theodore Peterson, *Magazines in the Twentieth Century* (Urbana, IL: University of Illinois Press, 1964), p.248.

32. *The New Yorker*, 12 November 1927.
33. *The Times*, 28 July 1926.
34. Letter of Leslie Howard to Gilbert Miller, dated 8 November 1926, from Great Neck. In the hands of a private collector, Elizabeth Adams, and kindly shown to the author. The provenance is not known, the letter presumably having been sold originally by Miller's heirs.
35. Marguerite Courtney, *Laurette* (New York: Atheneum, 1955).
36. Edward Doherty, *The Rain Girl* (Philadelphia, PA: Macrae, 1930).
37. National Archives, MI5 Report on Tallulah Bankhead. Dated 29 August to 3 September 1928. HW1/1709.
38. Sally Cline, *Radclyffe Hall: A Woman Called John* (London: J. Murray, 1997).
39. *New York Times*, 11 January 1927.
40. *The Times*, 11 September 1928.
41. *Evening Standard*, 17 October 1928.
42. *Evening Standard*, 17 October 1928; Tallulah Bankhead, *Tallulah: My Autobiography* (London: Gollancz, 1952); Lee Israel, *Miss Tallulah Bankhead* (London: W.H. Allen, 1972); Beatrice Lillie, *Every Other Inch a Lady* (London: W.H. Allen 1972); *Daily Mail*, 16 and 20 October 1928.
43. *Daily Herald*, 17 September 1928. The *Daily Herald* gave this particular weather report front-page coverage.
44. *Time*, 22 November 1948.
45. Axel Madsen, *The Sewing Circle* (London: Robson, 1996); Joan Schenkar, *Truly Wilde* (London: Virago, 2000). Beatrice Lillie's own memoirs, *Every Other Inch a Lady*, are amusing about the incident. She describes Tallulah as the 'Alabama peach', p.169, Mrs McPherson as, 'a charmer, with a tangle of bobbed auburn curls, a determined jaw and a nose that even I envied'.
46. *Evening Standard*, 1 June 1928.
47. *Vanity Fair*, July 1930.
48. *Vanity Fair*, July 1930.
49. Douglas Fairbanks Jnr, *The Salad Days* (London: Collins, 1988), p.158.
50. *New York Times*, 26 October 1927.
51. Leslie Howard, *Murray Hill: A Comedy in Three Acts* (London: S. French, 1934), p.29.
52. *The Times*, 7 March 1929.
53. For Leslie's affair with Jean Forbes-Robertson, see John Houseman, *Run-Through: A Memoir* (New York: Simon and Schuster, 1972). Her marriage reported in *The Times*, 2 September 1929.
54. See, for example, Brooks Atkinson, *New York Times*, 5 November 1929.

CHAPTER FIVE

1931–1939: Film Star

Towards the end of 1929 Leslie became enthused with a new play, *Out of a Blue Sky*, by a radical young Viennese author, Hans Chlumberg. Leslie was still enjoying the spectacular success of *Berkeley Square*, which was to continue playing in New York until May of the next year. He was therefore delighted to take a break from it with his own experiment. Chlumberg's comedy had been a success all over Europe and now Leslie provided a new translation from the German for its American debut. He gathered a first-rate cast, and an enthusiastic director and financers. One of the more anonymous backers turned out to be from the New York mob, who provided a sinister onlooker at rehearsals, to Leslie's horror.[1]

The play used the trick of actors involving the audience, with echoes of Pirandello and Molnar. Here the stage 'producer' has to call on the audience for actors when the 'real' ones are absent. The audience players are of course part of the cast, and play out their own little comedy. The trick didn't work in this case as the love-triangle drama within the play, concerned with a wealthy family's love affairs, had little interest. Somewhere the Germanic humour and manic energy of the original was dissipated and the production lasted only two weeks. But Leslie's translation wasn't entirely to blame – a later production in England using the J.T. Grein company version starring Nigel Playfair also flopped, and the play, originally *Das Blaue von Himmel*, virtually disappeared.

Perhaps it was the subject matter that failed to match up to the times. The competition from sound films and even more the Depression which followed the Wall Street crash of 1929 were rapidly dimming the brilliance of the theatre world. The darkening mood was unfavourable to yet more depictions of naughtiness amongst the rich and carefree, and theatre critics were becoming more politicized and intolerant.

Chlumberg himself may have felt some of this, as his next play, *Miracle at Verdun*, was a grimly cynical commentary on the First World

War (in which he had fought bravely)[2] where the ghosts of dead soldiers rise to arraign every establishment figure of Vienna society, including the rabbis. This play and its English translation achieved great success, but the Jewish author never knew. He died after a fall in the theatre, whether accidental or not (the play and the author being anathema to Hitler's Nazis, who were increasingly evident) just before its opening performance in Leipzig, at the end of 1930.[3]

Leslie had enjoyed taking *Out of a Blue Sky* right through from script to performance, and was not too badly upset by the failure. After *Berkeley Square*, New York took him to its heart in 1930 in a generous and uncomplicated way that would never be quite the same again. He attended parties and dinners given in his honour, spoke at cultural gatherings, played benefit and charity performances for out-of-work actors and hobnobbed cheerfully with New York society.

In the course of rehearsal readings for minor parts in *Out of a Blue Sky*, Leslie had dismissed an unsuitable young hopeful named Clark Gable. The part, 'German Play Reader', was an unlikely one for him and was eventually taken by William Gargan, who began a long friendship with Leslie. Mr Gable took his dismissal philosophically, in line with his easy-going nature. However, before the decade was out he was to achieve a complete if unintentional revenge, in the coming medium – sound films.

During the next few years the talents and energies of Broadway moved virtually en masse to Hollywood. Talking films, first seen in 1927, had enthralled the public even more than the original silents, as the shadows at last found a voice. But many new skills, artistic and technical, were needed to cater for them. Leslie was in the vanguard of the move, as his attractive voice and sophisticated playing were exactly the qualities required. Leslie had appeared uninterested in the new development, and even disapproving – he regularly included in any speech the idea that the public were now preferring bad movies to plays, and that the theatre had thereby lost its spontaneity and immediate appeal to its audience.[4] All the same, when his stage manager and friend George Fogel used his contacts in Hollywood to exploit Leslie's huge stage success, Leslie soon acquired an agent and a contract with Warner Brothers. Sound films were mainly their creation, and now they were anxious to improve their studio's prestige. They offered to make the film of *Outward Bound*, one of Leslie's former hits.

Leslie was due to visit Hollywood for the first time in early June of that year, when *Berkeley Square* finally closed its New York run.

After this he would have to fulfil his contract with Gilbert Miller to tour the play around America. Realizing that he would be travelling about for some time, Leslie sent his daughter home in the care of Miss Gospel, his housekeeper, and his sister Irene (who had been playing the part of the maid in *Berkeley Square*). And perhaps thinking that it was high time for a family home in England now that he could afford one, Leslie bought, sight unseen, an old English house called Stowe Maries in the Surrey village of Westcott.

As it turned out, the house might have featured in a horror film about the costs of renovating romantic old ruins. The final result, many months later, was a large family house with outward features of every century from the sixteenth onwards – one of the oddest houses now in that county. The interior was restored for Leslie in an Arts and Crafts style, possibly with the help of architect Oliver Hill, a pupil of Lutyens.[5] It was improved further by Leslie's insistence on central heating and 'American-style' bathrooms, now standard indoor bathroom suites, but then a novelty. There were also some acres of grounds, in which Leslie could keep and exercise his growing number of polo ponies. As a nod to his astonishing salary as an American film star, Leslie later added a swimming pool and a small cinema, complete with his own massive film camera. The Surrey house was eventually host to some very recognisable show-business names, who amused the locals by popping up in the improbable rural setting.

Leslie and his wife arrived in Hollywood in June of 1930 after a hot and dusty journey overland by train, as was usual then. They were given the traditional welcome by the sociable inhabitants, and had a chance to see the immense wealth on display in the stars' palatial houses, including the most impressive of all, that of Douglas Fairbanks and Mary Pickford, leaders of Hollywood society. Fairbanks' son, Douglas Junior, had a part in the film of *Outward Bound*, playing Leslie's Broadway role as one of the lovers rescued from death, while Leslie played what was originally Alfred Lunt's role, the young wastrel Tom Prior.

Leslie struck up a friendship with the much younger Fairbanks, whose naive and boisterous good humour was a welcome counter to Leslie's more serious moods. Long afterwards, Fairbanks' memoirs, which kept nobody's secrets but his own, told of their philandering adventures together. Leslie's wife Ruth might have sensed what was going on at the time, as she damped down the friendship by tactlessly suggesting to Fairbanks and his new wife, Joan Crawford, that their marriage would not last. This was a little too close to the truth to be tolerated and Fairbanks never forgot the incident. In return, he painted an unattractive portrait of Ruth as an overweight and overbearing matron in his autobiography, *The Salad Days*.[6]

The filming of *Outward Bound* must have been absorbing for all those involved. Hollywood's conversion to sound had taken place rapidly between 1927 and 1929, and had been enormously expensive and problematic. It was still very much in an experimental phase, and the new equipment was still being wrestled with. There were huge motorized cameras which could not be tilted or dollied, enclosed in stuffy sound-proofed booths, and uni-directional standing microphones which had to be concealed in unlikely places on the set. Editing the final film was also difficult because of discrepancies in the techniques of synchronizing sound and image. As a result, *Outward Bound*, like all early talkies, appears static and studio-enclosed. In fact plays which had first appeared on the stage were appropriate for the early filming limitations. For a short while Hollywood product turned into 'canned theatre' until technology improved and imagination broadened the varieties of artistic expression in the new medium.

Leslie's comments on the process were usual for the time. He reported that 'it was difficult to get ready for a scene on the command, "action" – it was too much like starting a race'.[7] He also missed the atmosphere and tension created by a live audience and found being on the set flat and enervating. Apart from these inconveniences, Leslie was immensely interested in every aspect of film-making. He investigated the new cameras and sound techniques and learnt as much as he could absorb, with the idea in the back of his mind that one day he would be producing his own work. In return Leslie could offer his own valuable experience of many years in staging, directing and acting techniques. In this case the film's director, Robert Milton, had plenty of his own, having directed the original play, and previously run an acting school in New York.

The result was successful, if not a smash hit. From a modern view-point, *Outward Bound*'s cinematography and sound are impressive, and the lighting creates the correct, spooky atmosphere. The acting, including Leslie's, is stagey but enjoyable, and the plot and dialogue still absorbing. One film review of the time took occasion to discuss Leslie's voice, an important point, as a 'standard' accent was then in transition. 'Howard speaks the English language without any of the disfigurements and affectations we are accustomed to hear in Britishers' attempts to speak their own tongue. It is free from the drawl, the clipped utterance

and the broadened vowel sounds ... it is the English of an educated gentleman, understandable in any country where English is spoken ... the
fountainhead of pure English.'[8] This was in contrast to contemporary
British sound films where leading men spoke with ultra-'refained'
voices in such a stuffy accent that it led to unintentional humour in
some cases.[9]

Leslie was at the beginning of a successful film-making career, and
once again he seems extraordinarily lucky to have been at the right
place and time with exactly the desired skills. In some ways Leslie was
limited in an American context – by his accent and bearing, which were
unchangeably English; and by his acting style, which though modern
and natural, was set by years of stage experience. America would soon
find its individual voice, and the limitations on expression in sound
films would be rapidly overcome. Almost all Leslie's classic films were
to be made in England, but it would not be true to say that Hollywood
never quite knew what to do with him. Leslie had much to offer at first
as a stylish foil for the studios' leading ladies, and because the American
image was not yet fixed, his next three films, unlike his plays, could have
American settings. As the 1930s moved on, there were plenty of good-
quality literary adaptations in Hollywood, and since Leslie negotiated
more control over his own work than almost any other actor, he had
some responsibility for the fact that he never quite scored an American
gold. Perhaps his nearest miss was as Sydney Carton in *A Tale of Two
Cities* (1935). Leslie's name was announced for the film, but at the last
moment his schedule was too tight and Ronald Colman took the part.
The film was an instant classic, and remains the definitive version. But
there were a number of silvers in the early years, where Leslie's
performance was better than the material – *Berkeley Square*, which
gained him an Oscar nomination, *The Animal Kingdom*, and *Of Human
Bondage*.

Whatever his successes in Hollywood, Leslie always had an eye on
British production. At the beginning of 1930 he had been approached
by theatre producer Basil Dean and asked to make a British film version
of his hit play *Escape*. Dean announced Leslie's appearance in the film
in both the British and the American press,[10] but finally Leslie decided
against it, having other commitments. Dean, despite his inexperience in
films, had ambitious plans to revive British production, which had sunk
to a new low with the advent of sound. At a time when virtually all
films seen in Britain were American, legislation had been introduced in
1927 (Cinematograph Films Act 1927) which called for an increase in

home production, so that up to 20 per cent of all films shown had to be British-made, with a British scenarist and at least three-quarters of the personnel to be British nationals. All that happened was that American companies, who wished to keep their hold on the British market, encouraged the making of 'quota quickies', rapidly and cheaply made films of poor quality, which could be used to make up the 20 per cent quota. These turned out to be so bad that they were only screened in cinemas during early morning hours. (There is an image, probably fanciful, of head-scarfed cleaning ladies, cigarettes dangling, being unheedingly entertained while they brushed the aisles and swept the seats.) By 1930, the quota quickies had become a public disgrace, and senior cinema and literary figures protested that while America and Europe were devoting every resource to the new artistic medium, Britain seemed indifferent.

Social divisiveness and prejudice played a part in the British lack of interest in film-making. In April 1931 *The New York Times* commented on the poor state of the British industry and quoted an (unnamed) influential observer of the scene: 'The type of men dominating the (British) industry are vulgarians with crude minds capable of little else than trying to copy the ideas of their betters.'[11] With this attitude, no wonder little finance was forthcoming to back production.

Dean had visited America in 1928, and returned with an agreement from the new RKO company to use their own sound process to make British films, and provide an outlet for them there. The implication was that the resulting films would be distributed in America, a prospect that would provide funding to revitalise the whole British industry. Dean founded his own company and built the first sound studios in Britain (later known as Ealing Studios) but the films he produced were too poor to make any impact. *Escape* was finally made with the ageing stage star Gerald du Maurier in the lead, instead of Leslie, but failed even in Britain partly because of its snobbish, upper-class air and exaggerated accents.[12] The irascible Dean sought revenge by including some comically unfavourable comments about Leslie in his memoirs.[13]

Back in California, Leslie moved to the prestigious MGM studio for his next pictures. The studio system was in full flow and under the leadership of Louis Mayer and Irving Thalberg, MGM was bursting with hyper-energised young men, full of enthusiasm, racing to turn out the product. Over the next three months, the spring of 1931, Leslie made three films: *Never the Twain Shall Meet*, *A Free Soul* and *Five and Ten*. The making of these partly overlapped, with one film shot in the morning and another in the afternoon, such was the pace. Nor did the actors have much power to protest at this time. Even worse for Leslie, his first director at MGM was 'One-Take' Woody van Dyke, whose rapid filming saved his bosses as much money as possible. There was also the fact that writers were treated even more contemptuously than actors and therefore storylines and scripts could be freely interfered with by directors, line producers or anyone who had power at the studio, with the results that might be anticipated.

Leslie reacted so strongly against these methods that he eventually gained the nickname 'Leisurely Howard' as a director of his own films. When the three pictures were finished, he switched to the new RKO studios for one more effort and then left Hollywood, exhausted, to return to England for a long summer holiday and a look at his new house. But the work had not been entirely negligible.

Never the Twain Shall Meet, like many of his films, exploited Leslie's sexy stage presence, starring him as a San Francisco shipping magnate's son who falls in love with Tamea, an amorous South Sea maiden. The father was played by his old friend Aubrey Smith. The story has Leslie following the child of nature to her Pacific island and proceeding to fall into dissipation, as apparently Western culture cannot cope with untamed passion. Leslie's co-star was the young and beautiful Spanish actress, Conchita Montenegro. He was to encounter her again, years later, on his last trip to Spain, and to the end of her long life she retained a great affection for him. Miss Montenegro was fresh and sparkling in this film, making her unlikely part believable as she cuts through the hypocrisies of white 'civilization'. Leslie, as the phrase goes, never looked lovelier, especially in the island scenes where the heavy make-up and mascara, which he hated, is dropped. Somehow, at the age of 37 he still had the bloom of youth, and there are naughty scenes of a nude Miss Montenegro underwater – a type of shot used again soon after in the film *Tarzan and his Mate* with Maureen O'Sullivan – and bedroom antics with Leslie beating Conchita, following this with a passionate embrace – the prohibitive Hays Code was yet to come. The most surprising aspect of the film today is the freedom of the woman to act as she wishes without being punished for her promiscuity by the fates. Leslie leaves Tamea to return home, but she is seen to go off happily with another lover at the end. It is alien to the 'ethics' of every film made after the Code, and which seem to linger even today. The unlikely tale holds the interest – 'One Take Woody' knew what he was doing, the acting is good enough to relax into moments of humour, and the film might be a minor classic in the style of *Red Dust* if it were not for the rather muddled racial ideas behind it. In retrospect it was probably influenced by the famous study of South Sea Island girls by anthropologist Margaret Mead, published in 1924. The study, now seen as questionable, had caught the spirit of the 1920s by portraying the girls as independent and free-wheeling in their love lives.

A Free Soul, starring Norma Shearer, was a more important production for the studio. Shearer's status as the wife of Irving Thalberg, MGM's head of production, provoked much envy and gossip from studio personnel, especially rival actresses. She was indeed in a favoured position, and her influence on this film led to a change of image for herself and a plot line that moved towards the unconventional. Shearer had feminist ideas and felt that women should be as free as men in every aspect of their lives.[14] Moving from her previous movie style as a respectable society miss, she turned in a performance of startling sexuality, with a plot that made it plain that she initiated guilt-free extra-marital sex. The film was made three years before the repressive Production Code censorship fell on Hollywood, and perhaps was one of the films that did something to provoke it.

The plot was taken from an overheated novel by Adela Rogers St Johns, another early feminist, and concerned a young society girl determined to live life on her own terms – the Free Soul of the title. Her actions lead to a fatal rivalry between her two lovers, one a member of the criminal underworld, the other from her own class, and to the death of her father, an alcoholic attorney. Playing the mobster was Clark Gable, and his tough, dominating role caught the American imagination. He leapt to stardom with this one film, his macho image setting the style for every subsequent all-American hero. Faced with these two vivid characters, Leslie made little impression, and his role as the gentle society lover fell into the background. He did, however, contribute a little to the pre-Code ambience by playing one whole scene with his hands on Norma's bosoms.

A Free Soul provoked enormous disapproval. *The New York Times* review spoke of a 'lurid and implausible' plot and denigrated every aspect of the film.[15] Many other critics expressed the same sentiments, but the film was a great success, and garnered three Oscar nominations, with Lionel Barrymore winning for his supremely hammy turn as the alcoholic father. *A Free Soul* has been seen in modern terms as proto-feminist, made while women still seemed to have an effective voice on film.

When Leslie had first come to Hollywood, he had ended his run of *Berkeley Square* with two weeks in a Los Angeles theatre. If he meant to showcase himself as an introduction to the film capital, it worked well. In the audience were many well-known names, and one of these was Marion Davies, famous as the mistress of multimillionaire newspaper baron William Randolph Hearst. Davies developed what she later called a 'theatre crush' on Leslie and since Hearst's influence on MGM was as strong as Marion's on him, she asked for and got Leslie as a leading man for one of her Hearst-financed films.[16] This emerged as *Five and Ten*, Leslie's next production. Once again there were the lavish production values of MGM, and their classic team, leaders in their field for years afterwards, including editor Margaret Booth, art director Cedric Gibbons, costumier Adrian, recording director Douglas Shearer, and cinematographer George Barnes. And once again an unlikely melodrama and patchwork script dimmed all their skills and the actors' talents together. Leslie and Marion at least seemed to enjoy making it, and reportedly amused themselves together off screen too, pursued as usual by a dubious Ruth Howard.

Leslie made one more film in Hollywood before turning back to the stage, where he at least had control of his own work. He changed to the new RKO studios, perhaps hoping for less tightly controlled working conditions, starring in *Devotion*, a pleasant enough love story and vehicle for Ann Harding, in an English setting this time; and this was a moderate success in America and Britain.

Three years later, again filming with MGM, Leslie gave an interview setting forth these experiences as an actor on the set:

> The movie actor rises at 6.30 a.m. or 7 a.m. – dashes to the studio – makes up and dresses while the assistant director and his emissaries are knocking on his door urging him to hurry. He rushes to the set. The moment he is there, nobody wants him any more. He sits and waits. Electricians, carpenters, painters, camaramen, property men fall over him as they go about their duties. It is too noisy to read. If he leaves the set he will be dragged back instantly. He has no idea what is going on. He tries to study the scene for the day. Then he is informed it will not be shot. He studies the submitted scene. It seems simple. Each of the two characters concerned has three lines apiece to say. The stage is finally set, but they have to wait for the leading lady who did not expect to work that day. By eleven o'clock she arrives looking radiant, accompanied by a retinue of make-up artists, hairdressers, costumiers and personal maids.

There is an interlude during which the leading lady's appearance
is discussed by the cameramen, the director and the retinue. Then
the lights are put out and the two rehearse the scene. They
rehearse it for a long time. The director is meticulous. They repeat
their three lines apiece many, many times. All the technical workers
who have been so busy now sit and wait. After the six lines have
been rehearsed fifteen or twenty times, and the actor is on the
point of screaming, the director mercifully announces he will
shoot the scene ...

Leslie's descriptions of delays, frustrations and the disjointed process of
film-making will still be very familiar to all in the business. Finally:

Our actor staggers to his dressing room at seven or eight in the
evening, removes his war-paint, dons his civilian clothes and goes
home to his wife, speechless with fatigue. He eats some food and
falls into bed, to be ready for his 6.30 a.m. call in the morning,
more exhausted from his three immortal lines than if he had
played Hamlet in the afternoon and Macbeth at night.[17]

Some of the problems Leslie complained of were part of the studio system
that was then in use. As a modern producer remembered, different studio
departments were practically autonomous, being only under the supervision of the studio head, and they followed their own set rules. This
meant that the editing department insisted every shot had to be 'covered':

it was mandatory for a scene to have a 'master shot' of the entire
scene, a medium shot, then over his shoulder to her, over her
shoulder to him, a loose single of him, same of her, close-ups ditto.
In this way, any line of dialogue or reaction could be used or elim-
inated. In addition to destroying any originality in the shooting
of a picture, this system put most of the strain on the actors,
because of the endless repetition and the seeming importance of
taking a puff on the cigarette on the same line for each of the eight
camera angles. Each of those angles would have numerous takes.
If an actor mismatched, the editor would often ignore a superior
acting take because his job was much easier if he used a take where
the cigarette action matched.[18]

Leslie left once again for England at the end of August 1931. He had
intended to do not much more than take a holiday, see how his new
house was progressing, settle his children's schooling and perhaps look
up his British theatre and film contacts. His plans were interrupted by

producer Alexander Korda, who had heard that Leslie was in Britain for some months and wanted his help for his first British prospect. Korda had developed a reputation for charm and persuasiveness, but Leslie was just as ready to hear of a project to give British film a boost. He would be paid £500 a week for the film, one tenth of his Hollywood salary. That autumn, he turned down a Hollywood studio contract because he did not like the methods of work, and wanted to remain a freelance. He commented, 'I intend to stick to the stage, but I hope also to take good film parts that appeal to me on their merits'.[19] Having turned down Basil Dean earlier in the year, Leslie must have been very impressed by Korda's background. The Hungarian-born producer had been a film critic and journalist in Budapest and Vienna, where cultural debate was meat and drink. Like Leslie he spoke many European languages, and he had experience of film-making in the Paris, Vienna, Berlin and Hollywood industries. He had most recently spent some years in Hollywood as a director, and like Leslie, he was unhappy with the conveyor-belt conditions. He had just made a sparkling and popular film in Paris, *Marius*, in a more European style, and this was to be a great success and advance to French sound films.

Korda was financed by the American Paramount studios, who were unhappy with the work coming from their British outlet. Korda was glad to accept a two-picture contract with them, hoping to establish his name in England and make some money to finance his own film company.[20] The new film, made at Elstree, was a sound remake of a popular Paramount silent, *The Head Waiter*, a frothy continental comedy. Paramount supplied Hollywood technicians and enough finance to achieve acceptable American production standards, so that the film could be released in both countries.

The result, *Service for Ladies*, released in 1932, was a success that evoked surprised admiration in both industries, and was much enjoyed by cinema-goers. It was Korda's first film in Britain, and was enough to establish his career, and an enormous boost for the home industry. Leslie's familiar name, his experience and his charming, expert playing certainly helped. Leslie afterwards commented,

> I found myself in perfect accord with Alexander Korda. We think alike, agree upon the same things, work the same way. He would make a scene, then throw the whole thing in the ashbin because he did not like it, and do it over again quite differently and very much better. That is why his work is so good. I would certainly like to do more work with him.[21]

The filming finished in November, and back Leslie went for his new Broadway play, *The Animal Kingdom*, a rather ill-tempered love story by Philip Barry set in Connecticut and Manhattan society. Bill Gargan, a New York born actor, who had become a friend of Leslie's, joined the cast as a comic butler. Rehearsals began in the first week of November, and straight away ran into difficulties.

Amongst the problems was a young Katharine Hepburn, who lasted for just six days of rehearsal and was then abruptly sacked by producer Gilbert Miller. Since the playwright, Philip Barry, had been attracted to her, it was both a setback to her career and a romantic rebuff, and Hepburn worried away at the incident for years. It was also not clear whether Barry had written the play with her in mind. She blamed Leslie, charging first that she was too tall for him (she was five inches shorter) and then that he was afraid she would run away with the play.[22] But it seems unlikely that Leslie could have over-ridden not only Gilbert Miller, his co-producer, but also the playwright, both of whom, as Miss Hepburn admitted, also thought her playing was not up to standard. Gargan agreed too, judging that she was too inexperienced.[23] A year later, playing on stage in *The Lake* (1933) her acting was so poor that she was savaged by all the critics, Dorothy Parker famously writing in *The New Yorker* that 'she ran the gamut of emotions from A to B'. With all this said, there is still a shadow of doubt about her dismissal. She had some of the qualities of the leading character, Daisy Sage, but equally she lacked her rather passive femininity. With Leslie's dire experience of dominating partners overshadowing his delicately etched performances, it is possible he didn't wait to let Miss Hepburn find her feet. She eventually triumphed in Barry's *Philadelphia Story*, a better play, but hardly more feminist.

The Animal Kingdom follows events in the life of a publisher, Tom Collier, who leaves Daisy, his bohemian girlfriend, for a disastrous marriage to the materialistic Cecilia. It seems to have originally been in two parts, the first showing Collier's life with Daisy, possibly from her point of view, the second part with Cecilia. After Hepburn had left, both Miller and Leslie worked on the play with the author, unifying the structure to explore Tom Collier's maturing understanding.

All the same, what finally emerged reads unattractively, with an unpleasant protagonist and a confused message. Collier leaves Daisy solely for Cecilia's sexual attractions, abruptly dumping Daisy because their sexual relationship has cooled. Since Collier is depicted as an intelligent and sensitive man, he might have worked out that this would also happen

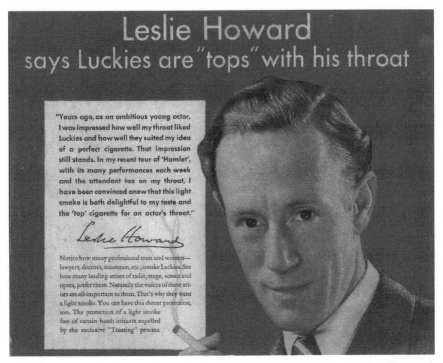

Leslie Howard
says Luckies are "tops" with his throat

"Years ago, as an ambitious young actor, I was impressed how well my throat liked Luckies and how well they suited my idea of a perfect cigarette. That impression still stands. In my recent tour of 'Hamlet', with its many performances each week and the attendant tax on my throat, I have been convinced anew that this light smoke is both delightful to my taste and the 'top' cigarette for an actor's throat."

Leslie Howard

Notice how many professional men and women—lawyers, doctors, statesmen, etc., smoke Luckies. See how many leading artists of radio, stage, screen and opera, prefer them. Naturally the voices of these artists are all-important to them. That's why they want a light smoke. You can have this throat protection, too. The protection of a light smoke free of certain harsh irritants expelled by the exclusive "Toasting" process.

Figure 18. Leslie, God forgive him, at least advertising products he used himself. From *Life Magazine*, 10 May 1937.

with his new love. Cecilia is blasted as a manipulative demon, using sex for blackmail and interested only in money. Again, why Collier would have married her in the first place seems questionable. And Barry has climbed a very high horse – remarks such as 'This book will make money – is that all he (Collier) cares about?' seem a little too noble for this world. In the final scene Cecilia is savagely humiliated, with the playwright assuming she is too stupid to notice the insults. After reading the play, it is difficult to know how it could be made into an attractive performance.[24]

In the event, Leslie's performance in *The Animal Kingdom* on Broadway in January 1932 was praised without stint – Brooks Atkinson describing him as 'a luminous actor … he has grace, precision and spirit'[25] – and the show was the hit of the season. Leslie showed a boyish lover turning gradually into a wiser man, finally impressive and commanding, and his poignant acting was enough to distract attention from all the misogyny, although some critics did note it. Leslie was also lucky in the choice of intelligent supporting players. Bill Gargan, playing a wise and comic servant in the ancient tradition, was the opposite physical type to Leslie, tall and strongly built, a working man from the Bronx, warm-hearted, funny and straightforward. Next to him Leslie seems all the more ethereal. Their characters in the play mirrored the real-life friend-ship which developed between the two men, and lasted until the end of Leslie's life. Gargan felt that Leslie had established his acting career, and afterwards named a son after him. He left a sardonically affec-tionate portrait of Leslie as a penny-pinching charmer and dressing-room seducer, in his memoirs, *Why Me?*

The play was such a success that it was turned into a film soon afterwards, without many changes from the original staging. *The Animal Kingdom* was made by RKO studios and released in 1932. In the film Ann Harding and Myrna Loy replaced stage actors Frances Fuller and Lora Baxter as Daisy Sage and Cecilia. Myrna Loy remem-bered the experience in her memoirs many years later:

> My maid ... fixed scrambled eggs laced with garlic sausage before I left for the studio. The test went well, but Leslie Howard seemed constrained, unusually stand-offish. 'What did Leslie Howard think of me?' I asked Ned. 'He thought you were very good,' Ned answered, 'but wondered if you always eat so much garlic.' Leslie was not only a fastidious Englishman, I learned later, but a vege-tarian, very persnickety about food. The smell of those sausages had made him quite ill, but of course he bore it like the gentleman he was. Oh, working with Leslie was heaven ... *heaven*. What a strong, brilliant actor, yet how easily he seemed to accomplish it, always taking time to encourage me, to ease me into a role that would be another big step away from exotica. We grew very fond of one another on that picture. I mean, it could have been a real scrambola – if I'd allowed it to be. Leslie was far more impetuous than his gentle screen image indicated. That cool, lean exterior belied a passionate nature, which manifested itself on the set. I resisted the temptation, so he stormed my house, imploring me to run away with him to the South Seas. He really wanted to chuck everything and take off. And don't think he wasn't persuasive. But he was married, and I didn't go in for that sort of thing. Besides, Arthur [Loy's fiancée], who happened to be in New York on busi-ness, returned in the nick of time. But, oh, I *loved* Leslie.[26]

As his name became familiar, Leslie settled into the social life in both New York and Hollywood. While the play ran on Broadway, he spoke at actors' guilds and societies, presided at charity matinees and attended events in aid of Depression-struck colleagues. One all-night ping-pong tournament at the Algonquin included most of the British actors in town, with Nigel Bruce, Edna Best and others, and was followed by a round-robin telegram from them all to British Equity, congratulating the actors' union in supporting the right of foreign actors to play on the London stage. It seems to have been Leslie's idea.[27] He also took time out to direct another Broadway play for his friends Geoffrey Kerr and Ilka Chase (*We Are No Longer Children*), but this lasted only a few weeks. Increasingly bored with the long run of the play *The Animal Kingdom*, Leslie also let loose in *The New York Times* with an article entitled, 'Why Must the Show Go On and On?' in which he asserted, 'twelve weeks I regard as the ideal run for an intelligent actor, and twenty weeks is the absolute maximum beyond which can only lie lunacy and stagnation.' Leslie went on to defend Noel Coward, whose play *Hay Fever* was also running on Broadway. Coward had acted in the play, but refused to prolong his stay, and had been strongly criticised by his producer. Leslie argued, 'Mr Coward is actor, writer, director and general man of the theatre, but he takes his work in small doses and lives in between so that he does not suffer the horror of routined art.'[28]

In the course of the long article, Leslie happened to cite, 'the unfortunate cases of first-class actor-managers such as Fred Terry, Julia Neilson and John Martin-Harvey, who for decades have toured the English provinces with the same plays because the public happened to be willing to go on seeing them again and again.' Leslie's views were no doubt a small talking point for the profession, many of whom agreed with him about long runs, and the article caused no particular ripple. However, a fortnight later an accusing ghost, not quite risen from the grave, replied to repudiate the charge. It was Sir John Martin-Harvey (aged 69), spluttering with indignation.[29] *The New York Times* gleefully highlighted his letter, but in view of the fact that he had previously boasted of appearing in the same play, *The Only Way*, more than 3,000 times, Leslie may have had a point. Leslie withdrew from *The Animal Kingdom* in June, and left for Hollywood to complete the film version, together with another production for MGM, *Smilin' Through*, a senti-mental vehicle for Norma Shearer.

He had also been asked by Mary Pickford to partner her in *Secrets*, her own production. Leslie later claimed that he was astonished to be offered this part – a rancher in the Wild West, shooting it out with ban-dits – and blamed local agent Mike Levy for negotiating it. But Miss

Pickford was held in great respect by Hollywood, and this was to be her last film. *Secrets* has great interest for her poignant acting, especially in the central scene playing a bereaved mother. But her powerful silent-film style unbalances the picture, and the original story had been unhappily reworked. The film did poorly at the box office, and Miss Pickford entered her long retirement. Leslie gained only a new agent, Mike Levy, (also known as Levee) well known in Hollywood, who became a friend and remained with him, helping to mediate Leslie's frequent dissatisfaction with the industry's ways.

Luckily, the film of *The Animal Kingdom* was as successful as the play, and in the doldrums of the Depression set a box office record that lasted for years. Leslie had looked rather fragile in the film, and indeed his habits of fussy eating and dieting, together with constant smoking to keep his appetite down, were beginning to affect his health. He was rescued by a new enthusiasm, or rather an old one that he now had money to indulge – polo, a popular sport amongst the wealthy stars in California. Leslie joined the Riviera club, starting with a handicap of zero (absolute beginners starting at minus two for some reason) and worked his way up to be quite a respectable player, in what was a strenuous and difficult sport. The club became a social centre, popular with the show-business world, notable other players including Spencer Tracy, Walt Disney and Darryl Zanuck.

Leslie was also a member of the Hollywood Cricket Club, which had been founded in 1931 by P.G. Wodehouse and his old friend Aubrey Smith as captain. It consisted largely of members of the 'British Colony' of actors in Hollywood. Leslie only joined to be sociable, as he had little interest in cricket and disliked the game, although it is doubtful whether he would have explained this to his craggy and imposing captain. In any case, he spent more and more of his time buying polo horses and involving himself in this sport. He and his wife also entertained moderately and enjoyed the sights and scenes of Hollywood, including a visit to San Simeon, the home of William Randolph Hearst, where Leslie adamantly refused Hearst's offer of another film with Marion Davies, and the company of British and American actors and their families, including Ronald Colman, Mary Astor, Herbert Marshall, Nigel Bruce, and the Gargans.[30]

Mike Levy hustled to move Leslie's career along, and arranged a contract with Warner Brothers which called for three pictures a year for three years. Leslie agreed to slightly less pay in exchange for a larger say in which films he would choose. He also grumbled at the commitment, but he was far luckier than other contract players, who had signed on for years and could have their time indefinitely extended if they refused a poor script. The contract was never completed, but then such contracts often were not, usually because the studio dropped the actor. In this case, Leslie simply refused to churn out poor product, and he never had time to complete nine films for the studio.

Early in 1933, Leslie started on a prestige effort for Warner, *Captured*, the story of a First World War prison camp, also starring Douglas Fairbanks Jnr. There was a huge publicity campaign for this, but when it was shown, it was clear that it had missed the public mood. The Depression-hit country had lost interest in the last war and no one wanted to hear about the atrocities in German prison camps (especially not the five million Germans who had come to the States between 1850 and 1920). An unlikely love triangle tacked onto the grimly realistic scenes (First World War survivors were on hand to advise) did little to improve matters, and the film eventually sank without trace, despite good reviews for the actors. Leslie himself enjoyed the change of pace, as an unshaven, machine-gun-toting, fist-fighting prisoner of war, and made a convincing enough show of it.

After this, he turned to a film of *Berkeley Square* (1933) for Fox Studios. This had been Leslie's great stage triumph, but the film version is disappointing. Without his magical stage presence, which has not translated to film, it gives evidence only of his ability to turn dross into gold. Leslie had made the play seem hauntingly otherworldly, but the film seems only aimless and vague. Good supporting character acting is missing, and the leading lady chosen for the film, Heather Angel, has none of the luminous qualities of the stage actresses Jean Forbes Robertson and Margalo Gillmore. As part of the film's press release, Fox researchers claimed to have followed a contemporary photograph of Berkeley Square found in the Smithsonian Institute. The diligence of the researchers seems dubious, as the film sets are around one hundred years out for the tale set in the 1700s, complete with lamp posts, first invented in 1820.

Leslie sailed back to London for the summer, having agreed to appear in Gilbert Miller's first attempt at film directing, and as it turned out, his last. This was *The Lady Is Willing* (1934) at Denham Studios for Columbia. Film production was picking up slightly in Britain as the American studios realized that better quality films there could be made profitable, and studios and technical facilities were slowly becoming more professional, but production was still split between quality and quota films.[31]

This film, however, turned out to be one where cast and crew have more fun than the eventual audience. Leslie played a private eye, complete with his favourite selection of false moustaches; other players were from a list of top English actors, Leslie's young brother Arthur joined the cast, and high jinks were had by all. Filming took place at Denham, Korda's studio, and Korda's austere production manager, David Cunynghame, watched the disaster develop without much amusement. Columbia, headed by the autocrat Harry Cohn, had insisted on two other directors, Cyril Gardner and Lewis Milestone, to keep an eye on the inexperienced Gilbert Miller. This was two cooks too many. In addition Cohn, not the most tolerant of the Hollywood moguls, had taken a break from his home operation and was prowling around Denham, supervising every penny of the budget.[32] Cunynghame kept a daily diary throughout his years with Korda, and the entries for *The Lady is Willing* are as follows:

> July 6th 1933. Had meeting with Harry Cohn and Gilbert Miller. Read script of their picture, *The Lady is Willing*. Thought it bad.
>
> July 19th. (1st day of shooting) Three directors, Miller, Milestone and Gardner making things a bit tough!
>
> July 20th. Milestone changed one of Gardner's set ups thus losing 1¼ hours of shooting time.
>
> July 22nd. Progress retarded by having both Milestone and Gardner assisting Miller.
>
> July 25th. Late start due to Howard's non-arrival till 9:45.
>
> July 26th. Binnie Barnes [the leading lady] wants to quit the picture because of too many directors.
>
> August 3rd. Continual script conferences eventually resulted in the picture being called off until Tuesday next in order to give time for re-writing. Cohn very tactless with weekly staff whom he wished to 'lay-off' for four days. He has only managed to save £2 on this.
>
> August 7th. In the evening attended a script conference on *The Lady is Willing*. Found chaotic conditions.
>
> August 15th (22nd shooting day). Becoming increasingly difficult to complete the picture owing to the lethargy of all concerned. The electricians are so far obdurate with regard to their 'knocking-off' time – walking out on us at 7:30 in between takes of a shot.
>
> Jan 2nd 1934. Attended trade show of *The Lady is willing*. I thought the picture terribly bad.[33]

A pity, as actors of the calibre of Cedric Hardwicke were wasted. It was also delightful comedian Nigel Playfair's last film appearance. The British cinema press tactfully said as little as possible, the film never reappeared after the trade show, and has now been lost to an indifferent posterity.

Leslie took much more trouble over the play he had been considering for some months, *This Side Idolatry*, by Talbot Jennings, a witty imagining of Shakespeare's life. This was given some fanfare, and the opening night was attended by a number of famous Shakespearian players such as Sir Frank Benson and Sir Philip Ben Greet. The first-night reviews included some impressive quotes from them, judging that it was, 'the finest performance' of Leslie's career. Whether this was the usual show-business politeness is not clear, as critical response was also good. But the production was not judged a success, and Leslie went back to America at the end of 1933 with little reward for his work in England.

A friend of Leslie, Robert Bruce Lockhart, visited him and Gilbert Miller back stage on the first night, recording in his memories, 'I had liked the play, but the astute Gilbert Miller knew at once that it was a flop. It was a blow to Leslie.' Lockhart described how enthusiastic Leslie was on the subject of the theatre: 'On this subject he could talk brilliantly, and I remember one evening when he told me with passion all the reforms he wanted to make'.[34] Some consolation awaited in America, as *Berkeley Square* was named as one of the best films of the year, and Leslie was one of three nominees for the Best Actor Oscar (won by Clark Gable for *It Happened One Night*).

Back in America for Christmas 1933, Leslie found Warner Brothers and the other studios coping with the double blows of the financial depression and the new Hays Production Code, headed by Will Hays, a politician and ex-postmaster general who was now appointed film arbiter. There were salary cuts all round, but they did not last long. The Code was a longer-term problem, but despite all the protests, something of the sort was needed. Although it now seems impossibly prissy in sexual matters, it was appropriate for the time. It also operated to repress scenes of violence, and one of the first films affected by it was *Baby Face* (1933), which had some brutal scenes and sexual sadism removed. The code bowdlerised many classics before it faded out, but contemporary critics may wonder how far the pendulum has swung.

Leslie's next film, *Of Human Bondage*, was never going to pass unscathed through Mr Hays' viewing room. The original novel was really poor film material, the interest lying more in Maugham's account of his own life, as protagonist Philip Carey, than in any striking story-line. Carey's doomed romance with Mildred, a cardboard monster, was transmuted from Maugham's own homosexual experiences. Mildred's ultimate death from syphilis while working as a London prostitute was just as unmentionable at this time.

But the difficulty of the original material cannot have been wholly to blame for the uninspired, slow-moving screenplay and awkward dialogue. No better use of the camera is found than to focus on hand-written letters to forward the plot, there are heavily telegraphed 'message' scenes and an intrusive musical accompaniment. Even a shot that makes the most of leading lady Bette Davis's enormous blue eyes is irritatingly done. The talkies were still young, but many productions did far better than this. Its only saving graces were the authentic atmosphere created, and the performances of the leading actors, which both gave the film interest, but for very different reasons.

Leslie had agreed to do the film early in 1933 for RKO, but was surprised by the announcement later in the year that Bette Davis, borrowed from Warner Brothers, had been chosen for his leading lady. None of RKO's leading ladies wished to play the deeply unsympathetic part of Mildred, a cockney waitress. Leslie thought that an American actress playing the part could never seem authentic. He was right, but in the event it didn't matter. He did make his feelings known at the start of the film, upsetting Miss Davis, who never forgot the slight. But Leslie rapidly changed his mind after he had seen the first rushes.

Bette had unmistakable star quality, and she made a career break-through with this film, but all the same, her heavily mannered style as the 'cockney' waitress sorts ill with Leslie's quieter playing. She has some well-realized scenes as her character ages and hardens, and achieved such a supreme hatefulness in the climactic scene as Mildred scorns Philip that contemporary audiences were said to have cheered at Mildred's death. No other actress had ever attempted such an openly vicious display of spite, and the scene is still shocking now. Leslie's Philip Carey seems to play ever more in contrast, and is the most gentle portrayal in all Leslie's films. His emotional points are made with economy, especially in a scene where the oversensitive Carey has to reveal his club foot to a crowd of medical students. Even so, Leslie seems a little shell-shocked at Davis' onslaught by the end of the film. The novelty of the performances earned the film some respect, and both actors received approving notices.

Bette played in two more films with Leslie, *The Petrified Forest* and

It's Love I'm After. Each time her acting was quieter and more confident, and the final film is the most light-hearted either of them ever achieved, although Bette always remained ambivalent in her memories of Leslie.

After a holiday break, Leslie moved on to *British Agent*, taken from a recent best seller describing a real-life spy's adventures during the Russian revolution of 1917. The narrator, Robert Bruce Lockhart, was agreeable to selling the film copyright to Warner Brothers. But he was not too happy at the usual Hollywood distortion of his book, which described actual historical events. As part of the discussion of the script, Lockhart met Leslie a few months before the film was to be made, and later remembered, 'I owed much to Leslie, whom I saw frequently in those days and who had been most helpful in preventing Hollywood from making a bigger travesty of my book than they did. He told me ... that at one time he had nearly thrown over his part.'[35]

Leslie and Lockhart became friendly and met several times in both America and England, but the film, shown in early 1934, was not a great success. It did worse business in England as the censor refused to pass a bogus but exciting scene of 'Lockhart' haranguing the British Cabinet and Prime Minister Lloyd George.

Leslie sailed home again for another Korda picture, *The Scarlet Pimpernel*, in the summer of 1934. On board ship was the playwright Robert Sherwood, who was helping with the script of the film. Sherwood was also pondering his next play, *The Petrified Forest*, and he and Leslie had some long discussions about it. The storm had been brewing in Europe. Hitler had been elected to power as a virtual dictator at the start of 1933. The Jews had always been targeted by the Nazis, but now viciously repressive measures were in place. Some news of the horror had been passed on by those immigrants who had sufficient funds to escape, but since doors to America and England had been closed at the end of the 1920s, there were not many. Among these last-minute immigrants were some famous names, including Arnold Schoenberg, Franz Werfel, Erich Maria Remarque and numbers of others prominent in the artistic world of Germany and Austria. Many had no particular interest in their Jewish background, but it made no difference. Fifty-nine German screenwriters, thirty-three directors and nineteen composers were helped to escape to Hollywood studios. Eventually there were questions from a hostile American Immigration Service. Of the studio moguls, Carl Laemmle helped 250 German Jews to come to the US until his affidavits were finally refused by immigration. Producer

Sam Goldwyn tried to get his sister and her husband out of Poland, but they died in Treblinka concentration camp.[36] Even Tallulah Bankhead stopped partying for a moment and used her family's diplomatic connections to help film producer Otto Preminger and his brother to safety.[37] But people who understood what was happening in Europe, and were willing to help, were few indeed.

Leslie had heard some of the stories. The Jews were helpless in the face of the violence against them. The Nazis stole their businesses and property, and Jews were no longer allowed to earn a living. Shops refused to sell them food or medicine. Faced with watching their children starve to death in front of them, unaided by their neighbours, many committed suicide. But most people in America and Britain simply could not believe what was happening. Astonishingly little was reported in the national press and even so most thought such 'atrocity stories' were exaggerations.

Alexander Korda, with whom Leslie would now make his film, had contacts all over Europe. He used his film scouts abroad to provide help for Jewish emigrants. Many brilliant technicians from the former Ufa studios in Berlin were helped to come over – actors, playwrights, anyone Korda could assist. Michael Balcon, and Isidore Ostrer of the Gaumont-British Picture Corporation, were doing the same. As in America there was an outcry against these arrivals, this time protests from British film workers, who resented potential jobs being filled by outsiders, no matter that the immigrants had much to teach them in skills and experience. As Leslie and Robert Sherwood worked at Denham, which gradually filled up with refugees, they were made aware of how desperate the situation was becoming.[38]

Others were more concerned about Germany's mass rearming. Winston Churchill MP, a lone prophet at this time, found his warning words in the House of Commons were hardly attended to. Leslie's daughter recorded some of her father's actions at this time, presumably using her mother's memories: 'In London Leslie met and talked with some of the few who believed in Churchill's warning. The people who had been to Germany and knew the fierce aggressive power growing there. Leslie went himself, and he too was made to fear. Late were the discussions of an evening round the fire at Stowe Maries.'[39]

Leslie's trip to Germany must have been very low key. Also mysterious are the men that Leslie met in London. There were few who supported Churchill, and most had to do so behind the scenes, as Churchill was not in office and not entitled to receive military or government information.

But he did.[40] One of his helpers was Robert Vansittart, permanent under-secretary at the Foreign Office till Chamberlain removed him in 1937, who had visited Germany himself and received information from that country. Vansittart had an estate at Denham village and became a close friend of Korda's.[41]

Other pro-Americans now known to be anti-Chamberlain and pro-American, some of whom secretly helped Churchill with information and other resources at this time, were politicians Duff Cooper, Anthony Eden, Dick Law, and Jim Thomas; public officials Lord Cranborne, Ralph Wigram, Rex Leeper and Robert Bruce Lockhart; American socialite Ronald Tree; and journalist Victor Gordon Lennox, who worked with American press representatives such as Vincent Sheean and Ed Murrow.[42]

Robert Bruce Lockhart, in his book *Friends, Foes and Foreigners*, describes his friendship with Leslie at exactly this time, just before Leslie was due to film *The Scarlet Pimpernel*. Lockhart was closely associated with Rex Leeper, head of information and propaganda at the Foreign Office. Leeper had been a close friend of Lockhart for years, since rescuing him from almost certain death in Soviet Russia. Both Lockhart and Leeper worked together later, during the war, in the Political Warfare Executive, concerned with aiming propaganda at the enemy.

At the end of 1934, Leeper managed to found the British Council, in the face of Chamberlain's complete opposition to a British anti-Nazi case being put to other countries – most importantly, in America. As Churchill and many others knew, America would be vitally important in the coming war. And America was being bombarded by Nazi propaganda and pro-fascist groups were forming in every city. The Nazi cause there had powerful advocates in well-known American figures.

Leeper's stated aim for his new British Council was 'cultural propaganda'. Leslie and Korda were just about to provide some. It is easy to speculate that both of them were asked to do what they could in this field. When Leslie went to London, the most likely topic was the one he was most qualified to give advice on – British propaganda in America. But both Leslie and any confederates knew that it was necessary to be extremely careful abroad. America was hugely averse to being warned about German ambitions, especially by the devious British who had 'tricked' them into the First World War. Rex Leeper was prepared to be unorthodox in his methods, and Bruce Lockhart, associated with secret service most of his life, even more so. It is possible that Leslie was encouraged to consider a prestige performance of the greatest play in the British canon – *Hamlet*. Or he could have been asked for his advice on setting up the Council, which came into existence at this time.

The English Speaking Union (of which Churchill was a founder) was another organization quietly promoting British–American friendship in America. They too at this time thought that Shakespeare plays from British actors were a good reminder of what had emerged from a culture now at risk. Leslie was later to speak from this platform in the States, as did other British actors respected in America. The ESU was open in its hatred of fascism (and communist dictators), in its opinion that British and American interests were the same, and that the two countries should draw together.[43]

For none of those named above, known to be in Churchill's orbit, does there remain any memoir, note, letter, or paper which contains the faintest reference to Leslie Howard in the early and mid-1930s. There is nothing in the Churchill archives. In fact many of the memories of that time seem absent or indistinct. The only connection that can be traced is that to Lockhart, who, after describing in his contemporary diaries his friendship with Leslie from 1933 to 1934, says that he never saw Leslie again, even though they were both working in the propaganda trade throughout the war. The editor of Lockhart's diaries states that some passages were removed from the published edition, in the interests of national security. Lockhart was certainly capable of factual economy, but there seems to be no reason why he would specifically state that he never had contact with Leslie after 1934 if this was not true.[44] There is therefore no evidence in existence, unless it remains to be made public, that Leslie was instructed by those standing with Churchill in the shadows, and yet, soon after, Leslie took on a very great responsibility in acting against Prime Minister Chamberlain's American policy. If he acted solely on his own initiative as a patriotic Englishman, it is remarkable that he did so.

It was clear from the start that *The Scarlet Pimpernel* had an agenda other than pure entertainment. On 26 July 1934 *Kinematograph Weekly* reported:

> *The Scarlet Pimpernel* starts filming this week. The English sequences of the film will show us a picture of England happy and opulent, contrasted with the seething turmoil of the rest of Europe at that time ... Alexander Korda says he is more interested in showing something of the unique position held by England at

that time than a mere catalogue of the Pimpernel's exploits in France.

The film equated the Terror in revolutionary France with that of modern Germany, but it was not a message anyone wanted to hear. It was Korda's longest and costliest production since his big hit, *The Private Life of Henry VIII* (1933). Korda took over at an early stage from its initial director, Rowland Brown, and thereafter supervised the film, although Harold Young was credited. The script credits went to Lajos Biro, a Hungarian playwright and novelist and Korda's great friend and mentor, followed by Sam Behrman, Robert Sherwood and Arthur Wimperis. Biro and Behrman (credited as Berman) were Jewish.

As a publicity note, Baroness Orczy, then living in England and the author of the original novel, was associated with the film, although she had nothing to do with the screenplay, and in fact was dissatisfied that the completed film differed from her book. There were a few alterations. For example, in the novel's climactic scene, the Pimpernel disguises himself as a Jew to help his wife escape, and is described as 'an elderly Jew, in a dirty threadbare gabardine, worn greasy across the shoulders ... he had the habitual stoop those of his despised race affected in mock humility'.[45] Instead of this portrayal, which was absolutely nothing out of the ordinary for the popular literature of the day, right up to the 1930s, Leslie and Korda inserted a couple of scenes, not in the book and apropos of nothing in particular. The Scarlet Pimpernel and the Prince of Wales are shown at an open-air boxing match, shouting for one of the fighters, 'Mendoza'. Following this, the Pimpernel is shown at home, describing the match to his indifferent wife Marguerite: 'Magnificent fight this afternoon my dear. Zounds, that fellow Mendoza has fifty lives. In the tenth round when Jackson had him down I shouted 'Get up Mendoza!' And damme he did! And sink me he won!'

Daniel Mendoza (1764–1836) was a real-life figure, a Sephardi Jew, and heavy-weight champion of England for most years from 1788 until 1795. Mendoza was a popular character who introduced a new 'scientific' style of boxing, and was famed throughout the country as a skilled and courageous fighter. A favourite of the Prince of Wales, he was the first boxer to be accorded royal patronage. He billed himself as 'Mendoza the Jew'.

Another complete departure from the Baroness was the final scene, in which the Pimpernel quotes John of Gaunt's speech from Shakespeare's *Richard II*:

Figure 19. Daniel Mendoza, Heavyweight boxing champion of Great Britain, 1792–95.

> This other Eden, demi-paradise,
> This fortress built by nature for herself
> Against infection and the hand of war,
> This happy breed of men, this little world,
> This precious stone set in the silver sea ...
> This blessed plot, this earth, this realm, this England!

It was a piece that set the tone for many later war films.

But the overall impression of this film is one of great fun – it is lavishly handsome, with costumes by Oliver Messel and settings by Vincent Korda. Leslie is unmatchably insouciant as the Pimpernel, Merle Oberon as Marguerite his wife is lovely if a little wooden, and Nigel Bruce as the Prince of Wales, Raymond Massey as Chauvelin and all the character actors play up merrily. Leslie's unique portrayal relies almost wholly on his voice, marvellously modulated and expressive,

Figure 20. *The Scarlet Pimpernel*, 1934. Leslie with Merle Oberon.

to convey emotion, while using hardly any facial expression or body movement. As a result he looks the coolest character on the screen, especially with Massey mugging away heavily as the dastardly Chauvelin.

On 21 December 1934 *The New York Times* correspondent in London cabled his paper that '*The Scarlet Pimpernel* is considered the best film ever to emerge from a British film studio'. The London *Times* unbent so far as to say that 'the spirit of the book is in it'. The film was a huge success in Britain and America (although Leslie's juicy playing of the fop, Sir Percy, gave rise to some rude catcalls in the more working-class cinemas). Korda allowed the film to be screened for free for American charities in some venues, to add to the goodwill.

Filming had taken place in a very unhurried manner throughout a sunny summer, during which Leslie performed his usual trick of falling in love with his leading lady, who seemed to reciprocate this time. As the two flaunted their romance all over London, Leslie's adoration for Merle Oberon became rather embarrassing for onlookers. David Cunynghame, Korda's head of production, asked them to lunch together and gently hinted that they might tone it down a little.[46] Robert Bruce Lockhart remembered seeing them together at a popular restaurant, and commented, 'we [he was with Michael Colefax] went round to Leslie Howard's table and had a talk – he was with Merle Oberon ... Leslie seemed very devoted to her'.[47]

Leslie was living two lives, as ever. His companion marriage had held for some years, and in a sense always would. But Leslie needed someone closer, both mentally and physically. His wife did not fully understand his new aims, and was not able to be the supporter or confidante he needed now. Merle had a quality that Leslie had first seen in his wife – she was self-possessed, she could stand alone. She was also intelligent, liberal-minded and very much opposed to the Nazis – but she was not a woman in love. The affair continued as they both returned to America for other work, but when Merle forced the issue by asking him to leave his family, Leslie demurred. It was a little late. Because they knew he had considered it, both his wife and his children were deeply hurt.

The Scarlet Pimpernel's scriptwriter, Robert Sherwood, sailed back to America on 26 September 1934, and gave *The New York Times* his truthful but not entirely tactful views on British theatre and film: 'The theatrical scene here is dull because the plays are listless, and the London Theatre is a pretty anaemic institution. Also the movie business in England is entering on a terrific boom, but that is because it is largely backed by American capital, so it cannot really be called competition.'[48]

Wilfred Noy, Leslie's uncle, also returned home at this time, looking towards his retirement after a long film career in England and
America. Interviewed in the *Kinematograph Weekly* of 11 October
1934, he gave his opinion that Britain needed most of all more skilled
technicians in order to catch up with America. Noy also suggested that
the encouragement of young screenwriters might be an idea for the
future, and some sort of training and education in the film trade would
be a good idea. No one took the slightest notice. They were busy
enjoying a boom – or so they thought – in British film-making, with
unprecedented interest and activity. Korda had led the way, starting
with his huge hit, *The Private Life of Henry VIII* (1933) which had at
last seen American acceptance for British offerings. Followed by *The
Scarlet Pimpernel* and others, the British industry, helped of course
by American money and expertise, seemed to be finally on its feet.
Financers were now eager to throw money at the film-makers.

It was a dangerous atmosphere, as there were opportunities for
exploitation by unscrupulous businessmen who could easily pull the wool
over the eyes of these new money men. Such a person was Max Schach,
another Jewish escapee, who would have better found another refuge. He
was trusted with large sums to found a new production company, and
managed to squander them all, disappearing after the ensuing scandal.
The Jews in the industry had to cope with the bad feeling, the last thing
they needed at this point.[49] Korda in his way hadn't helped, because
his lavish lifestyle – clothes from Savile Row, Rolls Royces everywhere,
lobsters and champagne all round at The Dorchester – helped to fuel
resentment and distrust. Perhaps all the over-consumption harked back
to his poverty-stricken childhood in rural Hungary. But there were
other problems. New legislation was due to tighten film quotas again,
and no one quite knew what the effect would be. As the financiers
realized with surprise that not every film made was going to be a success and make large sums of money, they lost confidence. Korda, the
only real British movie mogul, lost control of his own studio, Denham,
in 1938, as financial backing dried up.

So the boom would turn to bust in a few short years. After the new
Cinematograph Films Act 1938, production dropped sharply, but by
no means was all lost. A new industry had already been founded – not
enormous, but with some opportunities for the talent that was there in
abundance. There were more troubled waters ahead. Where companies
were owned by Jews, or were largely Jewish-run, they came under
attack from Nazi supporters, especially Mosley's Blackshirts. Jewish

distributors and studio and cinema owners were accused by Mosley of suppressing fascist views. After an incident where Paramount News Film interviewed Mosley, Herbert Morrison MP and the Reverend R.M. Zeffert to give their opposing views, Mosley's interview did not appear in the cinemas. Isidore Ostrer, owner of Gaumont British Company, was a particular target.[50]

Ostrer and other Jewish figures in the industry were faced with the choice of providing a platform for those who advocated their destruction, or being accused of giving a politically biased news information service in a democratic country. Ostrer eventually sold out all his interests and moved abroad, so that no one could accuse him of even backstage influence. By this time there were rumours without end, and without sense, of Jewish conspiracies in every sphere of life.

The American film industry faced a similar problem. Not only were most of the heads of the studios Jewish, but so were many executives, producers, directors and technicians. But they could not solve the issue by abandoning their interests. Without them the whole massive structure of the film industry, a huge American asset which employed thousands countrywide in all its ramifications, would collapse. They could hardly advocate an anti-Nazi course in a country which in the 1930s was largely isolationist and anti-Semitic. The heads of the American studios have since been blamed for not actively supporting the Jewish cause, but it was impossible for them to do so. They also had large interests in the German cinema, but if they had withdrawn them all wholesale there would have been an international incident and a huge outcry. They dared not make any political statement while America was neutral. More to blame were owners of radio stations and newspapers, who had no stake in the matter but were also silent on the Nazi treatment of Jews, and not for reasons of political objectivity.

The American studios could do nothing openly until March 1938, when the Rumrich spy trial in New York exposed the American Bunds[51] as proponents and spies for Nazi Germany, acting under Hitler's directions. The trial was given national publicity. At once the studios leapt into action, with Warner Brothers producing the film *Confessions of a Nazi Spy*, a very lightly fictionalized account of the events uncovered in the trial. The film was made in a documentary style, containing newsreel shots of Hitler and a highly unflattering impersonation of Joseph Goebbels, the propaganda minister. When the film came out, swastikas were painted on the film poster outside many cinemas. At the same time MGM dusted off Sinclair Lewis's *It Can't Happen Here*, Chaplin started

Isadore Ostrer, who is the Ras of Gaumont "British," the vast Jewish combine, which decides to what point of view British Cinema audiences may listen. The tentacles of Ostrer stretch out and cover most of the British Cinema industry and thus he is, to all intents and purposes, the film dictator of Britain. His reign will end when Fascism comes to power. Then only the British outlook will be placed before British audiences for their judgment.

Figure 21. Isidore Ostrer. From *The Blackshirt*, 31 October 1936, p.5.

on *The Great Dictator*, independent producer Al Rosen was working on a Hitler biography, *The Mad Dog of Europe*, and Paramount announced *Heil America*, the cast and director of which had to remain secret during production to save them from death threats from Nazi supporters.[52]

Leslie was looking for likely propaganda vehicles from the mid-1930s. It did not provide the best artistic motive, as he would learn. He sailed back to America and went straight into rehearsals for Robert Sherwood's new play, *The Petrified Forest*. On the way home, Leslie stopped off in Italy, where fascist dictator Mussolini was providing a gross imitation of Hitler.[53]

The Petrified Forest, when it appeared in January 1935, rather confused critics, as no one admitted to knowing exactly what the play was about. On the face of it, the message is clear enough – that men of action were needed for the times ahead, and the time for intellectual debate, pacifism and self-examination was over. The author, Robert Sherwood, had fought bravely in the First World War, and had suffered all the reaction from that horror. Pacifism seemed the only proper response for mankind then, and so he had believed for many years. Now that view was shifting. He eventually became a passionate advocate in the Allied cause. He also worked with the British Political Warfare Executive with Robert Bruce Lockhart and Rex Leeper, providing liaison to the Office of War Information, the American equivalent, and having the ear of Roosevelt. But Sherwood was still taking the first steps in his altered view. He never lost his hatred of war, and his contempt for those who would bring it about. But as this play states, 'Nature is proving that she can't be beaten – not by the likes of us. She's taking the world away from the intellectuals and giving it back to the apes.' At the time, Sherwood felt that he had not fully worked out his ideas. Of this play, he claimed that, 'I start with a big message and end up with nothing but good entertainment.'[54] Possibly he felt the need to be cagey about admitting a direct propaganda message.

The Petrified Forest follows the adventures of Alan Squier, a drifting poet and intellectual, who can find no particular aim in life. He is set against a background of rural America, at a lonely Arizona filling station on the way to a petrified forest in the desert. Squier arrives penniless, and meets a collection of American character types, more or less ineffectual or living in the past. The only bright spark is the young daughter of the place, Gaby, whose passion about literature and hopes for the future take Squier's interest. A gang of criminals on the run turn up to provide the means for him to help her. In an intensely romantic ending, Squier wills Gaby a last insurance policy (which he happens to have about him) in order to give her the chance to study and travel; he then asks the leader of the mobsters to shoot him. This man, Duke Mantee, is portrayed with some sympathy, as a decent man according to his lights. The whole was a wonderful formula for self-sacrificing hero-ism all round, and the references to modern (T.S. Eliot) and classic (François Villon) poetry added to the attractive mix.

The first-night premiere, on 7 January 1935, was a smash hit. Leslie of course portrayed Alan Squier, and the actor playing Duke Mantee was a young Humphrey Bogart. The critics loved it, the audience practically rioted, Leslie was mobbed outside the theatre by women determined to cut off his trouser buttons (fans seem to have been more direct in those days) and the show was set to run on and on. It was eventually nominated for a Pulitzer Prize, but rejected. The reason given was that the play was successful due to the acting, not the content. This must have enraged Sher-wood, but it is possible that the critics detected some propaganda behind the play, and strongly disapproved.

Leslie was co-producer, with a share in the profits, which was his custom when he partnered Gilbert Miller. He therefore was caught between making more money as the show went on, and experiencing his usual tedium at long runs. At least he did not have to tour, as he refused to do so. Sherwood wouldn't have been pleased with that either. Whether it was these annoyances, or a reaction to yet another burst of grumbling from Leslie in the press about how he disliked acting and long runs, Sherwood came out some months later, in a piece about the state of the theatre, with a perfect gem of malice:

> Katherine Cornell is devoted to the theatre and its art ... Helen Hayes seems to regard the theatre much as a champion mountain climber regards Everest ... Leslie Howard on the other hand, regards the theatre as a rather dreary factory in which the artist labours only long enough to make money to fulfil his true purposes in life, which are Polo and fox-hunting. Presumably the movies are preferable because with them fulfilment comes more quickly.[55]

Actually it was Leslie Ruth who enjoyed fox hunting, but this is not the voice of a friend. Nor a co-conspirator, if propaganda was their mutual aim. Sherwood amended his views a little in later years, and summing up his work with Leslie commented,

> Leslie Howard was a brilliant, sensitive, natural actor. He was also one of the most thoroughly unreliable artists that I have ever known.

> You could not count on him to show up for a rehearsal or even for
> a performance after the play had opened. Nor could you count
> on him, once the play had been established, to deliver the lines as
> written and not ad lib improvisations in order to relieve himself of
> doing the same things night after night. I knew Leslie for a long time
> – from his first arrival in New York to appear in *Just Suppose* in 1920
> ... I don't think I ever saw him give a bad performance.[56]

Sherwood's judgement on Leslie's professionalism was exaggerated. But
in this particular production, a certain sort of trouble was brewing. Merle
Oberon arrived in New York from Hollywood, where she had been making a film, *Folies Bergere,* on 26 January. A few days later, on 5 February,
Leslie was reported to be in hospital, too ill for that night's show. Merle
had wanted to know if their romance was anything more than a location
fling – would Leslie leave his wife, as he had no doubt vaguely promised? Leslie would not, but the nervous strain imposed gave him a nasty
outbreak of skin ailments – painful boils, bad enough to make him fever-
ish and need medical care. Not a romantic affliction, and Leslie continued to suffer from this for months. Merle took herself off, never much
moved by her affairs, leaving Leslie to repair the rents in his marriage.

Boils or not, Leslie was at the height of his fame and popularity. In
April he gave a press conference at the Broadhurst Theatre for 300 high
school and college journalists. Leslie seemed to be trying to reach out
to young Americans, as he did on his later *Hamlet* tour. He patiently
answered every question, although not with complete frankness, about
his acting ambitions and his opinion of films and the theatre. Asked if he
wished to play Hamlet, Leslie only replied that every actor does. The
most interesting question asked him was on propaganda. *The New York
Times* reported, 'He circled a discussion of propaganda by declaring the
theatre essentially a place for entertainment and relaxation, and took
occasion to register one vote against Sunday performances.'[57]

Leslie had to be exceptionally careful. It was an odd time – America
was happy to be harangued on many issues, including the rights of
Germany to *Lebensraum*, but if anyone dared to put the opposing case,
they were shouted down with horrified accusations of propaganda. The
word had then and still carries confusing associations, and its stigma was
used very cleverly by supporters of Fascism. Even so, Leslie did speak at
a Princeton meeting of the English Speaking Union, on 7 May 1935. The
ESU was very frank in its advocacy of an American–British alliance against
the Nazi dictators. It even ventured to speak of the oppression of the Jews.
But the subject of Leslie's talk was not reported by the newspapers.[58]

Leslie appeared at many venues at this time; for the Catholic and Episcopalian actors' guilds, at charitable performances, for Talking Books for the Blind. He continued to play polo, and was watched by an amazing 14,000 people at a match at Fort Hamilton near New York. He contracted for radio work, and he and his 12-year-old daughter Leslie Ruth gave a performance of Barrie's *Dear Brutus*, which was so popular it had to be repeated, unusual then. His interests were followed breathlessly by the press, and his hope to play T.E. Lawrence (Lawrence of Arabia) for Korda's company, for 'patriotic reasons', was announced in May. Warner Brothers reminded him that he still owed them eight films by contract, and acquired the film rights to *The Petrified Forest*, which Leslie agreed to start when the play ended. In June 1935 came the announcement that Leslie wanted to act in *Hamlet* and 'has expressed his desire to his associates'.[59]

In July Leslie closed *The Petrified Forest*, and the whirlwind activities came to a halt as he took his long-suffering family for a holiday in Bermuda. They must have needed it. Afterwards Leslie and the family returned to spend summer at Stowe Maries, and visit Leslie's family in London, as was their habit. (Ronald had been attending Tonbridge School in Kent and later went on to study at Jesus College, Cambridge.) At home Leslie was planning his production of *Hamlet*, hoping to put it on in New York in the next theatrical season. The scenarist Stewart Chaney came to London to discuss the project, and must have taken it very seriously as he then announced a visit to Denmark, to research early Danish architecture. Leslie gave notice in the London *Times* of his intention to produce *Hamlet* in November.[60] The announcement had already appeared in the American papers. Leslie hoped to warn and placate those members of his profession who might be somewhat surprised by his sudden classical acting ambitions, but unfortunately the tactic did not work.

Filming of *The Petrified Forest* continued into the following year, Leslie dealing dryly with Warner Brothers' attempts to simplify the play for the screen; the studio was dubious about audience reaction to the hero's death and tried to impose a happy ending. The debate received some publicity and *The New York Times* reported, 'Even Howard's 12 year old daughter (Leslie Ruth) has contributed. She says that Duke shouldn't have the nerve to kill Squier, so Squier borrows the gun for the purpose, captures all the criminals and collects the reward. Howard says she has been seeing too many movies.'[61]

The argument descended to bathos. After the Warner studio

suggested that a doctor intervenes to save Squier's life and Squier and Gaby go off together, Leslie replied that he would only do this on condition that they add a scene with Gaby at an easel in Paris while Squier sits at a typewriter, divinely happy because he is working for Paramount.[62] The film was made according to Sherwood's original ending.

Bette Davis joined Leslie for a second time to play a sweet and touching Gaby in the film, and Humphrey Bogart took the part of Duke Mantee. Leslie won another grateful colleague, as he had insisted on retaining Bogart instead of Warners' choice of Edward G. Robinson, even threatening to refuse the film unless Bogart had the part. Bogart, whose film career had been drifting, never looked back, (although his film performance did not match that of the play) and even gave the name 'Leslie' to his daughter with Lauren Bacall.

In addition to *Hamlet*, Leslie was contemplating another play of his own (he usually had one on the go) and more film projects, including a treatment for Bonnie Prince Charlie. Leslie was still speaking of playing T.E. Lawrence – another potentially patriotic subject, this time hoping that Warner Brothers might fund it. A more definite project was a film of *Romeo and Juliet* at MGM studios. Leslie wasn't keen – it was a vehicle for Norma Shearer and Leslie was her third choice of leading man. He was also nearly 40 years old, Norma was in her mid-30s and neither were suited to play classical teenage lovers. But it would be a prestige production, it would give him a chance to play Shakespeare, and it would certainly provide more funding for his *Hamlet* project. Whether he had cold feet about that and the new project was a chance to put it off, or whether he grew stubborn because Warner Brothers at first refused to allow him to go to MGM, Leslie made the mistake of agreeing to the film.

It was Norma Shearer's last chance at an expensive production for herself before her ailing husband, Irving Thalberg, lost his hold over the studio. The film was under Shearer's influence and no money was spared on the production. Talbot Jennings (who had written Leslie's earlier play, *This Side Idolatry*, about Shakespeare's life) wrote the screenplay, following the original closely. John Barrymore was engaged as Mercutio, Edna May Oliver as the Nurse, Basil Rathbone as Tybalt. Thalberg engaged Oliver Messel for the designs, but he was pushed out by Cedric Gibbons, who was annoyed at an outsider being used on such an important production. Gibbons designed colossal sets, very detailed, which dwarfed the actors; the centrepiece, meant to represent Verona, occupied five acres. Worst of all was the balcony set, a huge construction which overwhelmed the intimate love scene.

The resulting film was a muddle, without any overarching intelligence. George Cukor might have provided it, but directors had much less power then and it was not in his hands. The acting styles clashed, with John Barrymore's barnstorming Mercutio horribly at odds with the restrained, modern playing of Leslie and Norma. Neither story nor characters were realized and no one achieved a scrap of authority or credibility. Leslie did his gently charming best, as ever, but the sight of his rheumaticky knees running across the huge sets added nothing to engage the audience. The film apparently did not lose money, but remains one of the great turkeys of classical Hollywood. At the time critical comment was restrained, perhaps out of respect to Thalberg, perhaps because this was seen as one of the first serious attempt at Shakespeare on film.[63] (Hollywood had not always dealt so badly with Shakespeare – the previous year had seen Warner's innovative *Midsummer Night's Dream*, directed by Max Reinhardt.)

Filming ran into 1936, and Leslie's *Hamlet* had now been in the planning for over a year. In January Leslie announced his retirement from acting after he had finished *Hamlet*. He had been making serious attempts to found his own production company. In Britain he had set up United Players Productions with C.M. Woolf, a well-known film financier.[64] In America, *Bonnie Prince Charlie*, financed by Warners, was another abortive attempt. A year later he tried to engage Eugene Frenke, husband of actress Anna Sten, to form Frenke Productions, backed by California Oil, but this unlikely prospect also fell through.[65] Leslie finally managed a more hopeful arrangement making films in Britain for RKO, a studio already familiar with his work as an actor.

As the filming of *Romeo and Juliet* ran on, Leslie was forced to postpone his own project until October 1936. He finished filming in May, and returned to England for his usual summer holiday, apparently unworried by thoughts of his own acting preparation for one of the longest and most testing roles in the canon. He spent much of his time playing polo and horse racing. An unpleasant surprise was the announcement of John Gielgud's own production of *Hamlet*, due in America at the same time as Leslie's. Since Leslie's plans had been known for a year, some discussion resulted. Gielgud replied in *The Times* that he had already cancelled his own plans once, when Leslie's play was thought to be due in the previous May. It was clear that Gielgud, who had already given (according to his theatrical peers) the definitive Hamlet in 1934, was not happy to allow Leslie the fruit of his labours in the form of American theatre profits, which were the reward of every successful actor and production in Britain.

Gielgud had some cause to be annoyed. Leslie's sudden Shakespearian plans were really baffling. He was known to be fed up with acting, complaining a number of times in the press of how he found it tiresome and wished to give it up. He was making plans to be a producer, and really all his thoughts for some years had been of projects for his own productions. Even as he played *This Side Idolatry*, his friend Robert Bruce Lockhart found him talking, not of his own performance in the theatre, but of his ideas for theatrical productions. This expensive presentation of *Hamlet* would be financed solely by his own savings, at a cost of $90,000, another puzzling gamble, as Leslie was known to be careful with his money and was a shrewd businessman. There was to be an all-British cast, also an odd idea, as the American critics and audience would certainly appreciate the compliment of their own actors being presented – Gielgud's production of *Hamlet* in America had a mixed English and American cast. Most of all, Leslie hated touring, yet he had carefully arranged beforehand to play for only a limited time in New York and tour all over America, sometimes avoiding the larger cities in favour of theatres near universities and schools. After such performances, Leslie had arranged for students to come backstage and discuss the play with the all-English cast.[66]

Given all this, it is possible to speculate that this tour of *Hamlet* corresponded with the cultural propaganda ideas of The British Council. It is difficult to interpret it in any other way, and indeed John Houseman, whom Leslie had engaged to co-produce the play, was completely bewildered by Leslie's lack of preparation and relative indifference to Gielgud's production. Leslie could not of course enlighten him about any propaganda motive, as it was likely that Houseman would have indignantly demurred. In his memoirs Houseman describes his frustration, and can only suggest that Leslie's actions were due to 'a strange kind of fatalism' – actually the very last thing Leslie ever suffered from.[67]

Hamlet had a particular importance at this time, as Dover Wilson's new version of the text had been published in 1934, after a lifetime's study of Shakespeare. In addition, Wilson's *What Happens in Hamlet*, a fascinating commentary on the play and its enigmas, had just come out. The play was representative of all that Western learning and civilization had achieved.

Knowing that Gielgud's New York production would clash with his own, Leslie refused excellent advice to postpone his production to avoid any comparison. With farcical inevitability both went ahead, and the resulting debacle was all the gleeful press and public could have wished. Gielgud had opened on 8 October 1936. His production was half the cost of Leslie's, with a Jacobean setting that was thought to be rather dull by the critics. His notices were good if not unmixed, and in general it was considered a success. Leslie opened in New York on 10 November, having had successful out of town try-outs in Boston and Philadelphia.

Leslie never could have competed with Gielgud on his own ground. The great actor was entirely wrapped up in his art, lived only for the theatre and scarcely knew what was happening in the outside world, or cared. The fiasco was typical of Gielgud, but there was no doubt who was the greater classical artist. Leslie had no training in classical theatre, his voice was beautiful but he was unused to projecting high tragedy to the back of the stalls. He had not even had the kind of modern training which actors receive now, which requires them to use their own emotional resources in the expression of their characters. Such a thing was absolute anathema to Leslie, who rarely if ever indulged in such self-analysis. His style of playing was intricate and small scale, even more incongruous against his choice of setting – an impressive Viking background, including a great ship setting forth for England. Leslie's performance, despite intelligent playing and even moments of humour, was low key, dwarfed by the set, and disappointing; even his friends were dismayed. Noel Coward came backstage and urged him to try some over-acting for a change. Mabel Constanduros, an actress who had known him in his youth, felt that he had been too restrained, too afraid of being 'ham' and had thrown away the play's emotional climaxes.[68] It is possible that Leslie, given the enormity of the undertaking and the huge publicity, suffered from opening night terrors which contributed to his underplaying.

The critics decided to jump up and down on the corpse. Realizing they had seen and not quite appreciated a great Hamlet in Gielgud, they turned as one and savaged both Leslie's play and Leslie himself. As one critical observer concluded, 'the comments were viperish'.[69] Gielgud received renewed praise, and it was the comparison that made his success, with much fuller houses and greater press interest once Leslie's production had appeared.[70]

As embarrassment grew, with both Leslie and Gielgud feeling too aggrieved to laugh the matter off, Leslie decided to close the production in New York and go on to his tour. After a short holiday, this progressed

well and became an increasing success, setting box office records round
the country for the next four months, with hundreds having to be
turned away on many occasions. Leslie's English players received
praise, especially the aristocratic Pamela Stanley as a sensitive Ophelia
and Aubrey Mather as an authoritatively comic Polonius. Leslie's wife
Ruth accompanied him to help with the management, thoroughly
enjoying the sociability and the local interest from young people that
it engendered. As her daughter recorded, it was one of the most
enjoyable memories of her marriage. At least Leslie managed to recoup
all his money, but it must have been exceedingly worrying after the
New York opening. If propaganda had been the aim, Leslie had now
done for the moment all he could, to the best of his efforts and
resources.

Ignoring what might have been a crushing disappointment, not to
speak of the malicious press onslaught, Leslie shrugged it all off and
went straight back to some remunerative work. Wisely he decided on
a complete change, and it was the frothiest possible comedy that next
emerged to display his talents. *It's Love I'm After* (1937) for Warner
Brothers, is the most delightful of all Leslie's films. It is one for his fans,
as it seems to be about his own life, playing a philandering stage actor
pursued and pursuing one woman after another. There is even a skit on
Romeo and Juliet. Bette Davis plays his long-suffering fiancée, Olivia de
Havilland an enamoured young fan, hoping that Leslie can be enticed
into providing her with a fate worse than death, and comedian Eric
Blore his valet, with a simmering patience for the spoiled matinee idol's
zany impulses. At one point, as de Havilland pouts that her last crush
was on Clark Gable, Leslie replies 'Who is Clark Gable?'

The film got appreciative notices, although Leslie's career as an
American leading man was inevitably winding down. He followed up
with another in the screwball comedy genre, *Stand-in*, but this time he
made the mistake of trying physical comedy, which had never been his
forte. As *The Times* commented, 'Mr Howard is too dignified an actor
to try his hand at utter burlesque'. Receiving a tomato in the face, Leslie
doesn't throw it back, but simply wipes it off with a sad smile.

There had been a more important project in the wind. As far back
as May 1934 Alexander Korda had announced Leslie to play the lead
in a film of T.E. Lawrence, known as 'Lawrence of Arabia' for his
exploits in the First World War. But as with many of Korda's grand-
scale productions, it was delayed for one reason or another. Meanwhile
Lawrence died in a motorcycle accident in May 1935, and there were

problems with the copyright to his book, *The Seven Pillars of Wisdom* and other writings. In early 1937 Korda finally obtained the rights, and filming seemed imminent, again with Leslie announced to play.

Leslie, believing that the film would go ahead, gave an interview in *Film Weekly* of November 1937, outlining his thoughts. 'If the film was made at all, I felt that it must be made imaginatively by a serious-minded and expert craftsman. The picture must be free altogether of the Bengal Lancer aspect, it must have nothing Kiplingesque or senti-mental; above all it must have no shrieking Arabs riding across the desert in the manner of cowboys.'

Leslie was arguing for something a little more intelligent than the kind of Hollywoodized history that was common at the time. Winston Churchill, who had himself known Lawrence, was employed by Korda as a prestige scriptwriter, and had discussed the outline of the story with Leslie. Leslie went on to give a perceptive outline of Lawrence's complicated character. It might have been the part of a lifetime, but the Foreign Office were unhappy with the film. The Turkish armies would necessarily be portrayed in a most unflattering light, and 1937 was no time for Britain to be making new enemies. They prevented the film from going forward, and it could not be made until 1962, when the political scene had changed.[71]

After completing his *Hamlet* tour, Leslie had taken a long summer holiday with his family in Hollywood, following it with an even longer vacation at home in Surrey. Now he heard of plans, more or less advanced, to film one of George Bernard Shaw's most popular plays, *Pygmalion*. This caused something of a stir, as Shaw had made a well-known declaration never to grant the film rights to his plays, so disgusted was he with early Hollywood attempts. But businessman Gabriel Pascal had approached Shaw for the film rights, and this time they had been granted. It seemed a quixotic decision to many, as Pascal was of doubtful origins, a penniless eastern European, charming and very foreign, with the air of a Hungarian gypsy. Pascal himself claimed to have been orphaned as a baby, and brought up in the direst poverty by a troupe of gypsies, and his manners and temperament seemed to confirm this. He seems to have had an ability typical of aban-doned children – to instantly bond with any likely parental figure, and this had its affect on Shaw. But Shaw knew what he was doing. He was now over 80 years old, and this filming adventure promised new interests and excitements to brighten his life. Most of all perhaps was the realization that for once he could exercise a good deal of control over his own work. Pascal was solely reliant on Shaw, he had no other resources, no other base. Instead of remote and indifferent Hollywood studio executives, Shaw now had his material much more under his own hand.

So it worked out. With Shaw's blessing, Pascal raised the necessary financing while engaging the best team that were not under contract to other studios – Anthony Asquith to direct, promising editor David Lean and well-known British screen writers William Lipscomb and Cecil Lewis. Leslie was approached to co-direct with Asquith, and also to play the lead, Professor Higgins, who turns a cockney flower girl into a princess for a single night. They all came down to Leslie's house at Westcott in the autumn of 1937 to prepare the scenario. Leslie Ruth, then a schoolgirl on summer holiday, was fascinated by it all:

> Asquith spent hours at Stowe Maries with Leslie and the other people involved, thrashing out the plans for casting and script. Shaw had to be handled with extreme caution as he remained unapproachable and ready to withdraw his agreement at every turn. At first, no scenes were to be included that were not in the play, and this created a grave problem. Then with his usual flair for the unpredictable he gave in, and wrote them himself.[72]

Leslie Ruth remembered Asquith and Leslie working very well together, with Leslie's vague manner concealing his sharp concentration on day-to-day problems. Just before the film began shooting, Leslie took Pascal and Asquith on holiday to Austria with his wife, accompanied by his daughter Leslie Ruth and his sister Dorice. The Nazi takeover of Austria, the Anschluss, came just a few weeks later. While the others enjoyed a skiing holiday, Leslie took every opportunity to discuss prevailing political views with inhabitants sympathetic enough to talk to him. It was here he had his inspiration for some of his later films, especially after meeting radical artist Alfons Walde, who told him of the state of things in Austria – the doctors, teachers and pastors who had disappeared, the terrified atmosphere and the looming threat of Nazi takeover.

Filming of *Pygmalion* began as the Nazis marched into Austria. By contrast, the film was cheerful and humorous, although the backstage manoeuvring was different. Pascal was intemperate, overvaluing his own contribution. Asquith, with marvellous taste and intelligence, could be tremulous and uncertain, and David Lean was ambitious to take over some of the directing. Leslie held them all together, with great charm and the respect he effortlessly commanded. Without this team, Pascal's next filming of Shaw, *Major Barbara*, was a bad-tempered failure, and Pascal's career ran into the sands. His orphan's luck held however, and when the book that had been created for *Pygmalion* was made into a musical called *My Fair Lady*, he made a fortune from the rights without having to do anything further.[73]

Pygmalion was premiered with great fanfare in London in October 1938. The cast contained the best that could be obtained of British character actors; even wordless extras went on to become well-known names – Leo Genn, Anthony Quayle, Patrick Macnee. The only odd piece of casting was Wendy Hiller as the cockney ingénue. Shaw had picked her out himself, having seen her in his *Saint Joan* at the annual Malvern Festival. Miss Hiller came from a well-off background and not much effort seemed to be needed for her to emerge as the haughty princess at the consular reception; nor is there much sign of the spirited, pretty little street slut in her beginnings. However there was no denying her acting ability, and in any case, no actress since has convincingly portrayed both sides of Shaw's Galatea, no matter how much the accent and clothes are changed.

Leslie was not Shaw's choice for Higgins. Shaw's original description of the character was given in the introductory pages of the play in 1914:

> *Higgins ... appears as a robust, vital, appetizing sort of man of forty or thereabouts. He is of the energetic, scientific type, ... impetuous and eager... his manner varies from genial bullying when he is in a good humour to stormy petulance when anything goes wrong, but he is so entirely frank and void of malice that he remains likeable even in his least reasonable moments.*

It's not really too unlike Leslie. But Shaw disliked Leslie's matinee-idol attractions, which would tend to a more romantic finale with Eliza than Shaw wished.

The structure of the play stands up well after more than half a century and this version, close to the original, is still happily entertaining. Leslie makes the film fun, although it is hard to say exactly why. His contemporaries remember that he had a faster pace than any other actor, and would rattle off a speech without a single mistake after a few rehearsals, lending movement and lightness to the action. He runs round the sets, moving more rapidly than anyone else, chasing the stately Wendy Hiller up and down the stairs, flirting with her, popping chocolates first into his mouth then hers, making her practice with a mouth full of marbles and when she accidentally swallows one, ad-libbing breezily, 'don't worry – we have plenty more'. In this film, as in all his later British productions, he has a kind of magic, which he never lost, but which seemed to deepen with the years.

Pygmalion (1938) was a great success on both sides of the Atlantic, and again a great advance for British film. Leslie was nominated for an Oscar, losing this time to Spencer Tracy for *Boy's Town*, and *Pygmalion* had to remain a mostly British triumph. On the other hand, Bernard Shaw's Oscar for best screenplay, as if he was a newcomer, was a joke enjoyed on both sides of the Atlantic.

Something else had happened to Leslie while the film was in production. He had fallen in love again, this time with Pascal's personal assistant, a pretty secretary with an Anglo-French background, Violette Cunnington. She was something of a paragon, combining intelligence and practicality with very feminine attractions and great style. It was a combination that many men would dream of, and one that Leslie had been looking for with increasing desperation. Violette became his constant companion from then on, and rarely left his side wherever he was. Finally he had to set up two households, and as his wife and family became increasingly aware of the situation, try to keep both sides reasonably happy. He achieved a kind of compromise in the end, but not without unavoidable cost in unease and unhappiness all round.

Without much more in prospect in the British industry, and with the Munich crisis over and war fended off for the immediate future, Leslie sailed back to America, this time with Violette and without his family, to explore the possibility of producing British films with American backing. Leslie was offered an arrangement with RKO to produce pictures at Pinewood Studios in England where *Pygmalion* had just been filmed. At yet another press conference to discuss his ideas, Leslie elaborated, 'I like to make motion pictures, not act in them ... in pictures the actor gets practically no feeling of personal accomplishment ... the important persons are the men who make them'.[74]

Leslie felt that the potentialities of film had not been touched, and he could produce something more original for a reasonable cost. Many no doubt had the same ideas, but Leslie was determined to get his chance to try. He chose as his first film *The Man Who Lost Himself*, from a novel by H. de vere Stacpool, now long forgotten. The plans were well advanced, but this and Leslie's new company all fell to the ground in September 1939, when Britain declared war.

Meanwhile other film options were for the moment scarce, except for a part that had been long on offer, in an American historical production, *Gone with the Wind*. Leslie had not been in the least interested, but nothing else developed, and eventually he was sucked into the massive publicity campaign for the new blockbuster. Leslie was the popular choice for Ashley Wilkes, a confederate officer, and was duly approached by David Selznick, who was determined to recreate the best-selling novel on a massive scale. Other leading actors chosen were Vivien Leigh, Olivia de Havilland and Clark Gable. It has not been recorded whether Selznick's approach to Gable, by now deservedly acclaimed as the 'king' of Hollywood, was as crass as that to Leslie:

> Memo of October 14th, 1937: To Daniel T. O'Shea (Selznick's Chief Aide). Please open negotiations with Mike Levee (Leslie's agent) for Leslie Howard to play Ashley in *Gone with the Wind*. I suppose you do not need any coaching on sales talk or on attitude ... can you point out to Levee with complete accuracy that Howard has been a box-office failure in all his pictures of recent years without exception.[75]

This was nonsense even in 1937, and even less so after Leslie's great success in *Pygmalion*. But if it had been true, Selznick would still have got little reaction to this bullying from either Leslie or his very experienced agent. By the time filming had finally begun, at the start of 1939, the tone had changed somewhat:

> May 27th, 1939
> To: Mr Leslie Howard
> Dear Leslie,
> I send you herewith a copy of that book you ought to get around to reading some time, called *Gone with the Wind*. I think the book has a great future and might make a very good picture.
> Seriously, you will remember that you promised me faithfully not merely to know the paddock scene backward, but also to read those pages of the book from which it was taken, in order to get the true import of the scene, and in order to understand the full-length portrait of Ashley that these pages give. You won't have to read a great deal – only pages 525 to 535 inclusive.
> Promise?
> I'll check up on you!

Leslie was never really in tune with the production. Longing to get home, increasingly worried as war threatened, Leslie fretted as the endless schedule ground on. The only relief was the farcical attempt to keep not only Leslie's romance with Violette out of the press, but also that of Vivien Leigh and Laurence Olivier (both married to other people). Having met Olivier on the *Normandie* out to America the previous year, Leslie and Olivier had understood each other's marital situation. For a brief time during the filming they all shared Leslie's large home on Beverley Drive as a philandering foursome, behaving in a highly British manner about it all, except for Violette, who presumably took a very French attitude. In reality, they were all sheltered by the formidable press influence of David Selznick, as nobody would have profited by a scandal that marred the film.

In order to keep Leslie quiet, and possibly distract him a little, Selznick arranged for him to act as associate producer on another of his productions, *Intermezzo*, a remake of a Swedish film which had starred the newcomer Ingrid Bergman. Leslie also played the ageing romantic lead in the rather tasteless tale of a married musician's love affair. Leslie's assurance, and most of all Ingrid Bergman's freshness and talent brought off a moderately entertaining film, and Leslie had finally achieved what he most wanted, a production credit.

Leslie was saddened that summer as his mother, who had been such an influence in his life, passed away in July 1939, at the age of 69. Leslie had been very close to her, writing regularly and visiting when he could. He still had the support of his brothers and sisters, who indeed looked to him for guidance and help with theatrical careers, and Leslie did what he could. Leslie's father survived until after the war, when he died in July 1945 at the age of 83.

Filming finally came to an end in the summer of 1939, and Leslie sailed in August back to England. The premiere of *Gone with the Wind* was one of the biggest events in show business history and everyone was there – except Leslie. As much as Leslie had charmed the Americans, and delighted, entranced, and finally irritated and confounded them, Leslie had gone, from hearts and minds also, and he never returned.

NOTES

1. Leslie Ruth Howard, *A Quite Remarkable Father* (London: Longmans, 1960).
2. *The New York Times*, 15 March 1931, 'Who was Hans Chlumberg?'.
3. Email to author, 3 September 2007: 'Yes, he was born Jewish June 30, 1897 in Vienna, but he left Jewish faith in 1923. As far as I know he died by an accident in the theatre, but I don't have a source. He was buried in Vienna at Doebling (non-Jewish) Cemetery Dec 13, 1930.' Regards, Mag. Wolf-Erich Eckstein (Israelitische Kultusgemeinde Wien Matriken/Records,

w.eckstein@ikg-wien.at).

4. For example, see *The New York Times*, 22 January 1930.
5. According to the next owner, Mrs Ann Wickham. Communication to author, 2009.
6. Douglas Fairbanks Jnr, *The Salad Days* (London: Collins, 1988).
7. *The New York Times*, 13 July 1930.
8. *Washington Post*, 23 November 1930.
9. Rachael Low, *Film Making in 1930s Britain* (London: George Allen and Unwin, and the British Film Institute, 1985), p.89.
10. *The Times*, 10 January 1930, *The New York Times*, 9 February 1930.
11. *The New York Times*, 15 April 1931.
12. Low, *Film making in 1930s Britain*, p.150.
13. Basil Dean, *Seven Ages* (London: Hutchinson, 1973).
14. Michael Lasalle, *Complicated Women: Sex and Power in Pre-Code Hollywood* (New York: St Martin's Press, 2000).
15. *The New York Times*, 3 June 1931.
16. Marion Davies, *The Times We Had: Life with William Randolph Hearst* (London: Angus and Robertson, 1976); F.L. Guiles, *Marion Davies: A Biography* (London: W.H. Allen, 1973).
17. Interview reprinted in Stephen Watts (ed.), *Behind the Screen: How Films Are Made* (London: A. Barker, 1938).
18. Sidney Lumet, *Making Movies* (London: Bloomsbury, 1995), p.150.
19. *The New York Times*, 10 October 1931 and *Kinematograph Weekly*, 15 October 1931, p.55.
20. Charles Drazin, *Korda: Britain's Only Movie Mogul* (London: Sidgwick and Jackson, 2002).
21. Paul Tabori, *Alexander Korda* (London: Oldbourne, 1959).
22. Katharine Hepburn, *Me: Stories of My Life* (London: Viking, 1991).
23. William Gargan, *Why Me? An Autobiography* (New York: Doubleday, 1969).
24. *The New York Times*, 14 February 1932 notes the brutality of the treatment of both women.
25. *The New York Times*, 24 January 1932.
26. James Kotsilibas-Davis and Myrna Loy, *Myrna Loy: Being and Becoming* (London: Bloomsbury, 1987), pp.76–7.
27. *The New York Times*, 24 February 1932 p.24, and 27 February 1932, p.28.
28. *The New York Times*, 17 April 1932, p.XI.
29. *The New York Times*, 1 May 1932, p.X2.
30. See, for instance, Mary Astor, *A Life on Film* (London: W.H. Allen, 1973).
31. Low, *Film Making in 1930s Britain*, pp.116–97.
32. Cohn's abrasive personality was noted by most people who met him. See, for example, Bob Thomas, *King Cohn: The Life and Times of Harry Cohn* (London: Barrie and Rockcliff, 1967).
33. Contemporary diaries of David Cunynghame, private collection.
34. Robert Bruce Lockhart, *Friends, Foes and Foreigners* (London: Putnam, 1957), pp.174–5.
35. Ibid.
36. Michael Cohn, *Jewish Bridges: East to West* (Westport, CT; London: Praeger, 1996) p.87. For more information on numbers of immigrant Jews to America, and America's refusal to admit Jewish immigrants, see, for example, David S. Wyman, *The Abandonment of the Jews: America and the Holocaust 1941–1945* (New York: Pantheon Books, 1984). For Jewish emigration to Britain in the 1930s, see Bernard Wasserstein, *Britain and the Jews of Europe 1939–1945* (London: Institute of Jewish Affairs; Oxford: Clarendon Press, 1979). Email to author from Professor Bernard Wasserstein, 14 April 2009, 'About 65,000 Jewish refugees entered Britain between 1933 and 1939'. Figures for refugees reaching America are less clear. See also Bat-Ami Zucker, *Cecilia Razovsky and the American-Jewish Women's Rescue Operations in the Second World War* (London and Portland, OR: Vallentine Mitchell, 2008).
37. Christopher Reed, Ingo Preminger obituary, *The Guardian*, 13 June 2006, p.33.
38. For Jewish exiles in the film world up to and during the war years, see Kevin Gough-Yates, 'The European Film-Maker in Exile in Britain, 1933–1945' (PhD diss., Open University, 1990). See also Kevin Gough-Yates, *Somewhere in England: British Cinema and Exile* (London: I.B. Tauris, 2009). For conditions at Denham, in November 2000 the author interviewed Guido Coen, who was film producer Del Giudice's assistant for the Two Cities Film Company, working at Denham during the war.
39. Howard, *A Quite Remarkable Father*, p.199.
40. David Stafford, *Churchill and Secret Service* (London: Abacus, 2000) and Martin Gilbert,

Winston Churchill; The Wilderness Years (London: Macmillan, 1981).

41. Norman Rose, *Vansittart: Study of a Diplomat* (London: Heinemann, 1978).
42. Martin Gilbert, *In Search of Churchill: A Historian's Journey* (London: HarperCollins 1995), pp.108–35, Philip M. Taylor, *The Projection of Britain: British Overseas Publicity and Propaganda, 1919–1930* (Cambridge: Cambridge University Press, 1981) and Nicholas Cull, *Selling War: The British Propaganda Campaign against American "Neutrality" in World War II* (New York and Oxford: Oxford University Press, 1995).
43. *The Landmark* 1934–1939, Journal of the English Speaking Union.
44. Kenneth Young (ed.), *The Diaries of Sir Robert Bruce Lockhart 1915–1938* (London: Macmillan, 1973–80).
45. Baroness Orczy, *The Scarlet Pimpernel* (London: Greening, 1905), p.250.
46. Diaries of David Cunynghame, August 1935. Private collection.
47. Young, *Diaries of Sir Robert Bruce Lockhart*, p.303.
48. *The New York Times*, 26 September 1934.
49. Low, *Film Making in 1930s Britain*, 'Max Schach and the Aldgate Trustees', pp.198–208. Ms Low, who was Jewish herself, examined the financial documents of that time more thoroughly than anyone since. In her book she is tolerant of Korda's financial shenanigans, but can find no good word for Mr Schach.
50. *The Blackshirt*, 31 October 1936, p.5.
51. The German American Bund was an organization agitating in favour of the Nazi party in America. It operated from 1936 onwards. See, for example, Susan Canedy, *Americas Nazis: A Democratic Dilemma. A History of the German American Bund* (Menlo Park, CA: Markgraf Publications Group, 1990).
52. For a report on all these events, see, for example, *Time*, 15 May 1939, p.45.
53. *The New York Times*, 22 November 1934. Leslie returned to America from Italy, on *The Rex*, an Italian vessel.
54. Quotes from John Mason Brown, *The Worlds of Robert E. Sherwood, Mirror to His Times* (New York: Harper and Row, 1962), pp.311–14.
55. *Stage*, May 1936, p.38.
56. Quoted in Brown, *The Worlds of Robert E. Sherwood*, p.321.
57. *The New York Times*, 6 April 1935, p.17.
58. *The New York Times*, 7 May 1935.
59. *The New York Times*, 6 June 1935.
60. *The Times*, 28 November 1935, p.12.
61. *The New York Times*, 1 December 1935.
62. *The New York Times*, 1 December 1935, p.X9.
63. The film was released on 3 September 1936. Thalberg, Hollywood's most esteemed producer, died eleven days later, having been dangerously ill for some time. Thalberg's contribution to the film is not clearly known, but it came under his aegis. He rarely credited himself as producer.
64. Low, *Film Making in 1930s Britain*, p.215.
65. *The New York Times*, 15 August 1937.
66. Howard, *A Quite Remarkable Father*.
67. John Houseman, *Run-Through: A Memoir* (New York: Simon and Schuster, 1972), p.224.
68. Mabel Constanduros, *Shreds and Patches* (London: Lawson and Dunn, 1946), p.156.
69. Samuel L. Leiter, *The Encyclopaedia of the New York Stage 1930–1940* (New York and London: Greenwood, 1989).
70. Richard Mangan (ed.), *Gielgud's Letters* (London: Weidenfeld and Nicolson, 2004).
71. Andrew Kelly, Jeffrey Richards and James Pepper, *Filming T.E. Lawrence: Korda's Lost Epics* (London: I.B. Tauris, 1997).
72. Howard, *A Quite Remarkable Father*, p.228.
73. For events surrounding the filming of *Pygmalion* see Valerie Pascal, *The Disciple and His Devil* (London: Joseph, 1971), Kevin Brownlow, *David Lean: A Biography*, (London: Richard Cohen, 1996), Michael Holroyd, *Bernard Shaw: The Lure of Fantasy* (London: Chatto and Windus, 1991). For Pascal's manners and general ambience, see Kenneth Clark, *The Other Half: A Self Portrait* (London: Hamish Hamilton, 1977), pp.38–9.
74. *The New York Times*, 9 March 1939, p.19.
75. Rudy Behlmer (ed.), *Memo from David O. Selznick* (New York: Viking Press, 1972).

CHAPTER SIX

1935–1943: Leslie Howard – Secret Agent

No evidence has ever connected Leslie Howard to any intelligence agency, yet over the years a number of different accusers have named him as a spy. In June 1943 the Germans defensively announced that he was, 'a member of the British intelligence services'.[1] Historians in Lisbon, the place which Leslie was visiting then, even now describe him as a central European Jew, naturalised British, having come to Portugal to aid Jewish refugees.[2] But Leslie's mission there was a very public propaganda visit to Spanish and Portuguese film studios.

Allied sources too were convinced that Leslie somehow had secret work to do. Ronald Howard, Leslie's son, gave his opinion that Leslie had, by 1940, become a 'V-Personen', using the German term for those connected unofficially to an intelligence agency. Leslie's contemporaries in the film world had their suspicions about him.[3] Guido Coen, who was film producer Del Giudice's assistant and friend at Two Cities Films during the war, states that he and others thought that Leslie was involved in some secret work.[4]

Much of the early speculation about Leslie was put together by journalist Ian Colvin, in his book *Flight 777*, which purported to tell the true story of Leslie's trip to Lisbon in 1943.[5] Leslie featured sensationally in this as the seducer of a beautiful but mysterious female spy, a certain 'Countess Lila Miranda', who, overwhelmed with Leslie's charms, comes over to the Allied cause. Alas she is intercepted by German authorities and disappears, never to be heard from again. Ronald Howard, who carried out a thorough investigation into the circumstances of his father's death, took very little notice of all this. Ronald had many sources opened to him by sympathetic officials and witnesses who remembered his father with affection. While acknowledging some of the research in Colvin's book, Ronald remained sceptical about this story, for which there remained little, if any evidence. Colvin actually admits, in the Foreword to *Flight 777*, that 'the character described as the Countess Miranda is a synthesis of various qualities exhibited by known enemy spies', which is pushing the limits of journalistic romancing.

In the same year that *Flight 777* was published, an article in the American magazine, *Argosy*, (very aptly subtitled the 'fiction-fact' magazine) discussed Leslie's mission in portentous terms. Their version was a story entitled 'The Mysterious Death of Leslie Howard'. In it, the author stated, with no particular concern for references or supporting evidence, that Leslie was acting for MI5, with once again the lovely Countess Miranda to the fore.[6]

More journalists made a moderate splash with Leslie Howard speculation in the 1980s. Chapman Pincher, in his *Their Trade Is Treachery* (1981) and David Fisher and Anthony Read in *Colonel Z* (1984) took a new tack entirely and linked Leslie to secret work in America.[7] This idea has continued to surface occasionally, with Leslie featuring prominently in a 1991 *Observer* article about the secret wartime work of Alexander Korda.[8] Various sites have appeared on the Internet in recent years, with even the BBC describing Leslie as travelling back from Portugal on the 'spy plane', without bothering to give any provenance for this supposedly well-known gossip.[9] So was it possible that Leslie worked for the 'British Secret Services', or any secret agency operating in England or America in the late 1930s and the war years?

It seems unlikely. At the start of the Second World War, these agencies in Britain were in a more unprepared state than could be admitted for many years afterwards. MI5, responsible for home security, including British Empire territories, has been described as under-funded and short staffed in the late 1930s.[10] Its agents were often ex-members of the colonial police forces, and its officers were at the heart of the establishment, which had been most reluctantly anti-German for the whole of the 1930s. In addition, a report released in June 2000 from Whitehall's secret archives reveals that not only was MI5 in a shambles at this time, but its deputy director, William Charles Crocker, was a Nazi sympathiser completely opposed to the war with Hitler. Crocker was active in *Truth*, a journal openly supportive of Oswald Mosley, jailed leader of the British Union of Fascists. Crocker eventually left the agency in September 1940, after a critical report reached Churchill.[11] Right up to the war and beyond, MI5 had concentrated on a supposed internal threat from communist sympathisers. In 1940 it so mishandled the examination of recent foreign immigrants (many Jewish) that Churchill fired its chief, Vernon Kell.

With the start of the war MI5 expanded considerably, but it was not until after 1941 that the organization was in a state to claim some counter-intelligence victories. It seems unlikely that such a well-known but alien figure as a Hollywood film star, however patriotic, would have been of interest to them as an agent.

MI6 (responsible for foreign intelligence) had long had a network of agents abroad lightly disguised as passport control officers. This was known to the Germans and in 1936 Stuart Menzies, afterwards chief of MI6, started to build a parallel network – the Z organization – with the man who was later his deputy, Claude Dansey. This consisted mainly of ordinary businessmen settled in various countries, or having international interests, operating under cover. Unfortunately this suffered a serious setback in the course of the 'Venlo Incident' when two of these amateur agents were arrested at the German-Dutch frontier near Venlo in Eastern Holland by the Germans in November 1939. They were made to reveal all they knew of this network. MI6 had to begin again, using the contacts of Dansey and others, often on an ad hoc basis, and with the eventual help of supporters in the occupied countries, clandestine radio broadcasts, other agencies and the information gathered from ULTRA – German radio decrypts from the code-breakers at Bletchley Park.[12] From all evidence available, both MI5 and MI6 were hardly functioning as anti-Nazi centres during the 1930s and the early war years. They seem to have been hardly functioning at all, and were badly neglected and disorganized.

Other agencies operating in Europe by 1943 were SOE, the Special Operations Executive, concerned with secret sabotage, MI9, the prisoner-of-war escape and evasion service, and representatives of naval intelligence. None could have had any use in the field for Leslie. MI9 escape routes for British prisoners from German camps were reportedly not channelled via Lisbon,[13] which however was used as a stopover station for many long-haul flights.

One British organization which might have interested Leslie was the Political Warfare Executive, operational by 1941 and responsible for secret, rather than open, propaganda abroad. Working with it was an influential American representative, Robert Sherwood, well-known playwright and friend of Leslie's (he had written *The Petrified Forest* for him in 1936). Sherwood also later worked to coordinate the handover of British Security Coordination (BSC), the secret British operations in America, to the United States Office of Strategic Services (OSS). However, in none of his post-war memoirs does Sherwood mention working with Leslie at this time. Nor is there a word about Leslie in any of the many subsequent narratives of the Political Warfare Executive, BSC or OSS.

In 1940 Churchill secretly supported the mission of William Stephenson, a Canadian businessman, to covertly promote the Allied cause in America. Stephenson set up his headquarters in Washington and began a series of operations to counter German propaganda, sabotage any useful pro-German activities and intercept diplomatic mail. None of this was known to the FBI, which would have been furious had they discovered it, and in fact it remains controversial to the present day.[14]

These activities were organized by British Security Coordination, backed by Claude Dansey of MI6 and helped, surprisingly, by Alexander Korda, the British film magnate and friend of Churchill. Korda supplied a business front for the BSC's offices, helped with funding, and made a number of trips between England and America, under the cover of film-making, to provide briefings and instructions both ways. Korda, using his own company, London Films, may well have been a contact and helper of Dansey before the war, when the Z network was begun. The work of BSC was taken over by the Americans when they entered the war, under the title of Office of Strategic Services (OSS) and this developed ultimately, after the war, into the CIA.[15]

OSS developed its own secret organization throughout Europe from 1941. There were some clashes with British organizations, including one incident which demonstrated British suspicion of US agents with Jewish origins; one OSS psychologist found that a British assessment board had rejected help from many OSS propagandists as they were immigrants of Jewish descent.[16]

Leslie has been linked to Stephenson and BSC's activities, first by Chapman Pincher in *Their Trade Is Treachery*,[17] by Fisher and Read in *Colonel Z*,[18] and by decades of press rumours. The response to such allegations has not exactly been vague. In his introduction to *Secret Intelligence Officer*, by H. Montgomery Hyde, Stephenson simply stated, 'In fact, I never had anything to do with Leslie Howard'.[19] Stephenson, later written of as 'A man called Intrepid', has never been charged with keeping his wartime activities to himself. In fact he stands accused of the opposite fault – exaggerating his already considerable achievements.[20] In a final interview, he named a number of contemporary figures as helpers in covert actions, including Noel Coward, Merle Oberon and the Korda brothers.[21] If Leslie had been amongst them, there seems no reason to leave him out, and in addition issue a specific denial. In any case, Leslie was in England throughout the short lifetime of BSC. Alexander Korda could have acted as a go-between, but his brief and dangerous trips to England were on specific business in which Leslie was not involved. Korda is not known to have mentioned any contact with Leslie during the war years, when they were in any case based in different countries. Commander Kenneth Cohen, Dansey's deputy in the Z network, remembered Korda in his memories of this time. He never spoke of Leslie Howard.[22]

Douglas Fairbanks Jnr, another great friend of Leslie's, has written his own reasonably frank autobiography including events at this time.[23] In it he hints of his own efforts at passing on overheard snippets of information. In fact Fairbanks, a playboy socialite welcomed by high society, and apparently an amusing lightweight, increased his pro-Allied propaganda work after the war started in Europe, and was reporting direct to Roosevelt. Fairbanks later stated, in a 1990 interview with Professor Nicholas Cull, author of *Selling War: The British Propaganda Campaign against American 'Neutrality' in World War II*, that there was not much secret activity before the war amongst other actors in Hollywood – they lacked direction and leadership, and were under close scrutiny from American isolationists, both in the press and in Congress.[24]

Sharp-eyed hostility was directed, just before the war, at any American organization that was openly pro-British. Fairbanks in this interview mentions the English Speaking Union, a supposedly very innocent milieu, begun in 1920, and intended to aid cultural links between England and America. According to Fairbanks, it was 'often dismissed as a distraction for old ladies, where any discussion was punctuated by the rattle of teacups'.[25] Churchill was chairman of the ESU from 1921 to 1926. It remained innocent, but as the 1930s went on, its committee and anyone associated with it would be in the Allied camp. The ESU Journal became openly anti-Nazi and anti-isolationist from the mid-1930s, but had only a small circulation. In May 1935 Leslie appeared as the guest of honour at one of its meetings.[26] The ESU laid particular emphasis on the English Shakespearian heritage. The ESU (and Churchillian) phrase 'English speaking peoples' was also used by Leslie in his British broadcasts to America in 1940 and 1941.

Leslie did not have many friends or contacts who could frankly support such views. In the later 1930s, they could not be openly held in America without coming under strenuous attack from isolationists, who, if not in the majority, were certainly loud and aggressive.

During the course of his work for the White Committee in 1940, formed to defend America by aiding the Allies, Fairbanks was threatened with bombing and the kidnap of his children.[27] Once back in England, Leslie worked single-mindedly to promote the anti-Nazi cause. But before the war started and for some time after it, the secret services were in disarray, and the British government and Foreign Office had a long history of appeasement. Did Leslie find covert contacts to work with people promoting the views he supported? If so, who could they have been?

As is now well known, both Winston Churchill and Robert Vansittart (head of the Foreign Office from 1930 to 1938) had their own private and secret information sources in the 1930s – military, civil and political.[28] At the start of the 1930s Churchill was a member of parliament, but out of office, and deeply out of favour with the political establishment. As the decade wore on, he became a one-man opposition, hounding the appeasement government in and out of parliament. His centre of operations was Chartwell, his country house, where he nightly welcomed guests from every country and walk of life. Former colleagues, friends, civil servants and political well-wishers formed an unofficial network in defiance of government policy.[29] Some of these figures risked ruin, and even vicious personal threat from government figures, in order to keep Churchill secretly informed, particularly of what was happening in Germany.[30]

Vansittart was removed from office by Chamberlain in 1938 for his warnings against imminent German aggression, and his hostility to Germany, after which he continued his campaign both privately and publicly. He, like Churchill, had his own sources, but these were mainly from official military intelligence, and his friendship with Admiral Sinclair, head of MI6, and were centred on activities in Germany. Both Churchill and Vansittart had strong connections and sympathies with the British film industry. Besides the glamour of the film business, which attracted almost every member of the great and good of the day, the over whelming power of the new medium had been evident from its beginnings.

Alexander Korda also helped Churchill – who had weighty calls on his time and resources – financially. Churchill made most of his income from his books and journalism and Korda paid him large amounts of money over the years, ostensibly for developing scripts, although nothing came of them. Churchill loved the film world, and was regularly sent copies of British films to screen at Chartwell; in 1938, he personally welcomed Charlie Chaplin, to whom he had issued a special invitation.

Vansittart also had artistic ambitions, with a list of publications to his credit, including poetry and plays. He lived in Denham Place, a country house near the Denham Studios in Buckinghamshire, and in 1938, after the government had relieved him of office, Korda signed a contract with him to contribute to film scripts on imperial subjects.[31] Vansittart worked on the script of Korda's film, *The Thief of Bagdad* in 1939, and on the lyrics for the music with the composer, Miklos Rosza. Korda introduced Vansittart to Rosza, (one of many Jewish refugees of the day) saying, 'he is a fine poet, a good writer, and I think you will like him'.[32]

Rosza described the many weekends he spent with Vansittart in the summer of 1939, writing lyrics and music for Korda's film *The Four Feathers*. The two were at Vansittart's country house at Denham, and Rosza was aware of the constant flow of secret information around his host, which later became more open after war was declared (Leslie lived near Denham for much of the war).

Churchill and Vansittart kept in regular contact during the late 1930s in order to share and discuss intelligence.[33] In 1987, in his notorious work *Spy Catcher*, the former MI6 officer Peter Wright recalled that two of the most important sources for information at that time, Zu Putlitz (first secretary at the German Embassy in London, secretly working against the Nazis) and Klop Ustinov, his secret contact working for British intelligence, 'used to dine with Vansittart and Churchill, then in the wilderness, to brief them on the intelligence they had gained.'[34]

Both Churchill and Vansittart were of aristocratic family and could trace ancestors who had helped to rule the country back hundreds of years. They seemed to feel that theirs was the real heart of England, theirs the most realistic world view. They had good knowledge of what was happening on the continent, what German intentions were, and well understood the need for their own independent action, in spite of the views of the Chamberlain government in power before the war, and a large part of the British establishment.

Leslie himself knew Churchill casually, meeting him at Denham Studios, which Churchill visited to discuss scripts and film ideas. In 1937 in an interview about the possible filming of *Lawrence of Arabia*, Leslie said, 'I hope to bring in Winston Churchill to complete the scenario ... Already, in a number of informal conversations, Churchill has helped me considerably to round off my impression of Lawrence.'[35]

Vansittart was also associated with this script, having been asked by the Foreign Office to speak to Korda unofficially about it, with a view to minimizing references to Turkey which might give rise to offense and diplomatic difficulties.[36] But there is nothing now to show that Vansittart met or talked to Leslie, or that Churchill spoke to him of anything else but film business. Both Churchill and Vansittart had spy networks which only they knew fully, and only they coordinated.[37]

Whether Leslie was loosely or formally associated with any network is not now known. It is difficult to know whether such networks could best be described as a conspiracy, or as a consensus. Leslie's aim was to promote the anti-Nazi cause, and he had to do it very carefully indeed while the appeasement government and their agents and supporters held sway. In effect there was nothing he could do publicly until Churchill finally attained office in May 1940. Leslie spent some of the intervening time collecting his own evidence as to what was happening in Germany and Austria, through whatever English sources were open to him. Some of these were associated with Churchill, and might possibly have been accessed through Churchill's influence.

Churchill, until he became prime minister, had to use unofficial sources for gathering information and promoting the anti-fascist cause. He could not fully command government intelligence agencies when he was not in power, and even if he could have had access to them they were neither in a state to be used, nor in sympathy with him. So Churchill had to rely on forceful independents such as Korda, Stephenson and others, who were in a position to be of use, and could be trusted not to betray their cause to the fascists – or to the government and its agents, for that matter. The peculiar atmosphere for months after hostilities had been declared (the 'phony war') has been described by many historians. One termed the Chamberlain government as 'schizoid', still devout appeasers, still hoping that Germany could be placated.[38] The government issued instructions not to 'offend' Germany, and the head of the BBC, Lord Reith, had to deny airtime to any anti-appeasement spokesman.

One intelligence contact of Leslie's during the early part of 1940 was General Sir Noel Mason-MacFarlane, who was director of military intelligence with the British army in France, and later military governor of Gibraltar. MacFarlane had seen Germany's preparations for all-out war when he was military attaché in Berlin in 1939. He had done all he could to warn the government, but his reports had been negated by Sir Nevile Henderson, his own ambassador, and an appeasement supporter. MacFarlane had also been attaché at Vienna, and had witnessed the German army's entry into both Austria and Czechoslovakia. According to the actor Anthony Quayle, who served with MacFarlane in Gibraltar, 'he had developed for all politicians except Churchill a contemptuous loathing'.[39] Ronald Howard described how Leslie first met Mason-MacFarlane at the studio of Reginald Eves, a painter who had done several portraits of Leslie and was in 1939 engaged in painting a portrait of MacFarlane, amongst other top military personnel: 'Leslie ... was strongly attracted to [MacFarlane's] sympathetic and arresting personality ... They very readily saw eye-to-eye about the Nazis.'[40]

After war was declared in September 1939, the British Expeditionary Force (BEF) was despatched to join the French forces and meet the German advance on the continent. The BEF eventually numbered about 200,000 soldiers, with tanks, air and naval support. However, as time went on, Churchill became increasingly worried about the morale of the French army. In January 1940 Churchill was in France to look at French positions. At the same time, Leslie was sent to Paris to try to help in a proposed propaganda film effort. This, under the name of the Anglo-French Propaganda Council, was the work of Sir Campbell Stuart, director of foreign propaganda at that time.

Leslie was a good candidate to put forward for this, despite his own reluctance to appear in the political foreground. He spoke French, amongst other languages, loved the country, was well known as a film star and in addition had a most intelligent and elegant French woman at his side – his mistress, Violette Cunnington. Leslie had meetings with Jean Giraudoux, playwright and then French minister of information, and André Maurois, liaison officer between the French and British armies in the First World War, but unfortunately pro-Vichy at the start of the war. Noel Coward was also present, having been a friend of Sir Campbell Stuart, and appointed by him to help with propaganda in France. The idea of the meeting with Leslie was to discuss film-making with the French, sharing ideas, facilities and finance. Afterwards Leslie travelled to Arras, the headquarters of the British Expeditionary Force, to meet General Mason-Macfarlane, head of BEF intelligence. Leslie would surely have passed on his impressions of the French attitudes and work in progress.

Intelligence had been very difficult to organize for the BEF, due to staff shortages and diffuse army positions. Macfarlane's duties were many, including responsibility for all intelligence gathering, counter-espionage, and censorship of the press. He had to deal with many press representatives, VIPs from abroad, and most of all with the French.

The relationship between France and Britain at this crucial time was fragile, and was further undermined by the activities of some well-known

British personalities who were doing as much as they could to spread appeasement views amongst French society people. Leslie's
description of attitudes in Paris, especially from the government
representatives he had seen, must have been very welcome to Macfarlane.
In addition there was Leslie's influence and personality on the anti-
appeasement side, also good reason for his presence wherever he could be
seen and used effectively.[41]

Leslie went again to France in late April 1940 with Kenneth Clark,[42]
by then director of the Ministry of Information films division. The
earlier trip had ended with the proposal of a film starring Danielle
Darrieux and Leslie, to be directed by René Clair.[43] But by the time of
this second visit British and French armies were in retreat in the face of
the rapid German advance. A French surrender was soon to be forced
in June 1940. Nothing could now come of all these plans, which had
been left far too late.

As the war progressed Leslie quietly but openly visited some of the
neutral countries, Spain, Portugal and Ireland, ostensibly for discussions on film-industry cooperation and Allied propaganda. In April
1942 Leslie visited neutral Éire. Mr Nicholas Mansergh, who was then
working at the British Colonial Office with responsibility for relations
with Ireland, remembered sending Leslie over to Dublin: 'And after his
visit he wrote a very sensitive report on Irish feelings. We might well
have asked Howard to go back'.[44]

Ireland was a particular worry because its neutrality left Britain vulnerable to German attack through it, and also because de Valera, the
prime minister (Taoiseach), refused to allow use of certain very conveniently sited Southern Irish ports which might have shortened the Battle
of the Atlantic. Kenneth Clark (in late 1941) and subsequently Leslie
were wheeled out to promote good will, counter anti-British and pro-
German feelings in Ireland (of which there were plenty), to have
friendly arguments with the Taoiseach and to report back on prevailing
attitudes.

De Valera could not be influenced, but relations with Ireland were
considered so important that John Betjeman, later poet laureate, was
sent over as permanent liaison. Fifty years later the discovery that Mr
Betjeman and other figures prominent in cultural circles had reported
back to the Foreign Office on their friends and contacts' views was not
well appreciated by the Irish. But whether passing on other people's
public views and attitudes which are openly known counts as 'spying'
is surely arguable.

Leslie visited Spain and Portugal in May 1943. According to an unnamed source of Ronald Howard, he had a last meeting with his old security contact Major Mason-MacFarlane at this time in Gibraltar, on his way to Spain. Leslie might well have had a briefing with the governor of Gibraltar on conditions and attitudes in Spain, what kind of statements to make, help to offer, who was likely to be hostile, who could be relied on as friendly contacts. All this would have been entirely sensible and expected. Leslie may have been trusted to pass on messages to the governor in turn. However Ronald never produced any name or evidence for this meeting. In view of Ronald's other misleading speculations in his book, it will have to remain unproved.[45]

Leslie's own films contained propaganda for the Allied cause that was entirely public and emphatic. They display the most deeply felt acting of his career, and this period included his most productive and successful years. As for any other 'spy' work or activity as an intelligence agent – there are no known files in this country, or any official historical references to Leslie, by MI5, MI6, or any other British agency. There is no mention of him in this context in any history or biography of the time. In America, there is nothing in FBI or OSS files, as far as American authorities know or can say. In a communication of 2002, the National Archives and Records Administration stated that no record could be found of Leslie in the Department of Justice, the Index to Classified Subject files of 1921–36, or the Index to FBI records relating to the Second World War.[46]

Leslie was never a spy. How far his propaganda, or promotion for the Allied cause was covert work, remains arguable. When it began, in England or America, is also unlikely to be known for certain. And this is not only because official records are not or never will be available but because those who were witnesses have largely remained reticent, whether out of modesty, tactfulness or respect for those who actually laid down their lives.

NOTES

1. Ronald Howard, *In Search of My Father: A Portrait of Leslie Howard* (London: W. Kimber, 1981), p.229.
2. Letter to the author in 2002 from the British Historical Society of Portugal.
3. Howard, *In Search of My Father*, p.68.
4. Guido Coen, interview with author, 8 November 2000.
5. Ian Goodhope Colvin, *Flight 777* (London: Evans, 1957).
6. Maurice B. Long, 'The Mysterious Death of Leslie Howard', *Argosy* (April 1957).

7. Chapman Pincher, *Their Trade Is Treachery* (London: Sidgwick and Jackson, 1981), p.198; Anthony Read and David Fisher, *Colonel Z: The Life and Times of a Master of Spies* (London: Hodder and Stoughton, 1984), p.177.

8. 'Film Mogul Korda Was Secret Agent for Britain' *The Observer*, 3 November 1991, p.10.

9. See www.bbc.co.uk/pressoffice/pressreleases/stories/2003/05.

10. Nigel West, *MI5: British Security Service Operations, 1909–1945* (London: The Bodley Head, 1981), p.77; Nigel West, *MI6: British Secret Intelligence Service Operations, 1909–1945* (London: Weidenfeld and Nicolson, 1983), p.63; F.H. Hinsley and C.A.G. Simkins, *British Intelligence in the Second World War* (London: HMSO, 1970–1990), 5 vols, vol. 1, pp.45–9.

11. *Independent on Sunday,* 30 July 2000; Paul Lashmar, 'Wartime MI5 Chief Was on Side of Nazis'. See also David Petrie, 'The Security Service: Policy', National Archives, Public Record Office, (Pol F Series) Files KV 4/88 February 1941.

12. West, *MI6*, p.81. Hinsley and Simkins, *British Intelligence in the Second World War*, vol. 1, p.57.

13. M.R.D. Foot and J.M. Langley, *MI9* (London: Book Club Associates, 1979).

14. Nicholas Cull, *Selling War: The British Propaganda Campaign against American 'Neutrality' in World War II* (New York and Oxford: Oxford University Press, 1995); Susan Brewer, *To Win the Peace: British Propaganda in the United States during World War II* (Ithaca, NY and London: Cornell University Press, 1997).

15. Anonymous, *British Security Coordination. The Secret History of British Intelligence in The Americas 1940–45* (London: St Ermin's, 1998); Charles Drazin, *Korda: Britain's Only Movie Mogul* (London: Sidgwick and Jackson, 2002). Korda information based on an interview with Andrew King of MI6 in March 2001.

16. R. Harris Smith, *OSS: The Secret History of America's First Central Intelligence Agency* (Berkeley, CA: University of California Press, 1972), p.33; William J. Morgan, *Spies and Saboteurs* (London: Gollancz, 1955), p.111. Jewish volunteers of German origin were not accepted by OSS because their manner and speech was perceived as too Jewish for them to pass as Nazi Germans. On the other hand, British Intelligence rejected many OSS propagandists simply because they were of Jewish origin, which caused some friction between the two services.

17. Pincher, *Their Trade Is Treachery*, p.198.

18. Read and Fisher, *Colonel Z*, p.177.

19. H. Montgomery Hyde, *Secret Intelligence Agent* (New York: St Martin's Press, 1982).

20. David Stafford, 'Intrepid: Myth or Reality?', *Journal of Contemporary History*, 22 (1987), pp.303–17.

21. Bill Macdonald, *The True Intrepid: Sir William Stephenson and The Unknown Agents* (Surrey, British Columbia: Timberholme Books, 1998).

22. Author's interview 2002, with Colin Cohen, Commander Cohen's son.

23. Douglas Fairbanks Jnr, *A Hell of a War* (London: Robson, 1995).

24. Interview with Douglas Fairbanks Jnr by Professor Nicholas Cull, 9 March 1990, transcript kindly lent to author by Professor Cull.

25. Douglas Fairbanks Jnr interview.

26. *The New York Times*, 7 May 1935.

27. Douglas Fairbanks Jnr interview.

28. For Churchill's contacts, see Martin Gilbert, *Winston S. Churchill: Prophet of Truth 1922–1939* (London: Heinemann, 1976), vol. V, pp.874–84; William Manchester, *The Caged Lion: Winston Spencer Churchill, 1932–1940* (London: Michael Joseph, 1988), p.112–17. For Vansittart's network, see John R. Ferris, 'The Last Old Diplomat: Sir Robert Vansittart and British Foreign Policy – Indulged In All Too Little? Vansittart, Intelligence and Appeasement', *Diplomacy and Statecraft* 6 (1995), pp.122–75.

29. Martin Gilbert, *In Search of Churchill: A Historian's Journey* (London: HarperCollins 1995), p.109.

30. Manchester, *The Caged Lion*, p.113; Gilbert, *In Search of Churchill*, pp.111–16.

31. Andrew Kelly, James Pepper and Jeffrey Richards (eds), *Filming T.E. Lawrence: Korda's Lost Epics* (London: I.B. Tauris, 1997).

32. Miklos Rosza, *Double Life, The Autobiography of Miklos Rosza* (Tunbridge Wells: Midas Books, 1982).

33. Manchester, *The Caged Lion*, p.313.

34. Peter Wright, *Spy Catcher* (New York: Dell, 1988), p.86.

35. Kelly, Pepper and Richards (eds), *Filming T.E. Lawrence*, p.24.
36. Ibid., p.11.
37. For a thorough exploration of Churchill's secret networks, see David Stafford, *Roosevelt and Churchill: Men of Secrets* (London: Little, Brown, 1999).
38. Manchester, *The Caged Lion*, p.207.
39. Anthony Quayle, *A Time to Speak* (London: Barrie and Jenkins, 1990), p.311.
40. Howard, *In Search of My Father*, pp.67–8.
41. L.F. Ellis, *The War in France and Flanders 1939–1940* (London: HMSO, 1953), pp.64–5; and Ewan Butler, *Mason-Mac: The Life of Lieutenant-General Sir Noel Mason-Macfarlane: A Biography* (London: Macmillan, 1972), pp.104–10.
42. Sir Kenneth Clark was knighted in 1938. Although still young he was a highly respected figure in the British cultural world, having been fine arts curator at the Ashmolean Museum, and later director of the National Gallery. He was the youngest person ever to hold the post. *Oxford Dictionary of National Biography*.
43. Howard, *In Search of My Father*, p.69.
44. Bevis Hillier, *John Betjeman: New Fame, New Love* (London: John Murray, 2002), p.221.
45. Howard, *In Search of My Father*, p.69.
46. Letter to author from the National Archives and Records Administration, 29 January 2002 and an email to author from the same, searching the records of the Department of Justice, the Index to Classified Subject Files 1921–36, and the Index to FBI records relating to the Second World War, 1940–52.

CHAPTER SEVEN

August 1939–June 1941:
Pimpernel Smith

In late August 1939, Leslie travelled back to England with all his family, followed by his companion, Violette Cunnington, with whom he had already been living in Los Angeles. He continued to live mainly with her, visiting his family regularly at weekends and for short holidays and dealing, not entirely successfully, with the resulting complications. The family settled down at their house in Surrey, Stowe Maries, Leslie working there at times, but also living with Violette at a flat in Chelsea Manor Street, London.

Leslie began working at Stowe Maries on a report for the government, his *Notes on American Propaganda*, advising in it that care should be taken, as the Americans at this time were uninterested in a European war and sceptical of Britain's ability to take on the German war machine. A few months later, Leslie worked with Anthony Asquith on *The Film Industry in Time of War*, a report for the Ministry of Information. The report he and Leslie produced was detailed, covering training and instructional films, documentary ideas and even guidance on quota legislation and labour relations. Leslie was also looking about him at this time to see in what ways his work could best help. He used friendly and like-minded contacts for information on events abroad, and was able to obtain what must have been dismaying news from unofficial sources.[1]

Late in the summer of 1939, Leslie, his son Ronald, and Violette visited the house of Sir Eustace Pulbrook, chairman of Lloyds, at Woking, Surrey. There they met 16-year-old Paul Kuttner, one of the Kindertransport youths, rescued just in time from the concentration camps, and sponsored by Sir Eustace. Kuttner says that Leslie was 'fascinated by the horrors of the Nazi regime, about which I talked to him for hours ... The Howards and I became fast friends ... I still adore both men'.[2]

The Kindertransports had come about in the reaction to the attack on the German Jewish Community on *Kristallnacht*, 9 November 1938. British and American opinion was roused. The prime minister, Neville

Chamberlain, received a deputation of eminent British Jews, who asked that he permit the temporary admission of young children who were confined in concentration camps, or under threat, and who might later re-emigrate. Monetary guarantees would be given for all the children. After some hesitation, the plan was put into action and from December 1938 until the start of the war in September 1939, trains full of children separated abruptly from their families arrived in Britain. Wilfred Israel, a wealthy German émigré Jew, whom Leslie was later to meet, laid the infrastructure for the plan. Many people, Jews and non-Jews, gave their money and effort, and although there were problems and chaos, about 5,000 children were eventually saved. The older ones later joined war units. Most never saw their families again. Paul Kuttner would have been able to tell Leslie of all these things, and the terrifying conditions in Germany imposed by the Nazi regime.[3]

Leslie was actively looking for information on what was happening and had the luck to be helped by a neighbour of his, Jonah Barrington, the radio correspondent of the *Daily Express*. He took Leslie to Cherkley Court, country home of Lord Beaverbrook, the owner of the *Express* newspaper. Beaverbrook and the *Express* had been pro-appeasement all through the 1930s and even to the start of the war. (Eventually his old friend and rival, Churchill, talked him into becoming a very successful minister of aircraft production, from 1940.) Beaverbrook had set up his own short-wave receiving station at Cherkley, able to pick up broadcasts from much of Europe. From 1 September 1939 it was tuned to Poland, and interpreters provided instant translations of messages received, which were sent to the *Express*. They were also sent to the Foreign Office. Leslie listened to the last Free Polish people who had transmitters, while their country was invaded. Not only the Germans, but the Soviet Red Army invaded, allied with Germany under the Nazi-Soviet pact. On 4 October 1939, Poland capitulated, utterly overrun. No one had come to help them. The Polish government escaped abroad, and many thousands fled. 15,000 Polish officials and influential persons were murdered on the spot, or later in the camps. All Jews were segregated, organized for later mass murder by starvation, gas or shooting. German units would kill the mentally handicapped and the elderly who were in homes and hostels, and 'non-Aryan' children in orphanages – the buildings would be used by the German army. Concentration camps were built, starting with the mass destruction of 'intellectuals'. Leslie listened until the last free transmitter was silenced, and they heard the German announcers, speaking in Polish, announce that the Poles had lost.[4]

But in all his efforts to get things moving in the film world at the start of the war, Leslie came up against the blank wall of Chamberlain's administration and its recalcitrant officials. The will to move was still lacking. Leslie saw civil servants, wrote to Lord Halifax (then foreign secretary, later American ambassador) and sent his report, endorsed by prominent men in the film industry, to the government. The response was apathetic. Leslie's anger with arrogant and indifferent officials at this time was eventually translated into his film, but for months he waited while little apparently happened.

The Ministry of Information, which was to run the wartime film effort, had a dubious beginning. In the summer of 1939, Beaverbrook advised Samuel Hoare, the home secretary, on the setting up of the ministry. These two, and Chamberlain, the prime minister, still hoped to arrange a peace with Germany. Lord Macmillan was appointed to head the ministry, but the attitude was bureaucratic and cautious. Beaverbrook, a man at any rate of great energy and creativity, was later offered the position, but turned it down, saying that the ministry was apathetic and discredited.[5] Macmillan was replaced in January 1940 by Sir John Reith, formerly director general of the BBC.

On 10 May 1940 Chamberlain finally resigned, and Churchill was appointed head of a national government. Up till that time, the Ministry of Information had slowly evolved, under its different ministers, from passive to active, from provincial to balanced, from the haughtiness of its gentleman-amateur appointees, to cooperation with the British press and public. It was a sea change in attitude, experienced by the whole of officialdom as ideas on what the country was fighting for were debated and decided.

But at the start of the war, some of Chamberlain's appointments to the ministry were pro-appeasement, others were establishment figures who had no knowledge of, or sympathy with this work. Sir Joseph Ball was in charge of the Films Division until December 1939. He had been head of the research department of the Conservative Party in the 1930s and had some experience in the use of film as political propaganda. But he seemed disdainful of the film world, both the feature-film makers and the documentarists, and uninterested in taking any particular action to promote the war. He was an unpopular figure in the film world, but there was a further, more sinister side to him. Some historians have seen him as an *éminence grise* of the Conservative Party, with a history as an MI5 agent in some dubious political trickery. He was a great influence on and personal friend of Chamberlain, and active in promoting Chamberlain's views in the party and government. Ball was the owner of a weekly magazine called *Truth,* acquired in 1938, and he secretly had direct editorial control. After 1939 the magazine was used to smear anti-appeasers in the government, who were opponents of Chamberlain. It was Chamberlain's views that were expressed in the journal, the tone becoming more and more anti-Semitic and pro-German, with articles praising Hitler. Another director of the paper was William Charles Crocker, also of MI5, responsible for interning many Jews at this time. Sir Robert Vansittart later ordered an investigation into the magazine and its owners in 1942. His report concluded that Chamberlain, from the time when war was declared in September 1939, to his forced resignation in May 1940, was running a double policy; while openly at war with Nazi Germany, he was secretly in sympathy with it.[6]

Chamberlain's views were not representative of all the government, but there were a number who supported appeasement, as there were throughout the establishment. The new minister of information, Alfred Duff Cooper, a long-time critic of appeasement, who was to take over the ministry in May 1940, found that his views sometimes made him an uncomfortable target of former friends. His wife Diana later wrote of the atmosphere in late 1939:

> On leaving the Savoy Grill, lost in the blackout, we were nearly run down and kindly succoured by an outsize car in which sat the Duke of Westminster, the 'Bendor' I had once loved. It was an uncomfortable salvation. He started by abusing the Jewish race, a red-rag subject where Duff was concerned. When from this dangerous ground he plunged confidently on through some defences into praise of the Germans, rejoicing that we were not yet at war, and when he added that Hitler knew after all that we were his best friends, he set off the powder-magazine. 'I hope', Duff spat, 'that by tomorrow he will know that we are his most implacable and remorseless enemies.' Next day 'Bendor', telephoning to a friend, said that if there were a war it would be entirely due to the Jews and Duff Cooper.[7]

In January 1940, Sir Kenneth Clark, the youthful director of the National Gallery, with very little experience of the film world, was appointed head of the Films Division of the ministry. He had a benevolent attitude to the film industry but made a slip in referring to the 'non-British and Jewish element in the (film) Industry'. An apology followed, as it was pointed out in *Kinematograph Weekly* magazine that the film industry did not think of a man as non-British because he was

Jewish.[8] Clark eventually left, feeling that he had been one of the 'gentleman-amateur' appointees to the ministry, and from April 1940, Jack Beddington, of Jewish background, whose family had been English since the 1700s, took over as head of the Films Division.

Beddington had good experience of publicity and public relations, having been in charge of publicity at Shell. He developed a spirit of cooperation and openness to creative ideas, but had limited freedom as the Films Division came directly under the hand of Whitehall. He expanded the distribution of wartime films and supported the Crown Film Unit of innovative documentary makers, and their realist influence. In 1942 he formed an Ideas Committee, in which a number of directors and writers from film and documentaries met once a fortnight. This went on throughout the war, and included Leslie at times, together with Michael Balcon, Michael Powell, Sidney Gilliat, Rodney Acland, Charles Frend, Anthony Asquith and others. The Ideas Committee became the source of feature-film production ideology, where subjects and themes were discussed and checked against the ministry's information and propaganda policy. But the ministry always had the last word, holding absolute power over all aspects of communications during the war.[9]

The cinemas, which were closed very briefly at the outbreak of war in September 1939, were soon reopened, especially as nothing much seemed to be happening as far as conflict was concerned. Eventually, cinema audiences during the war grew to be larger than ever before, and films had a great influence on opinion. But British films would have to compete with some classic American productions. The first year of the war saw the release of more Hollywood classics than any other year – *The Wizard of Oz, Mr Smith Goes to Washington, The Hunchback of Notre Dame, Gunga Din, Wuthering Heights, Ninotchka, The Women, Stagecoach* and *The Young Mr Lincoln*.

In April 1940 Leslie himself was showcased with the British opening of the mighty blockbuster, *Gone with the Wind*. English film reviewers were never quite in tune with the inner workings of Hollywood, and some reviews of this three-hour effort were less than wholehearted. However *The Times*, always courteous, deigned to compliment the film on its 'extensive and miscellaneous information about the past ... the producer has even gone to the expense of having what seems to be a genuine daguerreotype taken of Mr Leslie Howard'. This review went on to praise the 'gusto and vitality' of Vivien Leigh's acting, and mentions especially Hattie McDaniel for her portrayal, saying that she acted everybody else off the screen. Leslie received faint praise, the paper excusing him by saying his part is 'too self-effacing to give his talent an opportunity'. This would not have amused Leslie, but the film was a giant success with the public, and as *The Times* admitted, 'no-one could quarrel with such luxurious entertainment'.[10] *Gone with the Wind* broke all records, and was shown continuously in London throughout most of the war, still playing in 1943, so Leslie was never to escape his most disliked role. But it provided constant publicity and a great boost for his personal standing.

Early in 1940, when the war seemed static, Leslie's thoughts began to centre round the production of his own film. The focus of his feelings would be the strongest message he could make against the Nazis; and his own energy and finances would have to push it into being. Since 1933 when they had come to power, Leslie had seen the Nazis remove Jewish citizenship, then Jewish homes and livelihoods, set up concentration camps and legalize brutal punishments for Jews and any anti-Nazis. The result of the oppression had been waves of emigration, first between 1933 and 1936, to other countries all over Europe. More came after the Anschluss, the Nazi takeover of Austria, in March 1938. A third wave followed *Kristallnacht*, in November 1938.

Leslie's film would make a statement about Nazi treatment of the German people. The genesis of the film was slow, and went through many changes, helped along the way by different talents. Leslie's son Ronald claimed the first spark of an idea came from the meeting with Alfons Walde, the Austrian modern artist whom Leslie had met on holiday in 1938. Walde had told him of anti-Nazi professors, doctors, teachers and artists who had been imprisoned, or murdered.[11]

It may be that Walde, who had spoken of his own difficult position, gave Leslie the beginnings of his idea. But there is no trace of this figure in the final production of the film *Pimpernel Smith*. Walde was not Jewish; ultimately he never left Austria and nothing much happened to him. The Nazis disapproved of his 'decadent', impressionist style, influenced by Schiele and Klimt, but he was not imprisoned.[12] Leslie used a character with similar sympathies to this radical artist in *49th Parallel*, the Powell and Pressburger production which was in the making at the same time and studio as his own film.

Leslie had conceived an escape film, and began writing a film treatment. For the next year, from the end of 1939 to the completion of the film in May 1941, Leslie would have to combine the promotion of his film and raising finance together with writing and rewriting until he had a finished script. It was a wearying task, and Leslie had to summon skills he had long neglected, of persevering despite one rejection after another, and enthusiastic socialising. Nor did the emotional force he felt sit well with his normally reticent character.

During this period Leslie was also working hard in other areas to promote the war effort. He was moderately popular as a broadcaster for the BBC, first being heard in America as a guest of J.B. Priestley in July 1940. He was to make twenty-seven broadcasts in a series called *Britain Speaks*, as well as appearances as a guest on other well-known shows. He also developed an early propaganda film with the Ministry of Information, *From the Four Corners* (also known as *Common Heritage*). This attempted to rally support against fascism from what was then the British Empire, now (in part) Commonwealth countries; but with the unspoken assumption that Britain was the 'home' country, it was bound to appear patronising.

In January 1940 Leslie and Violette made a trip to Paris on official business. They were to aid a joint British–French propaganda effort. The political atmosphere in France delayed any action, but in April 1940 Leslie tried again, accompanied by Kenneth Clark, then head of the Films Division. This time the proposal was more concrete – a film to star Leslie and Danielle Darrieux, to be directed by René Clair. These are famous names in film history, but not owing to this project, which could never be realized. Leslie and Violette took advantage of what was to be the last two weeks of France's freedom, for a numinous, dream-like holiday in Paris.

Back in Britain, Leslie sought for help with *Pimpernel Smith* in the small world of British film. He needed the 'look' of Germany at that time as settings for his story, and these could be well described by the foreign refugees with film backgrounds who had recently been helped to escape to this country. Some of these had worked at the famous German Ufa studios. At Korda's studio Leslie found among others Wolfgang Wilhelm, an ex-Ufa screenwriter with whom he had several meetings, and together they produced a film treatment; the script was something of a cooperative effort, with five writers eventually being credited, and had to pass scrutiny of the Ministry of Information, which was in overall control.

The novelist A.G. Macdonell, a friend of Leslie's, also lent a hand with the storyline. Macdonell had been working as a BBC short-wave broadcaster to the Empire and the United States in the summer of 1940, with a mildly comic commentary on German broadcasts monitored by the BBC. He was best known for his novel, *England their England* (1933), a satirical view of English society in the 1920s, which all the same ends with a romantic flourish and a celebration of England's rural spirit. Macdonell had recently married into a Viennese Jewish family,[13] who had escaped to Britain when Austria merged with Nazi Germany in 1938. He was handsome, quick-witted and always a ladies' man, and might have been a boon companion for Leslie, but unfortunately his experiences fighting in the First World War shortened his life, and he died of heart failure in January 1941.

The brooding home atmosphere was broken in April with the German invasion of Norway, but on 10 May 1940, reality exploded. Germany launched its western offensive with attacks on France, Holland and Belgium. Chamberlain finally resigned, and Churchill was appointed prime minister and also minister of defence. In effect he took charge equally with his military chiefs of staff. Three days later, speaking in the House of Commons, Churchill warned the British people, 'I have nothing to offer but blood, toil, tears and sweat'. He told the listening members of parliament, 'You ask what is our policy? I will say – it is to wage war, by sea, land and air, with all our might and with all the strength that God can give us; to wage war against a monstrous tyranny, never surpassed in the dark, lamentable catalogue of human crime.' The aim was, 'Victory, victory at all costs, victory however long and hard the road may be; for without victory there is no survival'.

The mood was grim, but Leslie was convinced of the importance of his work. In June his discussions with MacDonnell produced the role of Pimpernel Smith, using Baroness Orczy's character again, to give what seems to be a fusion of two of Leslie's most popular roles – the Scarlet Pimpernel and Professor Higgins of *Pygmalion*. Leslie was reluctant about grandstanding himself for once, but realized ultimately that his best asset was his own character, still held in great affection by his public. He also worried that associating his serious theme with the story of the Scarlet Pimpernel might trivialize it to some extent, but it was the best idea anyone could bring forward.

At the beginning of June came Dunkirk. France was overwhelmed, and the British retreat from the beaches had to turn into a mass rescue: 340,000 British soldiers were saved by any British ship that could sail across the channel. Leslie's daughter remembers the whole family standing in the fields beyond Stowe Maries watching the trains filled with the rescued soldiers and throwing them supplies of cigarettes, chocolate and fruit.[14] The family also did their best around this time to entertain and cheer locally based Canadian troops, with the 16-year-old Leslie Ruth herself a great attraction.

Leslie was trying to sustain both his relationships – with his family, and with Violette Cunnington, who was to be the love of his life. Everyone in the family was aware of what was happening, but for Leslie's sake, and the sake of his work, the tension held. All the same, the added stress on all parties, at a time when they (together with the whole country) were already under great strain, was eventually to prove disastrous.

At the end of June came the French armistice, and Britain stood alone. German bombers attacked the country as preparation for invasion. The RAF responded, and the Battle of Britain began. Leslie began his broadcasts to America, asking for sympathy and help. In August he visited Oxford, scouting locations for his film, but whatever he found there was not conducive, and he eventually used Cambridge, where his son Ronald was studying, as the academic setting for the early scenes.

Anatole de Grunwald was added to the strength of those working fitfully with the script of Pimpernel Smith. He had a background as a refugee, this time from Tsarist Russia, where his father had been a government diplomat. He was worldly and sophisticated, and had been educated at Cambridge and the Sorbonne. He worked with Wolfgang Wilhelm, already on board, and also with Roland Pertwee, English actor and another excellent dramatist. Together they sharpened up the script, improving the dialogue and moving the pace along. Leslie controlled all, handling the writers tactfully, and altering their work to his own specifications without ruffling feathers.

Finally, at the end of October 1940, Leslie managed to get a contract signed with British National Film Productions. He arranged finance with the company, which was owned by Lady Yule, patriotic widow of a multi-millionaire jute manufacturer, with enough money to risk in the uncertain business of films. Preliminary production began at the end of 1940. Leslie assembled a remarkable collection of talent – he had the opportunity, as the cream of the European film world was now camping out in England. His cinematographer was Max 'Mutz' Greenbaum who, being Jewish, had been helped by Balcon away from the German film industry in the early 1930s. He later demonstrated the first use of deep focus cinematography in England (pioneered in 1941 by cameraman Gregg Toland in *Citizen Kane*) and used by Greenbaum in *They Flew Alone* (1942).[15] He had extensive experience of the expressionist style in Germany, and Leslie was to make eloquent use of his chiaroscuro lighting. In the finished film, this contributes much to the nightmarish atmosphere, contrasting the normality and humour of the English world with the dark horror of contemporary Germany.

The film editor was Sidney Cole, who later had a long career with

Ealing Studios, and was associated with the Documentary Film Movement, which aimed for greater realism in film. He remembered of that time:

> I worked on a series of interesting films, perhaps the most outstanding was working with Leslie Howard on *Pimpernel Smith* in 1941 at Denham. Leslie Howard had a great sense of style. He was starring, producing and directing. He was a very pleasant man to work with. He was also very practical and down to earth. He had not directed much before so he liked to surround himself with all the technical aid he could summon. I was made supervising editor on the picture and he asked me to be on the floor all the time so he could ask my advice. Even when he was directing a sequence which involved music he had the music director there ... I found it very stimulating to work with Leslie. I think that picture and another which he later did, *The First of the Few*, on which I was also supervising editor, I found very rewarding because Leslie had considerable style both as an actor and a director, you took this as the keynote of the way you edit the film. If you took the rhythm of Leslie's performance, that was the rhythm you did as an editor to carry the whole stylistic approach into the final film. And that was a contribution to the war effort because it was about a modern Scarlet Pimpernel rescuing people from the Nazis.[16]

Production of *Pimpernel Smith* got slowly under way between January and February 1941. Leslie and Violette, bombed out of London by the Blitz, moved to a large house near Denham Studios, which became one of the main centres of film production during the war. The others were Ealing, headed by Michael Balcon, and later, in December 1941, Pinewood Studios, which the Government opened as the headquarters of a new nationally sponsored propaganda drive, jointly housing the Army Film Unit, The RAF Film Unit and the Crown Film Unit of the MoI, as well as some commercial film-makers. Other studios also operated sporadically, but mostly making minor films – often comedies with much-loved stars of the day. These were meant to cheer the spirit, but their portrayal of Nazi figures as schoolboy nuisances was also an index of the obliviousness of the British to the storm of evil in Europe. Despite this, wartime films went on to become some of greatest achievements of the British industry. There were major works from some inspired individualists, such as the Boulting Brothers, Launder and Gilliatt, David Lean, Anthony Asquith, Carol Reed, Michael Powell and Emeric Pressburger.

While making the film, Leslie and Violette were not alone in their house, which was the property of Anthony Havelock Allan, aristocratic film producer, and his wife, actress Valerie Hobson. It was also a home for others such as Harold Huth, the film's producer; Irene Howard, Leslie's sister, who helped with casting; and Mary Morris, Leslie's female lead, who slept in an adjoining bedroom to Leslie and Violette and had to creep past their sleeping forms every morning she was on set.[17] Violette also appeared in the film, briefly playing a French shop assistant, listed under her real forename as Suzanne Claire. The scriptwriter Sidney Gilliat (later director and producer) remembered visiting Leslie at this house to discuss a propaganda film for Empire audiences, during which an air raid took place, while Leslie valiantly kept everyone's spirits up:

> Leslie Howard and I were supposed to discuss this Empire film. I found him charming. I suppose that by origin he was Jewish-Rou-manian; but in manner he was very English. There were eight or nine people at dinner, including Roland Pertwee, and we all washed up and dried the dishes, Howard included. And then he sat down at the piano and played – rather badly but spiritedly – old music hall songs, and we all sang them. It was a most surpris-ing evening to me. I don't think we ever discussed the Empire film – but it was made. It was called *From the Four Corners*.[18]

Nearby stood Denham Studios, created by Alexander Korda, who had later lost control of his own company after financial difficulties. He spent most of the war based in Hollywood, but made frequent trips to England. Korda's last major film at Denham was *The Lion Has Wings*, made on his own initiative in September 1939. Korda meant it both as a patriotic morale-booster, at a time when Britain's war capability was under question, and a promise that the British film industry would par-ticipate to the fullest in the coming propaganda war. The film was put together hurriedly, and although it did well at the box office, extolling the RAF, it was also widely criticized for its 'too blatant' propaganda.

Although Korda was gone, the atmosphere he had created at Denham remained. Korda had helped many Jewish refugees, funding their escape from the Germans, and finding jobs for them in England. Denham remained a centre of anti-Nazi feeling and exchange; refugees, many like Korda, Hungarian, still haunted the studios for financial help, fellow-feeling and emotional support in the turmoil of the times.[19] Denham had been a modern, art-deco show place when it was built in 1936, and an atmosphere of fame and glamour hung about it. At this time during the war, there was less glamour, but a feeling of tremendous solidarity amongst those working there. Ronald Neame, who worked with Leslie (and is alive at the time of writing, aged 94) said of Denham during the war years, 'it was a very close, friendly time, very warm. Everyone helped each other. There was a little group of independent film makers and we all knew each other. I worked with Leslie – he was always everything that was charming ... We didn't think of him as Jewish, but then we didn't bother about that at all.'[20]

The resolute atmosphere at Denham and the content of the films then being made had their effect on a political controversy of the day. On 4 March 1941 a news story broke that a number of actors and musicians, including the actor Michael Redgrave, had signed the manifesto of 'The Peoples' Convention', a political movement which called for, amongst other popular and socialist measures, 'a people's peace that gets rid of the causes of war'. The grouping was backed by the Communist Party, whose line at this time was pacifist, although this changed in the course of the war. The BBC's political policies were carefully vague, but they drew the line, according to a spokesman, at 'inviting any person to the microphone whose views are opposed to the National war effort'. Redgrave and other signatories were banned from performing on the BBC.

Amongst the first people to respond to the BBC ban were Leslie and the others at Denham. According to the *News Chronicle* the next day, 'Leslie Howard and several actors and actresses in *Pimpernel Smith* and *49th Parallel* at Denham studios drew up a resolution ... protesting vehemently against ... this action, which was sent to the BBC'. Leslie saw the point at issue before anyone else, which was simply that censoring an artist's work because of his private political views was part of the fascist doctrines being fought against.

Over the next few days, following Leslie, a chorus of individuals and groups, including a petition of forty MPs, put the point loudly to the BBC governors. Michael Redgrave's letter stating that he was not a pacifist, and was in fact just about to join the Royal Navy, was published prominently. Finally, on 21 March, Churchill announced in the House of Commons that the ban would be lifted. During this debate, one MP had put to him the *reductio ad absurdum* case – would a pacifist conductor have his music banned? Churchill's reply: 'no, but I think we should have to retain a certain amount of power in the selection of music, as spirited renderings of *Deutschland uber alles* would hardly be ...' was interrupted at this point by a roar of laughter in the House, and the matter ended in good humour and good will.[21]

Leslie was in unchallenged control of his film once the Ministry of Information had passed the script. He took his time in making it, even getting up late and refusing to allow a hurried atmosphere on the set, and ignoring financial constraints. One observer noted, 'Leslie Howard was the producer, director and star, and he had a good deal to say about the script as well'.[22] This was David Tomlinson, later a well-known actor, playing one of Professor Smith's students in the film. Tomlinson also commented,

> He certainly wasn't the romantic ethereal character people thought him to be. He was actually quite tough, although he had enormous charm; on the set he would stand for nothing less than perfection. He would set up the scene meticulously and then, at the very last minute before shooting began, he would step into the shot and play his part, making it seem the easiest thing in the world.[23]

Pimpernel Smith, after all its evolutions, received its British premier on 26 July 1941. It was seen in America in February 1942, but of course nowhere in Europe, except in private showings in the neutral countries. What emerges most strongly from the film is Leslie's anger. The mood is emotional and forceful. Ronald Howard later described it as 'the most virulently anti-Nazi film ever produced'.[24] The film reflects

Figure 22. Leslie as *Pimpernel Smith*, 1941.

Leslie's gathered experience of what was happening in Europe, his disgust with the appeasers and the isolationists, and his frustrated efforts to make something happen, dealing with the recalcitrant bureaucrats of the time.

The film opens with a written dedication to 'those unfortunate people of many nationalities who are being persecuted and exterminated by the Nazis'. The setting is spring 1939, in Berlin, where a medical researcher is miraculously rescued by a shadowy figure – Pimpernel Smith. The scene moves to foreign journalists at the Berlin propaganda ministry telephoning news of this escape. A Nazi official tells them all that the story is false, and ends by stating firmly, 'in Nazi Germany, nobody can hope to be saved by anybody!' This sequence ends in Professor Smith's Cambridge study, amongst ancient academic buildings, where the rescued scientist is seen with the professor, preparing a 'serum' for the good of mankind.

Leslie may or may not have been thinking of a specific individual here. Certainly many well-known Jewish scientists had managed to get away from Germany, but the character in the film is strongly reminiscent of Ernest Chain, the later Nobel Prize winner. Chain found a means of turning penicillin into a usable drug, the first antibiotic, saving thousands of servicemen's lives during the war. He had left Berlin in 1933 and worked at Cambridge during the war. In the film, this character remarks to Smith, 'You and I are not men of action'. Leslie replies, 'No, I hate violence'.

In the next sequence, Smith succeeds in extracting 'the world's greatest pianist' from Germany. When asked why he risks his life for such rescues, Smith replies, 'when a man holds the view that progress and civilisation depend upon the hand and brains of a few exceptional spirits, it's hard to stand by and see them destroyed'. Smith adds, in words that seem personal to Leslie, 'I'm not a very spectacular person. In fact a natural capacity for melting into the landscape has proved very useful.'

Most tellingly, Leslie mocks the Foreign Office and the establishment with a very English, monocled, aristocratic figure identified as 'The Earl of Meadowbrook'. This buffoon-like character, in answer to any question or comment, such as 'and what have you been doing so far?' loudly repeats, 'Absolutely nothing!' Smith finally manages to get him arrested by the Gestapo. Leslie even includes an attack on American isolationism and the pro-Nazi German–American Bund. Disguised as an American journalist visiting the German Ministry of Propaganda, Smith says, 'I'm Wodenschantz, the one who got the Nazi party those nice headlines in America. I put the Nazi-American Bund on the map

... I'm nursing the American (press) correspondents. They can tell the U.S. not to believe what they hear about the camps!' Smith goes on to name particular American newspapers – the *Chicago Tribune*, the *Baltimore Sun*, the *New York Herald Tribune*, and the *Boston Transcript*.

These were all real newspapers: the *Chicago Tribune* was the leading American isolationist newspaper, supporting Hitler on the grounds that he was a bulwark against Communism. The *Boston Transcript* had written an editorial on the Nuremberg Laws in 1935, explaining that they had been brought in due to the failure of 'measures already taken to keep the German Jews in subjection'. The American press throughout the 1930s dismissed Nazi persecution of minorities as exaggerated, or somehow justified. Even during the war the true events were similarly treated, with the millions of deaths played down or obscured. Leslie's judgement here on the foreign correspondents of the US newspapers, mostly based in Berlin, was not true for all US journalists. Some tried to pass on what was actually happening, but were beset on both sides – the Nazi regime increasingly harassed reporters throughout the 1930s who did not follow their party line, and in any case lied about their policies, while the US newspapers were unwilling to publish all they were told.[25] Leslie did not say so, but the British press had not been much different.[26]

The character of 'Wodenschantz' may or may not be a reference to General Bodenschatz, of the Nazi military command. But the scene strikes the modern viewer with foreboding. The use of realistic figures in what was really a romantic film added to the impact. Similarly with the actor parodying Goering, Francis Sullivan, who was an imposing and rather frightening figure in real life. These direct, but scornful images of the Nazis were a dreadful challenge. The Nazis were not likely to forget them, and they were vengeful.

In the film Smith continues his rescues, aided by some of his Cambridge students, and in the process falls in love with a young Polish woman, whose father, a newspaper editor, he has already rescued. Several of those rescued in the film have Jewish names – Josephs, Meyer, Blumenfeld, but are never explicitly identified as Jews. As the film ends, Smith is at a French border station, in danger of being captured and killed by the Nazis. He confronts von Graum, the parody figure of Goering, and principal Nazi villain in the film. Von Graum tells him that the Germans intend to invade Poland that same night. Smith replies,

> Tonight you will take the first step along a dark road from which there is no turning back. You will have to go on, from one madness

to another, leaving behind you a wilderness of misery and hatred. And still you'll have to go on, because you will find no horizon, you will see no dawn until at last you are lost and destroyed. You are doomed, Captain of Murderers, and sooner or later you will remember my words.

Von Graum shoots at Smith, but in the darkness he escapes across the border to Switzerland, his voice-over finally whispering, 'Don't worry, I shall be back – we will all be back.' But too late, as Leslie didn't add.

One of the surviving anecdotes about the making of the film demonstrated how far Leslie was prepared to go in pursuing his own individual efforts in the face of what seemed far too much apathy. The atmosphere at Denham had attracted Albert Meltzer, a member of the British anarchist movement, and who was playing an 'anarchist prisoner' in the film. In his memoirs of this time, Meltzer tells a romantic tale of a courageous German Jewish girl, who approached Leslie for help with action against Hitler. Many years later, as records were revealed, the story was confirmed. As Meltzer later described,

> I put [Leslie] in touch with Hilda Monte and the Birmingham people and they suggested an international resistance group located in Lisbon. It is hard to know what came of it though I know he managed Hilda Monte's attempt and persuaded Military Intelligence to let her get on with it. I guess that if this was the case, they took the attitude that if a Jewess was prepared to risk going back to Germany, and she was a spy, there was no risk to them.[27]

Hilda Monte was a young German woman very active in federalist and anarchist movements on the continent. These parties were in opposition to the Communist Party, giving an even more radical interpretation to the works of Marx. Monte, originally named Meisel, was of Hungarian Jewish origin, although she had lived in Germany from childhood, and was passionately anti-Nazi. She had come to England permanently in 1936 and was determined to do all she could to carry on the battle.

The dates of documents at the National Archives are in accordance with Albert Meltzer's statement. In SOE Files HS9/1118/3 Hilda Miesel (*sic*), Hilda Monte is recorded as a member of SOE – the Special Operations Executive. This was a branch of the Secret Services formed in July 1940 and urged by Churchill to 'set Europe ablaze' with sabotage and hidden resistance. Leslie's film was made at Denham from the beginning of February to April 1941. On the 27 February 1941 MI5, the home intelligence service, in overall charge, received a 'trace'

Figure 23. Hilda Monte. From Annedore Leber, *Conscience in Revolt* (London: Vallentine Mitchell, 1957).

request, to investigate and clear Hilda Monte's background. On 17 March her file reads, 'X2 advised that it is intended to employ (Monte)'. And on 29 March, 'X2 advised that (Monte) is being employed by X section, and will leave for Lisbon on Tuesday, April 1st.'

'X' was the code letter in SOE files for the German and Austrian section, 'X2' one of the men in charge of it at that time. Hilde was given the codename 'Crocus', which in the Victorian language of flowers means 'joy', 'gladness' and 'keep from harm' – there was a strain of sentiment in the midst of the horror.[28] As Meltzer stated, SOE was criticized later for its employment of Jews by those who did not understand (or did not want to) that there were some who would rather die in battle than watch passively while their whole people were destroyed.[29] Leslie was to have other connections to SOE.

Meltzer wrote that Leslie backed Monte and her anarchist colleagues financially, with an idea that they would 'have a go at Hitler' – try an assassination attempt. Others had suggested this, but such proposals had been rejected by Lord Halifax, who stated that he could not condone assassination in favour of diplomacy.[30] Such a response showed the gap between Leslie and British upper-class and government opinion of the time. To most of these Hitler was a statesman with a legitimate, if extreme, political model. Leslie knew enough to see him as a vicious madman who had blighted a nation. The isolation of this stance had followed Leslie all through the 1930s, and even into the war, and accounted for his determination to take his own action now.

There is plenty of evidence about Hilda Monte; she studied at the London School of Economics, published three wartime books and some poetry with Victor Gollancz. She was praised by Jennie Lee (Labour MP and later arts minister) for her idealism and bravery in rescuing refugees from the Nazi regime.[31] But SOE's German section was inactive until near the end of the war – the Nazi terror gripped the country too tightly for agents to achieve much. Evidently Monte's work at Lisbon came to nothing. In 1942 SOE merged resources with the American secret agency OSS (Office of Strategic Services, a forerunner to the CIA). In 1944 the OSS, with somewhat greater reserves of personnel, energy and optimism, took over most operation attempts in Germany. Monte's links with the determined underground radical groups in Europe made her valuable. In late 1944 she was one of the first agents flown out with the aim of starting an intelligence chain in Austria, and carrying news of its progress back through Switzerland. Monte succeeded in doing just this, and returned carrying information to the Swiss border in April 1945.

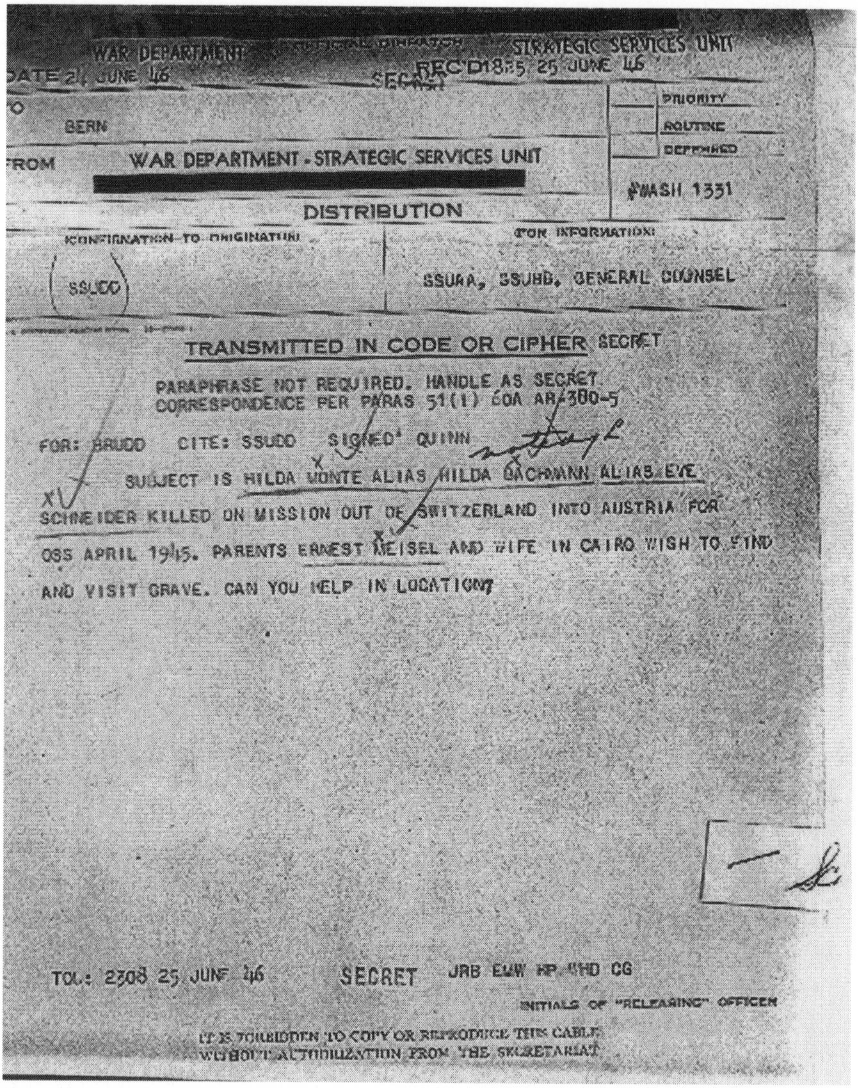

Figure 24. Hilda Monte's death. Telegram kept at the archives of The National Archives and Records Administration, USA.

As she was about to cross the border, 'Hilde Meisel stumbled into an SS patrol. An expert marksman brought her down with a shot that shattered both her legs. Before the Germans could reach her, Hilde bit into her 'L' pill, a capsule of cyanide, which killed her instantly.'[32]

It is not surprising that Monte's passion, youth and idealism appealed to Leslie's romantic imagination. The unlikely meeting seems to have also had an effect on the film itself. There is a scene at an embassy party in Berlin, with Leslie, as Pimpernel Smith, palming an invitation to evade the minister of propaganda. This is very close to Monte's own experience: 'A female member of (Monte's) German action group before the war had somehow acquired an official invitation to a Nazi reception which Goering was scheduled to attend, and smuggled in a pistol concealed in her handbag. For some reason Goering failed to appear and the opportunity (for a murder attempt) was lost.'[33]

Leslie was at the limits of independent action in supporting such a dangerous attempt. Later in the war, behind Churchill's leadership, his actions were less self-determined. But at that time, at the beginning of 1941, Leslie was at the height of his resolve, and Monte's wide-eyed idealism was a match for his own.

By the time *Pimpernel Smith* was finished, much of Europe was overrun by the Nazis. The governments in exile had escaped to London, the last resource. Britain had been bombed continually for six months, with the loss of thirty thousand civilians. London was in ruins, one third of its streets impassable.[34] In April 1941, the Hungarian prime minister had committed suicide after the regent joined the country to the Nazis. Two weeks later the head of the Greek government did the same, in despair at the country's defeat and demoralization. There were rumours of mass killings in the east. Even Churchill began to sound a little desperate.

The British were listening to *ITMA*. Somehow British morale remained high; they were determined to keep fighting. Without bravado, an indomitable spirit had taken hold, and the British people felt the war was their cause. And in the meantime, they listened to their favourite comic radio programme, the utter silliness of the humour seeming to be the most sensible thing happening in dark times.

Pimpernel Smith provided another minor distraction, but a successful one, achieving one of the top box-office totals of the year in 1941.[35] Whether the British viewers at the time took in the points Leslie made is a different question. The romantic story and Leslie's personal charms may well have provided excellent entertainment, certainly for female cinemagoers. Not only that, but Leslie's drive and energy affected everyone working on the film, and every aspect of it was as polished as possible, with an immensely stylish result. *The Times* gave a favourable review while neglecting the film's message, saying of Leslie: 'He is adept at the art of appearing to flick sentiment and feeling away from him at the same time as he is cunningly arranging them in his button-hole'. Concerning the meaning of the film, *The Times* said only, 'Mr

Howard's ... set speech towards the end carries (the message) that there is rather more at stake than the rescue of individuals'.[36]

The exact influence of the film in England can never be recovered. However, one viewer who certainly got the point was Raoul Wallenberg, a Swedish diplomat who saw the film in the British embassy in Stockholm. After seeing *Pimpernel Smith*, he told his sister that he would like to do the same thing. In 1944, as an official of the War Refugee Board, established by Roosevelt, Wallenberg saved thousands of Hungarian Jews from deportation to death camps, both by issuing protective Swedish passports and negotiating money gifts in exchange for their freedom.[37] There is no doubt that Leslie's film did influence Wallenberg, although of course it was not the sole reason for his action. Mrs Nina Lagergren, Wallenberg's sister and close companion in those times, told the story to a biographer:

> Nina got a hint of where Raoul's feelings were taking him when she went to see a film with him during the winter of 1942. It was called *Pimpernel Smith* ... a takeoff of the Baroness Orczy novel ... In the American [*sic*] film an absentminded professor, played by Leslie Howard, manages to save Jews from the Nazis. The sister and brother both took great delight in the movie, and when it was over Raoul confided in Nina that he'd like to emulate the Professor. She took it as a passing fancy. But Raoul was by that time profoundly concerned.[38]

If one film could have such an effect, other strong messages of outrage from the civilized world might have been cumulative. But more such messages were sparse.

Discussing the genesis of his father's film, many years later, Ronald commented, 'Leslie never cared much for the finally selected title of *Pimpernel Smith*, finding it catchpenny and trivial. The story of the rescue from the guillotine of persecuted aristocrats and Huguenots in the 1790s seemed to Leslie to have little to do with Hitler's racial proscriptions terminating in the gas-chambers of the 1940s.'[39] This seems an unequivocal statement on the meaning behind of the film. And Leslie dedicates the film to 'those who are being exterminated by the Nazis' in the very first line.

Leslie was surrounded by Jewish influences – the refugees at Denham, many colleagues, and many others in the film business and the refugees of that time, MacDonnell's wife, Hilda Monte, Paul Kuttner. He also had in Vienna, where he had grown up, friends of his own family in the

Jewish community. He had an international rather than a parochial British viewpoint, but was politically naive when it came to opinions in Britain. But even in mid-1941, Leslie could have known little of mass Jewish deaths. Historians have found evidence that British intelligence knew of large-scale executions of Jews by September 1941. This was reported in the British press at the end of 1941.[40] The official acknowledgement did not come until 17 December 1942, when a joint British and American declaration denounced Nazi killings of Jews and the House of Commons stood to observe a moment of silence. But at this point, Leslie knew only of years of persecution and outrage, not the facts of mass extinction.

All the same, knowledge of what might happen was not exactly obscure. In September 1939, the well-known political commentator George Orwell reviewed Martin Block's new history of the Gypsies, *Gypsies, Their Life and Customs* with this summary:

> The terrifying thing about modern methods of persecution is that we cannot be sure, as yet, that they will not succeed. The Inquisition failed, but there is no certainty that the 'liquidation' of Jews and Trotskyites will fail. It may be that the wretched gypsies, like the Jews, are already serving as a corpus vile, and it is only because they do not have friends who own newspapers that we hear nothing about it.[41]

'Corpus vile' means a thing worthless except as an object of experiment. Astonishingly, as time went on, warnings about Nazi persecution became even rarer, and Leslie's film remained the most direct media reference to the Nazi persecutions. *Pimpernel Smith* was unique, and remained so throughout the war. There was a particular reason for this. The Ministry of Information had a very careful policy during the war concerning the direct mention of the subject of the Jews. In effect the word was forbidden, on the grounds that it would aid German propaganda, or promote anti-Semitism. The ministry's own researchers and pollsters found anti-Semitism reported constantly.[42] The establishment also considered their own type of public-school anti-Semitism was the general feeling, although this was far from being the case.[43] Many people were outraged at the Jewish plight, and the opinion that Britain should do more to help became more vocal as the war continued. Unfortunately, establishment figures had plenty of political reasons why such opinions should be neither heeded nor aired in public: fear of provoking even more anti-Semitism, wariness of exaggerated tales of terror, and many others.

In July 1941 the Planning Committee of the Ministry of Information considered whether 'atrocity stories' should be lifted out of the context of general propaganda and given more emphatic treatment as part of a campaign to combat apathy. It was suggested that such stories would just repel people: 'In self-defence people prefer to think that the victims were specially marked men – and probably a pretty bad lot anyway. A certain amount of horror is needed but it must be used very sparingly and must deal always with treatment of indisputably innocent people. Not with violent political opponents. And not with Jews.'[44]

Churchill allowed the ministry to go its own way throughout the war. Amongst other things he seems to have had a stronger connection to the British people than the ministry officials or the Foreign Office, and a greater trust and belief in their understanding and will to fight. He generally left home propaganda to look after itself, except in a few particular cases. The behaviour of the Foreign Office, really in control of all that could be used as foreign propaganda at this time, has been seen as most responsible for this policy, which applied to films and the BBC. One author concluded, 'The real issue was one of passive anti-Semitism within the British establishment – sometimes not so passive'.[45]

In 1993 the BBC itself broadcast an examination of its own conduct during the war, including some interviews with those in charge at the time. It also examined contemporary Foreign Office documents, released in the early 1990s.[46] The programme showed that anti-Semitism in the higher ranks of the Foreign Office and the BBC during the war led to a policy which suppressed facts about the extermination of the European Jews. Both these agencies believed that their low opinion of the Jews was shared by the public. Both Home and European broadcasting services during the war had their coverage limited concerning what was known. Jewish sources of information were thought of as suspect; identifiably Jewish broadcasters were barred.

A very few broadcasts were made on the BBC Foreign Service to Germany, in late 1942 and 1943, describing the facts of mass killings in the very low key BBC style. It was the Political Warfare Executive, who had responsibility for foreign propaganda that was the main pressure group behind these broadcasts. It is possible that Robert Sherwood, Leslie's old friend, had some influence here, as the American representative and a close confidante of Roosevelt. His views were liberal and sympathetic to the Jewish cause. On one of the few Home Service broadcasts on the subject, Robert Vansittart spoke openly and shockingly in September 1942. He told how thousands of Jews, including women and children, were being murdered daily by poison gas. BBC officials were outraged at his plain speaking, and he was never allowed to broadcast again.

Even from the start of the war in September 1939 the BBC said little about the widespread persecution and harrying of German and Austrian Jews. At the end of 1940, Leslie seemed to criticize the BBC on their policy of keeping quiet about events, being one of very few people with such sympathies who were in a position to do this. Even he had to make his attitude known indirectly. But the subject of this anecdote, broadcast on 16 December 1940, would have been clear to those at whom it was aimed:

> Even in our Home Service radio news bulletins the announcers all contrive to speak with a uniform, unemotional anonymity of voice, and, on those occasions, as recently, when they have had victorious news to proclaim, and have permitted a tinge of human excitement to creep into their delivery, I feel sure they have been afterwards severely reprimanded for being momentarily carried away into a method both un-English and melodramatic. I remember in Hollywood, a well-known actor and friend of mine, Roland Young, used to give an imitation of an English radio commentator describing the running of the Derby (horse race). It was a remarkable affair in which the commentator described everything except the race.[47]

Leslie at first appears to be criticizing BBC style, but it is actually the content of broadcasts that the anecdote refers to. Leslie's comments on official attitudes were often to be delivered in this indirect way, most of all in his later film, *The First of the Few.*

Leslie had an accepted position as a propagandist and film star with the highest figures in society: Harold Nicolson, then parliamentary secretary at the Ministry of Information, wrote in his diary for 2 April 1940:

> Dine with Kenneth Clark. Willie (Somerset) Maugham, Mrs Winston Churchill and Leslie Howard are there. We have an agreeable dinner and talk mostly about films. Leslie Howard is doing a big propaganda film and is frightfully keen about it. We discuss the position of those English people who have remained over in the United States. The film stars claim that they have been asked to remain there since they are more useful at Hollywood, but we all regret bitterly that people like Aldous Huxley, Auden and Isherwood should have absented themselves. They want me to

write a Spectator article attacking them. That is all very well, but
it would lose me the friendship of three people whom I much
admire. I come back with Leslie Howard and he continues to talk
excitedly about his new film. He seems to enter into such things
with the zest of a schoolboy and that is part of his charm.[48]

A misleading note in the book by its editor, Nicolson's son, Nigel, states
that Leslie was discussing *The First of the Few*. But that film was made
two years later, as a celebration of the Battle of Britain. This meeting
was five months before that battle started, and the film Leslie was making and discussing so eagerly, which Nicolson so lightly dismissed, was
Pimpernel Smith.

Harold Nicolson had joined Oswald Mosley's New Party in 1931.
But he did not support Mosley's British Union of Fascists, and in 1935
he entered the House of Commons as a National Labour MP, joining the
Ministry of Information in Churchill's government in 1940. Nicholson
later wrote that although he had rejected fascist views, he could never
overcome his own aversion to Jews, a view typical of many of his
background. Clark, with whom Nicholson is dining, was director of
the Films Division for the ministry at this time.

Leslie at this point seems to be almost a magical figure in the landscape. Charming, successful, beautifully mannered, he is here courteously
accepted by those of the highest social status – and at the same time
treated entirely as a lightweight, so little meaning is given to what he is
trying to say. Leslie knew that his ambiguous identity helped him to put
over some of what he wished to say – but it also operated to obscure his
message. Given the certain fact that the Ministry of Information would
have checked his script closely, it is remarkable that Leslie managed to
say even as much as he did.

In this he may have been helped by Duff Cooper, head of the ministry while *Pimpernel Smith* was produced, and up till July 1941. As has
been seen, Cooper's attitudes were not anti-Semitic. In addition he was
a leading anti-appeaser and had the energy (and a well-known temper)
to oppose his unwilling civil servants – for a time. At the end of 1939
he had made a trip to America with the express purpose of promoting
anti-German propaganda, despite sinister warnings against doing so by
Neville Chamberlain.[49]

In his memoirs he commented on the partiality of the Foreign Office
and its disfavour towards the Jews, and his own contrary opinion.[50]
Duff Cooper's disagreement with the prevailing views in his ministry
was part of the reason why he was dismissed – but he also lacked a

'common touch' and managed to offend too many people by his high-handedness. However his successor for the rest of the war was Brendan Bracken, a man in Churchill's confidence to be sure; this time one with the same common prejudices as others in the establishment.

A large proportion of the British film community were of Jewish background. Not only had that been true from its inception, it was also true of some of those most responsible for its development in the 1930s, even to the building of the cinemas themselves.[51] In addition these ranks were swelled with refugees from all the film industries in Europe, as the Nazis gained influence. So much so that there were protests from British film workers, even though the newcomers' expertise was to be vital in the British film industry's flowering.[52]

Since Leslie's film remains the most direct confrontation of Nazi ideology, there is the question of why the Jews in the British film industry themselves said little or nothing at the time, on film or in public about this and the treatment of the Jews. Korda never wrote his memoirs, nor publicly revealed his Jewish background, although it was an open secret at Denham, where he had helped rescue many Jews in various film industries to escape from the Germans. Korda and his brothers never even spoke of it to their children, who learned of it years later from Korda's biographer. This was far from unique; for example Miklos Rozsa, Korda's associate and film-music composer, published his autobiography in 1982 without once mentioning his Jewish background, even though this had determined the whole course of his life.

The memoirs of Michael Balcon, head of the other wartime centre of production at Ealing, are also opaque on the subject. Balcon's reactions throughout the war were entirely as a patriotic Englishman. He did not publicly mention the Holocaust at that time or afterwards, nor Jewish reactions to the Nazi threat. Nor did he say why he then made no attempt to denounce Jewish persecution on film. During the 1930s Balcon had attempted to put forward a positive image of Jewry, in the face of the storm of prejudice, in his film *Jew Süss*. The Germans were infuriated by the film and the German ambassador in America tried to stop it being shown there. Balcon made a special trip to the States and enlisted Einstein's help, amongst others, to get the film shown.[53] By early 1940 he had the Nazi's brutal response – *Jud Suss*, a hate-filled distortion of the tale which compared Jews to rats. This film was shown all over Germany and Europe – enough to quiet even the most courageous propagandist.

Balcon had gone so far as to criticize those people who escaped to

America as Britain seemed about to be invaded, even having a personal argument with Korda on one occasion, whose trips to America included secret government work, and who had no intention of settling there. But he also criticized non-Jews who had gone to America, such as Alfred Hitchcock, with whom there was an acid public correspondence. Leslie had nothing to say on the subject. But Balcon was especially sickened, as his lifelong friend Victor Saville, also Jewish, had left for Hollywood in 1939. Saville enjoyed a long and successful career there, but Balcon never spoke to him again.

Such flights were something more than shameful at the beginning of the war – any suggestion that British Jews were cowards or traitors risked losing sympathy for them all at a time of their imminent discovery and destruction by invading Germans. However, at the moment when it seemed the Germans were on the point of invading, the alternative to taking flight for Jews was to accede to the deaths of their families as well as themselves. Once a German regime was in place the Jews would have been segregated and sent away to 'work camps' or whatever euphemism was used, and murdered. The Nazis still had their supporters in Britain, and they already knew where all the Jewish communities were.[54] Balcon seemed to want to say something of his past films in his 1969 autobiography:

> My final thought on this part of my life (the 1930s) is one that has nagged at me for a long time. I realise that the preceding chapters of this personal story have been played against a shadowy background of world events – some world-shattering. Alongside them the then important-seeming struggle and internal conflicts for the control of Gaumont British, ending with the disappearance of the Ostrer regime and the rise of the Rank empire, were relatively trivial. Those were for example, the days of Mussolini's Abyssinian War, the Civil War in Spain with all the implications for the future, and now that events can be seen in their historical perspective, one cannot escape the conclusion that in our own work we could have been more profitably engaged. Hardly a single film of the period reflects the agony of those times.[55]

And this is all Balcon has to say in general on all his work. The same applied throughout the whole film world. But the Jews of the British film industry were not silent. They were, whether through malice or mistaken policy, silenced. Leslie, uncrowned king of Denham, Balcon, in charge at Ealing, Jack Beddington, head of the Films Division throughout the war, all of Jewish background, said nothing further. But Leslie had said all he could, knew, and believed. And he had said it with all the force and passion of his life.

The atmosphere of the time was a sort of paralysis. Clouds of fear, hatred and secrecy surrounded the subject of the Jews worldwide. Poisoned rumours and endless convoluted conspiracy theories about the Jewish race were published in fascist newspapers such as *The Blackshirt*, and spread in Britain. Even the most decent, honest and intelligent people were not proof against such prejudice. Those who dared to mention the subject were at deadly risk, as Britain stood alone against the terrifying power of the German army as it cut through Europe.

Pimpernel Smith criticized British officialdom for doing nothing, and the American press for saying nothing. It also made a direct and emotional appeal for those endangered by the Nazis to be rescued. How Leslie got away with saying even so much, given the ministry's policy and overall control, was a result of his convictions, his determination and energy, his equivocal identity, and not a little luck. As the war continued, the focus of propaganda shifted to other themes which emphasised the military battle and the fight for the country – themes of the land itself, an idealized rural England, the heart of the countryside; and the people, the essence of their character.

In 1941 it was hardly realized that there were two battles to be fought. One was that of the British people against German military might. The second was against Nazi genocide. One was won, and amidst the rejoicing the fact that the other was lost was left to history to lament. Leslie took a moral lead, and tried to deal with both, because he thought they were the same battle. But as the war continued it became evident that they were not. No other film ever repeated his message.

NOTES

1. Ronald Howard, *In Search of My Father: A Portrait of Leslie Howard* (London: W. Kimber, 1981), pp.54–73.
2. Leslie's meeting with Paul Kuttner, who came over with the Kindertransport. Confirmed by telephone conversation between Mr Kuttner and the author 3 August 2004. See also the Kindertransport site at www.kindertransport.org.
3. M.J. Harris and D. Oppenheimer, *Into the Arms of Strangers: Stories of the Kindertransport* (London: Bloomsbury, 2000).
4. Howard, *In Search of My Father*, p.60.
5. A.J.P. Taylor, *Beaverbrook* (London: Hamish Hamilton, 1972), pp.392, 396, 399.
6. R.B. Cockett, 'Ball, Chamberlain and *Truth*', *The Historical Journal* 33, 1 (1990), pp.131–42.
7. Diana Cooper, *The Light of Common Day* (London: Hart Davies, 1959), p.46. John Julius Norwich, *The Duff Cooper Diaries 1915–1951* (London: Weidenfeld and Nicolson, 2005), entry for 3 September 1939.

8. Kevin Gough-Yates, 'The European Film-Maker in Exile in Britain 1933–1945' (PhD diss., Open University, 1990).

9. Anthony Aldgate and Jeffrey Richards, *Britain Can Take It: The British Cinema in the Second World War* (Oxford: Blackwell, 1986). Jeffrey Richards and Anthony Aldgate, *Best of British* (Oxford: Blackwell, 1983).

10. *The Times*, 18 April 1940.

11. Howard, *In Search of My Father*, pp.63–4.

12. Alfons Walde remains a well-known and respected Austrian artist. He died in 1958.

13. 'On 22 June 1940 he [Macdonell] married Rose Paul-Schiff, a Viennese, whose family was connected with the banking firm of Warburg Schiff and had come to England just before the Anschluss.' *Oxford Dictionary of National Biography*, Life of A.G. Macdonell.

14. Leslie Ruth Howard, *A Quite Remarkable Father* (London: Longmans, 1960), p.250.

15. *Kinematograph Weekly*, 27 November 1941.

16. Interview with Sidney Cole. BFI BECTU tape 7, from interview on 9 September 1987 and later transcribed for the British Film Institute.

17. Howard, *In Search of My Father*, pp.96–7.

18. From an interview with Sidney Gilliatt by Bevis Hillier, 1989, quoted in *John Betjeman: New Fame, New Love* (London: John Murray, 2002), p.163.

19. Author's interview with Guido Coen, producer Del Giudice's assistant at Denham, 8 November 2000.

20. Telephone interview of author with Ronald Neame, 12 December 2005.

21. *The News Chronicle*, 4–21 March 1941 particularly followed this story, although it was reported elsewhere in the national press.

22. David Tomlinson, *Luckier Than Most: An Autobiography* (London: Hodder and Stoughton, 1990), p.68.

23. Ibid., p.68.

24. Howard, *In Search of My Father*, p.99.

25. Deborah Lipstadt, *Beyond Belief: The American Press and the Coming of the Holocaust 1933–1945* (New York: Free Press, 1986).

26. 'Beyond belief' is also the only description for the British press reporting of Nazi treatment of Jews. A few words in an end column on the back page about 'transfer of Jewish population' was the only note that a nation's Jews had been obliterated. For this example, see *Evening Standard*, 26 September 1942. In general, see D. Stone, *Responses to Nazism in Britain, 1933–1939: Before War and Holocaust* (Basingstoke: Palgrave Macmillan, 2003); F. Gannon, *The British Press and Germany 1936–1939* (Oxford: Clarendon Press, 1971).

27. Albert Meltzer, *I Couldn't Paint Golden Angels: Sixty Years of Commonplace Life and Anarchist Agitation* (Edinburgh: AK Press 1996), p.96.

28. National Archives, Public Record Office, SOE Files HS9/1118/3 Hilda Miesel (*sic*).

29. Nigel West, *Secret War: The Story of SOE, Britain's Wartime Sabotage Organisation* (London: Hodder and Stoughton, 1992), pp.241–5.

30. Anthony Cave Brown, *The Secret Servant: The Life of Sir Stewart Menzies, Head of Intelligence* (London: Michael Joseph, 1988).

31. Annedore Leber, *Conscience in Revolt: Sixty-four Stories of Resistance in Germany* (London: Vallentine Mitchell, 1957).

32. Joseph Persico, *Piercing the Reich: The Penetration of Nazi Germany by OSS Agents During World War II* (London: M. Joseph, 1979), pp.74, 83, Monte's death described p.89.

33. Reported by John Olday, Hilda Monte's husband, in *Anarchist Review*, 1978.

34. Martin Gilbert, *Second World War* (London: Weidenfeld and Nicolson, 1989), p.181.

35. Aldgate and Richards, *Britain Can Take It*, p.64.

36. *The Times*, 2 July 1941.

37. Michael Nicholson, *Raoul Wallenburg:The Swedish Diplomat Who Saved 100,000 Jews* (Watford: Exley, 1989).

38. Elenore Lester, *Wallenberg: The Man in the Iron Web* (Englewood Cliffs, NJ: Prentice-Hall, 1982), p.53.

39. Howard, *In Search of My Father*, p.78.

40. Richard Breitman et al., *U.S. Intelligence and the Nazis* (Cambridge and New York: Cambridge University Press, 2005), pp.10–44.

41. George Orwell, review of Martin Block, *Gypsies, Their Life and Customs*, translated from

the German, *The Adelphi* XV (Oct 1938–Sept 1939), p.137.

42. Ian McLaine, *Ministry of Morale: Home Front Morale and the Ministry of Information in World War II* (London: George Allen and Unwin, 1979).

43. For example, see Richard Bolchover, *British Jewry and the Holocaust* (Cambridge: Cambridge University Press, 1993), Preface.

44. Secretary of State for War to Prime Minister, 12 June 1941, Churchill, Papers of the Prime Minister, PREM 4/99/3. Quoted in McLaine, *Ministry of Morale*.

45. Richard Breitman, *Official Secrets: What the Nazis Planned, What the British and Americans Knew* (London: Allen Lane, The Penguin Press, 1999), p.244. And see also Bernard Wasserstein, *Britain and the Jews of Europe, 1935–1945* (London: Oxford University Press, 1979); Louise London, *Whitehall and the Jews 1933–1948: British Immigration Policy, Jewish Refugees and the Holocaust* (Cambridge: Cambridge University Press, 2000). See also Breitman *et al.*, *U.S. Intelligence and the Nazis*, pp.10–44.

46. *Documents: The Unspeakable Atrocity*, Radio 4, 26 August 1993. See also Jean Seaton, 'Reporting Atrocities: The BBC and the Holocaust', in *The Media in British Politics* (Aldershot: Avebury, 1987).

47. *Britain Speaks*, 16 December 1940. From programme transcripts at BBC Written Archives Centre, Caversham, Reading.

48. Nigel Nicolson (ed), *Harold Nicolson: Diaries and Letters 1907–1964* (London: Weidenfeld and Nicolson, 2004), p.238.

49. Alfred Duff Cooper, *Old Men Forget: An Autobiography of Duff Cooper (Viscount Norwich)* (London: Hart-Davis, 1957), pp.268–74.

50. Norwich, *Duff Cooper Diaries*, entry for 22 May 1948.

51. Allen Eyles, *Oscar Deutsch Entertains Our Nation: Odeon Cinemas* (London: Cinema Theatre Association, 2002).

52. Gough-Yates, 'The European Film Maker in Exile in Britain 1933–1945'.

53. Monja Danischewsky, *Michael Balcon's 25 Years in Film* (London: World Film Productions, 1947), Introduction.

54. German broadcaster 'Lord Haw-Haw' sometimes addressed British Jews directly in his radio broadcasts from Germany – for example, the author's mother, living in Manchester, remembers hearing, 'you Jews of Cheetham Hill we know where you are – we are coming to get you'.

55. Michael Balcon, *Michael Balcon Presents ... A Lifetime of Films* (London: Hutchinson 1969), p.99.

CHAPTER EIGHT

July 1940–April 1942: Propaganda

Leslie made BBC radio broadcasts from July 1940 through till February 1943. The bulk of these were on the Foreign Service, made before December 1941, and aimed at America and Canada, with the purpose of engaging American sympathies and countering Nazi propaganda there. They reflect the changing British attitude to America: from the start of the war, when his broadcasts sounded like despairing appeals, to after the Battle of Britain, when they became a little more confident and less importunate. Leslie was also occasionally heard on the Home Service, with talks aimed more at entertainment and support of the home war effort, and on *Answering You*, a sort of quiz show dealing with the problems of the moment for British listeners.

The talks as a whole had one significance which Leslie never realized; they comprise his memoirs – the only ones he ever produced. Because his style was aimed at being direct and straightforward, in line with that of the BBC generally, he often spoke informally and personally about events that had happened to him. He also interviewed both his children on air, and in doing so revealed more of his feelings towards them than perhaps he intended. All the *Britain Speaks* talks were broadcast to America.

He spoke on many subjects, from urging America to fight, to describing the problems of the British film industry. He discussed what the word 'propaganda' meant and how he felt it applied to him. He made an attempt, as did many others, to characterize 'the British People'; tried to put into words what people thought they were fighting for; described the atmosphere in the streets and pubs and bomb shelters; and said that the British wanted something more than victory; they wanted radical change in their own society.

One of Leslie's earliest talks to America in December 1940 discussed the problem of propaganda, especially whether any attempt at it should be made from the British side. That there should be no such attempt, and that German propaganda should go unanswered, was quite a prevalent view – a hangover from the excesses of First World War propaganda and atrocity stories. This amounted to allowing only one side of the case to be heard, as Leslie suggested:

> The radio programme on which I am talking to you is entitled *Britain Speaks*. It is addressed, primarily, to North America; to Canada and the United States, that is to a staunch ally and a friendly neutral. It is one of many broadcasts from this country to all parts of the world. In common with them it is certainly classified by our enemies, wherever they be, as British Propaganda. I should like to spend a few minutes discussing the implications of the word. I suppose propaganda in its modern sense means advertising – whether it is for the purpose of selling a motor-car, a tooth-paste, a film company, a cause or a country. Now the fact is that most English people are very shy of advertising – or propaganda – and are not, by nature very good at it. They take the view that ... constant proclamation of the virtue of any idea is tiresome and defeats its own object.
>
> Our enemies, on the other hand, believe profoundly in propaganda and have organised it to a unique degree ... Eventually if you are thorough and patient, which no one will deny the Germans are, the lie will be believed. Indeed, you may end by believing it yourself.
>
> The result has been that, during this war, the belligerents have conducted their advertising campaigns in a nationally characteristic manner, the Nazis vociferously, and the British, to a degree which has been the despair of their friends and the astonishment of their foes; cautiously, politely, and with painstaking rectitude. Even in our Home Service radio news bulletins the announcers all contrive to speak with a uniform, unemotional anonymity of voice ...
>
> ... To all those who regard this country with an unfavourable eye, my remarks may seem but a long-winded way of persuading you that my little chats in the *Britain Speaks* series do not properly belong in the category of propaganda. Well, I don't think they do – not in the Goebbels sense. I didn't come to England to be a publicity agent. I've spent an awful lot of my life dodging that kind of thing. And I don't care a hang either way. I say to hell with whether what I say is propaganda or not.[1]

Leslie had always impressed all sorts of people with his charm. The radio broadcasts may or may not have possessed some charm, but they were neither tactful nor diplomatic. Leslie, despite the hand of the censor, took a swipe at all sorts of people; neutral countries, including the US, who were living in 'houses filled with dynamite'; the 'corrupt' French regime that failed to oppose the Germans;[2] the British appeasers;[3] his own complacent middle class, who never examined the damaging mores of their own society;[4] even the complacent English aristocracy, who originated from 'an illegitimate Norman pirate called William the Conqueror, who stole the land from the original inhabitants!'[5]

All this was not propaganda; in fact it is possible that he made more enemies than friends. Leslie did begin more mildly, in his first broadcasts to America. But perhaps in line with Britain's successful defiance, he became more angry, more confident and more direct as time went on. He began with a rather naive appeal for help to America:

> America ... is very much in our minds today, probably more than since the Declaration of Independence aroused the consciences and admiration of all liberal Englishmen. Though more than forty million free people in this island are again involved in the eternal fight against European domination, their eyes are towards the West ... For there lives the biggest group of democratic peoples in the world today.[6]

By November 1940, this has changed to:

> You (in America) think we here are in a jam, fighting against the most terrific odds and feeling pretty bad about it, anxious to be friends in a day of difficulty with those whom we treated rather snobbily in the days before the war. If you think this is the reason [we are trying to appeal to you] you are making a mistake. To tell you the truth we don't feel too bad about this war. The people in these Islands do not feel themselves in a desperate condition. We don't like War, we know war is a black and brutal and bloody business. But we all feel we are going to win this particular war and that we have now in the last month or two set off up the long mountain road to victory.[7]

Brave words, but it was not just the triumph of the Battle of Britain which made this change. In America, Franklin D. Roosevelt had just been re-elected president, but this time with a smaller majority. Leslie therefore had to counter the German propagandists who argued that Roosevelt's anti-isolationist stance only doubtfully had the support of most Americans. He also had to say that Britain was happy to stand alone, or that in any case Wendell Willkie, Roosevelt's defeated opponent, would have had a similar attitude to the Allies. Britain now had Roosevelt's support for supplies of arms and other resources, but direct help from America in the battle, it was clear, would not be forthcoming. After one or two more broadcasts, in which he warned that no country would be able to stay neutral,[8] Leslie dropped his appeals to America and concentrated on film-making. His talks almost certainly had little effect on American actions, or even attitudes, unless it were to annoy more people than he persuaded. But Leslie remained faithful to his ideal America. Later his friends would note that Thomas Jefferson was Leslie's hero, and he wore a scarf on which was printed the Declaration of Independence.[9] Leslie went so far as to say publicly, 'All this emphasis on nationality has always seemed nonsense to me. I feel equally a native of Great Britain and the United States. I'm all for dual citizenship for everyone.'[10]

Leslie's other themes during his talks were by no means unique to him – the meaning of democracy, the history of the British people and land, the cultural heritage of the West – were all being explored, as topics in the continual discussion of 'why we fight', mostly aired by writers such as George Orwell and J.B. Priestley, a more experienced speaker than him. But Leslie sometimes hit home by reason of his simple and direct style. Here he talks of his recent experience with others in the air-raid shelter he generally used during the Blitz:

> The shelter is the basement of an old, grey London building. We call it the Catacomb. As we have from twenty to thirty people dossing down there you can guess that by the time the All Clear [siren] sounds in the morning, there is quite a fug ... We sleep on small camp beds which lift us about six inches off the brick floor. In our Catacomb we are fairly safe from blast, but if a heavy bomb hit we should be for it ... We are a mixed lot in the shelter. Apart from myself, there is a journalist, working men, city men, a soldier or two, or sailor or airman, passing through London. On the other side, separated by a passage and screen are the women – the secretaries, wives, mothers, and Lillian the servant girl of an hotel. It would have been impossible in the old days for the housemaid to sleep in a dormitory, on terms of agreement, with the mistress who paid her wages. Today all over Britain, that sort of class consciousness and snobbery is disappearing. It hasn't gone yet, by any means. It clings on in odd corners of our national life like barnacles on a ship's bottom. But it is fair to say that it is on the run. I do not believe it will ever be restored here again.[11]

Elsewhere Leslie discusses people he had spoken to and admired in the course of his travels. Just after the Battle of Britain he gave a talk on the Observer Corps, thanking them for what had been vital help from amateurs in the face of official neglect:

> At more than a thousand posts throughout the British Isles members of the Observer Corps are permanently on duty day and night, listening with trained ears, watching with trained eyes for every sort of aerial activity. What they see and hear they transmit quickly by telephone to some forty observation centres where other members of this little corps sort and plot the information passed to them ... When the last War was over and the world was safe for democracy, [the Government] abandoned the Observation Corps as they abandoned most other forms of defences and armaments because [*this sentence has been censored by the BBC.*] The League of Nations was in charge, peace was here forever and the only way to preserve it was to throw away all arms and methods of defence and rely upon the natural goodness of mankind ... So the few cynical groups of the Observer Corps hung on, trying to perfect their system of observation and they scraped along with little funds and no thanks from anybody ... Today their intricate network covers every inch of Great Britain, they number 35,000 trained observers and the Fighter Command of the Royal Air Force does not know what it would do without them.[12]

In a talk given on 5 August 1940, Leslie speaks of the Free French, members of the French Army who found themselves in England or who escaped to it after the fall of France. By this time General de Gaulle was their leader. Leslie seems to have visited them 'in a camp in the south of England'. Presumably he made some connections here, perhaps with the help of Violette, and these connections were kept up in a friendly way later in London. Leslie retells their experience of flight by ship from Brest, with the German army due to arrive at any moment:

> The ship on which my [Free French] friend found himself was packed with troops and refugees. As it steamed slowly out of the harbour, someone started to sing *The Marseillaise*. Instantly, others began to join in and then all of a sudden the great French song died away. People remembered what the song of the men of Marseilles had meant in the great days of France and they had not the heart to sing it with the Germans overrunning their country.

Life was not like the films, apparently. In *Casablanca* (1942), French refugees escaping from the German regime sang *The Marseillaise* spiritedly, drowning out a German rendering of *Die Wacht am Rhein* – though there was a little more cause for hope by that time.

A talk on 2 December 1940 spoke of the many peoples who had by then been driven from their own countries: 'In Poland, France, Belgium, Holland, Norway, people like you have been turned out of their houses at half an hour's notice, without food, or money or warm clothing, in the depth of winter, and told they could walk to a town twenty, fifty, or a hundred miles away if they wanted shelter.'

At the end of December, Leslie made his only attempt on radio to speak of Nazi racial policies. It tends to fail as propaganda, both because it is too wide-ranging historically and because Leslie speaks of the German people in other times, which loses the listener's interest. During the course of the talk Leslie mentions the Jews twice, both times tangentially and not in the context of being persecuted: '[the British can be] as stubbornly enduring of all vicissitudes as the Slavonic or the Jewish race', and 'we have spread our Christian faith which sprang from Judaism'.[13] Which was two more references than any other BBC programme, including news and current affairs.

Leslie's broadcasts freely mention his own life and feelings. Perhaps the most startling example is his admission (finally) that he saw no action at all during his time in the army in the First World War: 'during most of the last war I was a very junior officer in a cavalry regiment; however, long before I got anywhere near the battlefront, everybody there had settled down into trenches, and as horses are useless in trenches, I found myself near Divisional Headquarters, pretty bored but pretty safe.'[14]

Glimpses of his life at the time of these broadcasts come in his anecdote about walking out of his family home in Surrey after some sort of argument, and making his way to the nearest pub to cheer himself up:

> [I felt] my share in the war effort which I'd come specially to do was negligible. I was in a fine state that Saturday evening. I may say my family did not want me either. So I went out into the night in solitary state. I walked down to the village, dodging Army lorries in the blackness, and being cursed for flashing my torch in the wrong direction. The guns were popping away at the German raiders on their way to London, and the searchlights were flashing on and off. I hated the raiders; I hated the guns; I hated everything. I didn't like myself much.[15]

Leslie eventually found solace in the local pub, where the atmosphere of cheerful solidarity amongst all classes of people succeeded in reassuring him.

It was Leslie's custom at the beginning of the war to spend weekdays living with Violette in London, and most weekends with his wife and children in Surrey in the family home. It was a practice which satisfied nobody entirely, although they all managed to tolerate it for Leslie's sake. A very strong bond had grown up between Violette and Leslie, forged by their mutual understanding of what was being fought for. Ruth was stoical, having had to put up with similar situations throughout their married life, and knowing Leslie would not ever entirely desert her.

Leslie's son Ronald was now in his early twenties, and was soon to enter the Royal Navy and be posted away for much of the war. For this short time, he and Leslie had a warm friendship, and saw a lot of each other both in London and the country. Leslie Ruth had a more difficult time perhaps. She adored her father and had believed that nothing could come between the special relationship they shared. But Violette was now foremost in his affections. Jealousy and feelings of sadness, however hidden, surrounded Leslie when he came home to Surrey. Both children married quite young during the next two years, but then many people were doing so, hoping to have children before the husband might be killed in the battle.[16] Leslie's feelings did not change, and he fondly inserted both his children into appearances in his films and his broadcasts wherever he could.

Ronald was interviewed for one broadcast in the autumn of 1940, which proudly described how Ronald had joined the navy as soon as he could, seeing some early action escorting merchant ships and on antisubmarine patrol, and even sinking a U-boat. The broadcast, agreed by the Admiralty, was meant to provide some publicity and recruitment material for the navy, but gives a strong impression of the affection between father and son.[17] To even things up, Leslie interviewed his daughter a couple of months later. This time a slightly more adversarial relationship was revealed:

> Speaking personally again, not only is the boy born in 1918 [Ronald] bearing arms again, as we were 22 years ago, but the girl born in 1924 [Leslie Ruth] is equally exposed to destruction at the hands of the enemy ... In view of this fact, I thought it might be interesting to have a little interview with a young English girl of the new generation and elicit her feelings about this unbelievably

dreadful war ... I now hope you will not object that the young lady, who is sixteen years of age, happens to be my own daughter ... As you know, for more than a year I've been trying to persuade you to go back to California, where you could have been living a normal, amusing, and above all a safe existence. You have obstinately refused to go, and have preferred to remain here under war-time conditions which make life dull, difficult and increasingly perilous. Why?

[Leslie Ruth] I'm surprised you should ask me that, but if you must know I suppose it is because I should be miserable anywhere else. I want to be part of it all. I shall almost be disappointed if the war ends before I'm old enough to be accepted for a real war job. Meanwhile I do what I can. And life isn't dull here – it's exciting to see our country getting stronger every day in spite of the air-raids, and when bombs have fallen near our house, perhaps one has helped to defeat Hitler by refusing to get panicky. I'd like to be here for the victory. And, in case anything did happen to my family, I'd like to be here too – instead of six thousand miles away. Do you want any more reasons?

[Leslie] Miss Howard, the first time you ever smiled, you smiled at me, and I have never since been able to argue with you. I only reserve the right, from time to time, to be a little anxious. Now be a good girl and say good-night to those who have patiently listened to us.[18]

As Leslie continued his broadcasts, he was called on increasingly by the Ministry of Information Films Division to provide more material, or help with other people's work. He was also the first choice to provide any voice-over or commentary, and this he did for *In Which We Serve* (1942), a propaganda film which was made at Denham a little later than *The First of the Few*. He also spoke in *The White Eagle* (1941), about Polish airmen, *Yellow Caesar* (1941), about the life and crimes of Mussolini, and *War in the Mediterranean* (1943, now lost), a history of the region back to classical times, and which was then trying to fight off German occupation. At that time, as Ronald Neame recalled, there was great cooperation between all the film-makers at Denham; Pat Jackson, associated with the Documentary Film Movement, also remembered this spirit and recalled how Leslie had helped him with some difficult technical footage while both were filming.[19]

In August 1940, Leslie's broadcast included a mention of the American-Canadian border, and its lack of defence: 'The North American radio beam does not differentiate between Windsor and Detroit, between Niagara and Niagara Falls. And the beam is right, because the boundary between the United States and Canada is an imaginary line, thirty-five hundred miles long and completely undefended on either side.'[20]

This view on Canada may have been publicly expressed first by Leslie, but it had occurred to many people. Wherever it was first discussed, the notion started a train of thought that resulted in Powell and Pressburger's film *49th Parallel*. Leslie's part in it was filmed while he was at Denham making *Pimpernel Smith*. Its makers intended their film as propaganda aimed at America, and it was an expensive waste of money in that sense, as by the time it opened in the States, in March 1942, the country was already at war. However, it did eventually achieve other aims – to pay tribute to the Canadians, and to provide an account of 'why we fight'. It also later won an Oscar, the Americans sympathizing with its aims.

The film was very long in the making as Michael Powell (director and cinematographer) and Emeric Pressburger (scriptwriter) slogged out to Canada and then across the country, searching for settings and plots. It is recorded by Pressburger's grandson that the plot of the film was already settled by autumn 1940, by which time they had returned from Canada; work on the sets at Denham began in February 1941.[21] The film mirrored a real incident, although neither Powell nor Pressburger's memoirs mention this.

In January 1941, Franz von Werra, a Luftwaffe pilot who had been taken prisoner in England, then transported to a POW camp in Canada, turned up in New York. He had escaped from the train which was taking him to the Canadian camp. There were eight other escapees originally, but he was the only one who had made it across the border. There was a great deal of crowing about this feat; von Werra was the talk of the town, German propagandists made a hero of him, and Hitler publicly awarded him the Iron Cross while he was still in New York. For three months Canada tried to have him returned, but while the legal wrangles continued, von Werra was smuggled back to Germany via South America. He later wrote a triumphal book about his escape, which received a lot of attention. Whether the plot of *49th Parallel* was written to combat this very successful propaganda coup is not known. Von Werra's story was filmed in Britain after the war in Roy Baker's *The One That Got Away*, in 1957.

However late it was, *49th Parallel* was a strong statement, demonstrating Michael Powell's brilliant visual imagination, but it does seem that a fully comprehending mind behind their propaganda was missing. Pressburger was the ideas man of the duo. He had arrived in England in 1935 as a terrified and harried refugee, rescued by Korda. He had some experience with Ufa, the German film company, as a story writer, but was hardly the sophisticate, steeped in European culture, that some liked to present. In reality he was a Jew from a small village in Hungary, who just managed to scrape into college in Germany and study a subject he had little vocation for – civil engineering. Escaping from the Nazis in 1933, he always regretted being torn away from his beloved High German culture. In May 1944 his mother, aged 73, was taken out of her home to be gassed. Pressburger never recovered, and never seemed to reconcile his experiences. His ambivalent feelings are evident in his later film, *The Life and Death of Colonel Blimp* (1943) whose opaque plot, at the start of the film, celebrates old Germany and its culture as if Nazi ideology had never been embraced.

Leslie's contribution to *49th Parallel* was a small cameo part as ethnologist Philip Armstrong Scott, encamped in the Rockies with his local native helpers. He is first seen fishing in a lake, and encountering the escaping Nazis, who are trekking over the mountains. Scott at first affects to be above the fact that Canada is at war with Germany; 'from up here it all seems unimportant'. He explains that he is working on a book describing the indigenous peoples of the area. He takes the Nazis back to his tent, and shows them some impressionist paintings, and books, including Thomas Mann's *The Magic Mountain*, that he keeps with him.

All this is anathema to the Nazis, who despise this 'decadent' culture and Scott's pacifism. Scott further infuriates his guests by comparing Nazi customs to those of primitive warlike tribes. At the conclusion of this sequence the Nazis POWs attack him, and destroy his paintings and books, claiming 'the war is right here in your tent'. Roused at last, Scott storms after them unarmed and manages to capture them. Scott comments, 'Well, he had a fair chance – one armed Superman against one unarmed decadent democrat. I wonder how Dr Goebbels will explain that?'

The biography of Emeric Pressburger written by his grandson, Kevin Macdonald, records Pressburger's annoyance (from his contemporary diary) with Leslie's determination to speak against the Nazis. 'Arrived at set ... Howard on it. They were shooting an entirely unknown text to me from a bit of paper. Slow and bad ... new lines, twisted the wrong way. Lurid and bad'.[22] Years later, a film historian asked Pressburger in a personal interview whether he though the propaganda in *49th Parallel* was a little 'over the top'? Pressburger disagreed, saying that the Nazis really were like that. Given what had happened to Pressburger in his life, and in fact to all the Hungarian Jews, it seems a somewhat bizarre question to have put to him.[23]

In June 1941 Leslie began a film to celebrate the victory of the Battle of Britain. This was to be *The First of the Few*, and had developed from a story about R.J. Mitchell, the designer of the Spitfire planes famously used during the Battle. Mitchell had died in 1937 after a wearying four-year struggle with cancer, managing to achieve his original designs for the Spitfire mostly between 1934 and 1936. The origin of the work began with a story by author Henry C. James, who obtained an agreement with Mitchell's widow. An outline for a film was later created from this by Miles Malleson, an experienced scriptwriter, who suggested it as a vehicle for Robert Donat, a leading actor of the day. Donat had other work on hand, and the project went into limbo for a time. Leslie heard of the story, became interested, and began to research an outline of his own. Eventually Leslie was to produce and direct it, as well as starring as Mitchell.

Arthur Rank's company, as usual, was approached to finance the project. This was not a difficult decision, as considerable excitement was generated when it became known that Leslie was preparing the film. Contemporary magazines and newspapers commented on his every move and progress. Churchill chimed in and provided a 'go anywhere' pass which enabled Leslie to ask for help from anyone he needed, including the Royal Air Force military and technical staff. As time went on, Leslie had responsibility for a most prestigious work, holding the efforts and enthusiasm of the country and its most admired fighters in his hands. Even with all this, triumphalism was the last thing on Leslie's mind, and the film that finally resulted is decidedly subdued compared with later war films.

The Battle of Britain had begun in July 1940, with Germany's air attack on the country, aimed at smashing defences before an oncoming invasion. But from the start, the Luftwaffe were surprised by the skill and determination of the defending pilots. The RAF, with the help of the Polish, Czech and Canadian fighter pilots who had joined, fought them off. Over the next few weeks, German losses of planes and men were heavy, those of the British much less. As the British fought on alone, some hope came with the support of Roosevelt, who promised a supply of arms for the future. On 19 August 1940, Churchill spoke in the House of Commons, famously paying tribute to these airmen and their successful defence at the country's most desperate time: 'Never in the field of human conflict was so much owed by so many to so few.'

Not surprisingly, the RAF took on the nickname of 'the Few'. The German air bombardment continued, but wave after wave of German bombers were repulsed and shot down. On 8 September, it seemed that the German invasion would come, and church bells rang out a warning all over Britain. It never came. By October the German air force had mostly withdrawn. Their costs were too high and Hitler's battle for Britain was lost.

The storm subsided, and for the moment, the danger of invasion was put off. But Britain still stood alone until June 1941, when Germany invaded Russia. A long, bitterly fought battle between these two ensued, with no definite result for the next two years. Churchill supported Stalin to the greatest extent he could manage, thankful for one ally that might turn the tide. Perhaps the idea for the film emerged from this breathing space. The whole nation was following events closely, and it began to be realized how much the Spitfire had contributed to the decisive battle. On further exploration, the figure of R.J. Mitchell emerged, the genius inventor who had worked until his death, aged only 42, to ensure the production of the plane.

Leslie spent a long time researching the history of the Spitfire development, much of which was hidden by the great secrecy necessary for rearmament in peacetime. Even now, Leslie's sources are not known, and many of the facts of this story themselves remain uncertain. Mitchell's work at the Supermarine Engineering Company had been kept intensely secret, even more so when the firm was taken over by Vickers. Concerning this background for the film, one of Leslie's biographers, Ian Colvin, said that, 'the official material was dry, the story of the widow insufficient'. Colvin states that Leslie finally learnt the true story through informal contacts, the trail leading to 'one of Vickers top scientists, then working on cathode-ray tubes ... They sat and talked for hours. Leslie learnt the amazing story of Mitchell, the £6 a week draughtsman who became absorbed in aerodynamics and studied the shape of birds in flight, in his search for the plane that could outfly the new fighters that Germany was building.'[24]

Ian Colvin gives no provenance for his information. Like much of Colvin's work as an historian and journalist, it may be a mix of inside knowledge of the time and his own suppositions. But Colvin did have reputable contacts. One of his informants was Frank Foley, who held an important position in MI6 during the war, and later gave Colvin a number of leads, including the first clues to the story of *The Man Who Never Was*.[25]

Leslie forcefully makes the point in *The First of the Few* that aircraft development was frustrated by the appeasers in the mid-1930's British government. Mitchell is shown, fired by a trip to Germany, arguing for money for the new fighter plane, but is refused by government minions at Whitehall. Throughout this scene there is in the background a huge poster across a nearby building declaring, ironically, 'Trust Baldwin', then prime minister and supporter of the appeasement policy.

Colvin wrote that as Leslie had gradually uncovered this story, 'he heard of incredible delays in Whitehall, before it was realized that there was genius in Mitchell, (and) of an official minute written on his proposals, "this man must be mad"; of stupidity and perhaps worse in the Contracts branch of the Air Ministry.'[26] Again, Colvin supplied no documentation for this. On the other hand, Colvin's book *The Chamberlain Cabinet*, telling the story of government discussion in the pre-war years, is an accepted standard work for historians to consult. The subject of how far the appeasers of Hitler purposely blocked Britain's rearmament – and why – is still under discussion. Leslie clearly had his own view at that point: Mitchell's dying words in the film are to tell Crisp, 'make sure you get all the planes you need – don't let those Whitehall boys put anything over on you'. Leslie had shown Mitchell working on the Spitfire design in spite of the government's delays and refusal to supply funding. Vickers was of course a private engineering and armaments firm, and they could do as they liked, up to a point, providing they could find the money. The film suggests that the scientists and engineers of the day, particularly Henry Royce, worked semi-secretly, around government opinion, cooperating with each other and getting the work done somehow – 'the money would find itself'.

By the end of autumn 1941 Leslie and his scriptwriters had put together the main draft. Location filming began with the RAF. Leslie filmed some exteriors at Polperro and interiors were filmed at Denham from December 1941. On 7 December, the Japanese bombed Pearl Harbour. Four days later, Germany declared war on the United States. America had been neutral in Europe, but had now been drawn into a struggle in the Pacific against enormous odds. The Atlantic, and the struggle on the continent of Europe, was half a world away. The Americans came into the European battle gradually – first their warships, then their warplanes, and finally their armies came, to the great relief of Britain and its allies.

Neither location nor exterior work on the film were finally to be completed until June 1942. It was a complex and technical work, with the additional difficulties of filming a military unit while it was still engaged in a daily battle. *The First of the Few* was finally presented in England, complete with music from classical composer William Walton, in August 1942. Leslie had expert filming help from Georges Perinal, cinematographer and escapee from France, (again, helped by Korda) where he had been well known in their industry. Jack Hildyard, Leslie's favourite camera operator, his old friend Adrian Brunel, and his usual production manager, Phil Samuels assisted. Sidney Cole, an expert film editor, is listed as technical advisor. He remembered being in demand:

> I'd been approached to become editor at Ealing. I did this and then Leslie Howard was about to make *The First of the Few*, so he rang up Balcon and asked for me to be supervising editor on that film. I was in demand both by Michael Balcon and Leslie Howard, which was gratifying. On the film, I was in charge of the cutting room. One would look at the rushes and discuss the approach to the editing. Sometimes take a sequence and do the final cut oneself. Generally overseeing everything that went on. For some reason, Leslie could not be at the running of the film with William Walton, so he told me beforehand very elaborately what he wanted from the music. Walton listened to my version of all this very carefully and then said, 'Oh I see, Leslie wants a lot of notes', and he went away and wrote the Spitfire Fugue.[27]

Walton was not generally interested in the film industry, but this was to be a national effort.

The well-known actor David Niven partnered Leslie in the film, playing the test pilot for Mitchell's planes. Niven was at this time in the army himself – he had originally joined the Rifle Brigade, but transferred to Phantom, a highly trained Commando signals unit that was to coordinate the locations of the Allied armies. He ultimately rose to the rank of Colonel, and was present at the Allied landings in 1944. Niven wrote in his memoirs that he was given 'four weeks special duty, with a radio transmitter in my dressing room from which I controlled "A" Squadron'.[28] However, his biographer afterwards found that he had been given five months' leave to work on the film.[29]

Niven has a star role to play as Geoffrey Crisp, a composite figure representing a number of real persons, including Mitchell's test pilots and technical advisors. Crisp conforms most closely to Beverley Shenstone, a Canadian with a degree in aeronautical engineering who spent many years with Mitchell, and who was responsible for some of the work designing the Spitfire wing. He had also spent time in Germany, and was aware of developments in the industry there. There was also an element of Vickers' chief test pilot, known as 'Mutt' Summers. Niven himself gave some form to the character, which is played as a handsome, witty womanizer.

Leslie found Rosamund John, an inexperienced but fresh young actress, to play Mrs Mitchell. Miss John, long afterwards, had some playful comments to make on how she was chosen for the film: 'I was living in a house with Robert Donat at the time, and I think I ended up with the part because Violette (Leslie's partner) knew about this, and knew I wouldn't be a rival for Leslie, who was known to be very interested in his leading ladies!'[30]

Violette had a speaking part in the film, credited as 'Suzanne Clair', and playing a rather uninhibited married lady distracted by David Niven's test pilot. She is very much in evidence in a scene at a German dinner party, sitting between Leslie and Niven, while Rosamund John is out of shot, sitting opposite. Leslie provided a speaking part for his attractive young daughter Leslie Ruth (although she insisted it be uncredited) as a nurse looking after Niven. Leslie's son also appeared as an extra.

The scriptwriters had to invent some material to give interest to the characters of Mr and Mrs Mitchell, about whom they knew little. This was made more difficult as Mrs Mitchell and her son Gordon were on the set during much of production. Leslie and Rosamund John had to be extremely careful. Mrs Mitchell had no real knowledge of her husband's work, or the struggle with officialdom to get the Spitfire into production. Indications of the part that she played were shaded in rather than emphasized. One odd scene shows the Mitchells entertaining Crisp to dinner, together with his rather embarrassing new girlfriend. As she chatters on inanely, Mitchell and Crisp leave the ladies to it and go out in the garden to discuss their real interest – the new design of plane. The scene seems pointless, unless it is an indication of how little anyone, including Mitchell's own family, was informed about his work. In fact throughout the film Mrs Mitchell is portrayed as unaware of any technical or political development, remaining closeted and naive.

The film begins with an introductory voice-over from Leslie, who gives a summary of the course of the war up to the end of 1940.

He shows German boasts that England would soon fall, American commentators who believe that the British Empire could not win the battle, and most sarcastically, Goebbels stating that 'The hour is here. Britain will be erased from history'. The introduction ends with the title 'Zero hour, 15th September, 1940'.

An air force control room is shown tracking pilots over Southern Britain. A battle takes place unseen, and the pilots are shown emerging from their planes afterwards. These brief speaking parts were played by actual participants of the Battle of Britain – Tony Bartley, and some said Peter Townsend, Douglas Bader and John Cunningham, although these are hard to spot on the film. Tony Bartley also did the flying stunts needed for the film.[31] More remarkable today is the extreme youth of the pilots with the silk neckties and the silly moustaches. Some of those who gave their lives for their country were barely out of their teens.

The pilots discuss the Spitfire plane which is winning the battle and ask their station commander (Niven) about its history. A flashback to 1922 begins, as the history of Mitchell's background as a seaplane designer, sharpened by the desire to win the Schneider speed trophy, is related. Mitchell is seen on a cliff top, gazing at the flight of gulls over the sea. He dreams to his wife, 'someday I'm going to build a plane that'll be just like a bird – all in one – wings, body, tail, all in one'.

Mitchell sketches a simple and revolutionary design for a new seaplane, back in 1924. Much of the film becomes his personal battle to get his work realized. The elegance of the radical design needed both genius and artistry, and Leslie refused to let Mitchell's character remain too stolidly down-to-earth. Mitchell's new design for Supermarine's seaplane was known as the 'S4'. It needed technical developments and was at first outing a failure. However, the 'S5' and finally the 'S6 B' in 1931, with the addition of a Rolls Royce engine, won the Schneider trophy outright for the best designs of seaplane, leaving all the rest obsolete. The techniques used by Mitchell in designing these seaplanes were to be used by him for the Spitfire and the development of the Rolls Royce Merlin engine. Vickers, the major aviation company of the day, took over the firm Mitchell designed for, Supermarine, with Sir Robert Mclean taking over as chairman, and becoming a devout believer and backer of Mitchell. Even with his help, the development of the S6 was in doubt before the 1931 Schneider competition. At this point in the film there enters Lady Houston, an actual millionairess, a fierce opponent of the appeasement government, who defied them to fund further aircraft research.[32] She gave a secret gift to Vickers of

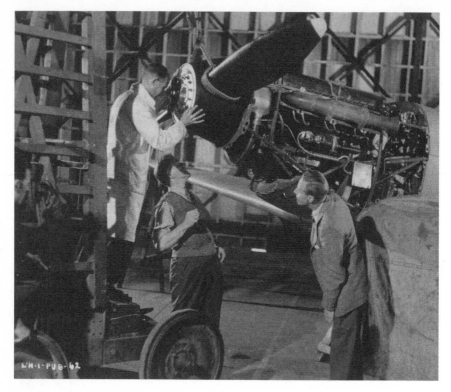

Figure 25. *The First of the Few*, 1942.

£100,000, a startling amount then from any individual. With this extra help, the winning S6B plane was developed, and from it, the Spitfire was on its way.

Mitchell was, in real life, diagnosed with cancer in 1933. The next year, he underwent an operation and spent some time in Germany to recuperate. In the film he is shown experiencing the militant fascism that is brewing there and the aggressive nationalism behind German aircraft design, even being introduced by his German hosts to Herr Messerschmidt. Some of this was dramatic licence. But some of Mitchell's close colleagues did experience something like this. Gordon Mitchell remembered,

> Mutt Summers, the Vickers chief test pilot, was a source of much useful and disturbing information about what the German aircraft industry was doing in the 1930s, since he had many personal contacts holding high positions in that country. Although some were inclined to dismiss what he said, saying in effect that his job was to

be a test pilot, not a sort of unpaid spy, others nevertheless took serious note of what he was saying and there can be no doubt that many people, such as Sir Robert Mclean and Mitchell, had a pretty good notion of what was going on in Germany. They recognized the need for Britain to re-arm, and realised that one of the weapons sorely needed was an improved and modern fighter aircraft.[33]

Sadly by this time, Mitchell's story is nearly told. In real life he worked on until his death, knowing he had a fatal illness, never sparing himself. But work on the Spitfire design was mostly finished before his death. For a more dramatic ending on screen, Mitchell, told he has eight months to live, is still working on the Spitfire. He replies, '(the Spitfire) has got to do 400 mph, turn on a sixpence, climb 10,000 feet in a few minutes, dive at 500 mph without breaking, carry 8 machine guns ... a curious sort of a bird, which spits out death and destruction'. Which of course is an accurate description of the plane that was produced to win the Battle of Britain.

In a poignant last scene, Mitchell is shown resting in his garden, the work done. As the camera pans to the horizon, a seagull is shown soaring to the skies, representing the passing of his spirit. A Spitfire squadron flies past, and as the tide of battle turns, they fly into the setting sun. Churchill's tribute to the fliers concludes *The First of the Few*.

On the film Leslie leaves in view a signed note as the last shot – 'a Leslie Howard production'. In it there have been no triumphant scenes, no stirring marches, no violence, no battle action at all. The film is very different from the full-blown, romanticized style of Hollywood. There was the influence of the wartime documentary movement, which had gained very well-received showings of real action. Leslie also made some political points, perhaps because he had spent so much time researching the background of the story. The deaths of the young pilots in the Battle of Britain was a sickening loss to the country, and yet another one that it could barely afford to make. No wonder that the mood of Leslie's nearly contemporary film was less one of celebration, more of angry questions being asked. Leslie had done wonders in bringing together the film industry and the RAF to create the film during wartime, and in giving a restrained and intelligent portrayal of a key event in history. There is Leslie's reticent, perceptive personality, projected as R.J. Mitchell, and his light touch as a director. The low-key but determined British mood is caught perfectly and there are moments of humour which turn gradually to darkness as German war plans are understood. The film stands as Leslie's masterpiece. *Pimpernel Smith* had been much enjoyed, but it is not clear that its message was fully perceived. *The First of the Few* expressed not only a renewed national confidence, but the widely felt anger and questioning that western civilisation should ever have hung by so thin a thread. *The First of the Few* was the top-grossing British film of 1942. *The Times* commented, 'the casual under-statement, the off-hand approach, the artlessness which conceals hard work and perfect timing ... is here successful, for it perfectly fits the theme and title of the film'.[34]

At some point in 1942 Leslie was asked by the Foreign Office and the Ministry of Information to undertake a delicate propaganda trip to neutral Ireland, which would rely on his skills of charm and diplomacy. Southern Ireland (Éire) was neutral throughout the Second World War. Eamonn de Valera, the prime minister (Taoiseach) and acknowledged leader of his country, had to tread a narrow path between Irish nationalism, which at this time meant hatred of Britain and therefore pro-German attitudes, and the realities of the war. In early 1942, Britain's anger about Irish neutrality had been curbed somewhat, but there were still two main points at issue. One was Ireland's southern ports, which would have been extremely useful to Britain in the desperate naval Battle of the Atlantic, where thousands of lives were being lost. The ports had always been thought vital to Britain's defence, and during the war could have brought British and American sea power hundreds of miles closer to the operating areas of German submarines. In 1938 Chamberlain had ceded them entirely to Ireland. De Valera would not allow Britain back. Another worry was that Irish sympathies could aid Germany in an invasion through their country.

Whoever realized that goodwill might play a larger part than threats or anger in the struggle for Irish hearts (possibly Brendan Bracken, Minister of Information, of Irish origin himself), by 1942 a cultural and charm offensive was well under way. John Betjeman, who had been working at the Ministry of Information, was sent out as 'cultural attaché' to the British minister in Ireland in January 1941. He liaised directly back to Britain with Nicholas Mansergh, official in the Colonial Office and described as 'a one-man Irish office' for the MoI. Betjeman was immensely cultured, charming, eccentric and as a poet, more admired in Ireland perhaps than in his own country. He worked doggedly in Ireland to find, as he put it, 'friends for Britain', sway opinion away from Germany, and secretly, to report back carefully on attitudes at all levels and recommend the best political and propaganda moves. He would oversee Leslie's visit.[35]

Leslie flew in to Dublin on 10 April 1942 with Violette, listed officially as his secretary. On that day, *The Irish Times* carried a front-page story that Leslie was visiting the country to 'make a personal appearance on behalf of the Newspaper Press Fund' in aid of its charity. In an interview Leslie threw out some smoke trails, including mention of a 'constantly postponed dream to produce a film version of *Hamlet*' hinting at a cultural exchange behind the visit. One whopper was a supposed Irish connection in his own family: 'As a small boy I often passed through Dublin to spend summer holidays in Ennis, County Clare, with an aunt.'

Leslie also managed a tricky propaganda point by insisting that British film distributors would not stop films going to Ireland because they objected to Irish censorship. As he said, 'I cannot believe that anyone wants to foist on a country propaganda that it does not want to see.' The censorship was extremely strict, and in fact was at such a level that little information of any sort was passing between the two countries, except what could be brought out in person. Although the Irish press mentioned *Pimpernel Smith* and *The First of the Few* as Leslie's films, neither were allowed to be shown there, nor were any of Leslie's later works.

Leslie sailed along, apparently making no particular point and doing his best to engender some goodwill over the next week. A report of his activities on 12 April, which included a lecture (about *Hamlet* again), a cultural evening and a radio interview, was headed, 'Leslie Howard's winning charm'. Describing his lecture, the *Irish Independent* praised him for his beautiful voice and unforced style:

> He came on the stage and chatted to the audience in such an intimate manner that his conversation might have been addressed to them individually rather than collectively ... subtle preparation could hardly have improved on the winning reference to Dublin as 'the city of beautiful manners', those graceful tributes to the Press, the nice selection of revealing incidents he chose to relate.

These hymns of praise from the press hint strongly at where their sympathies lay. Leslie's radio interview was also described in very friendly terms, Leslie mentioning his Irish friends in Hollywood, William Gargan and J.M. Kerrigan.

The next day Leslie made an official visit with John Betjeman to the residence of the Irish president, and was received by his secretary, Michael McDunphy, who, besides asking for autographs for his children, also spoke to Leslie and John Betjeman. Mr McDunphy later wrote, 'Mr Howard came with Mr Betjeman on 13 April. They remained an hour. I found Mr Howard extremely interesting and very friendly towards all things Irish.'[36]

On the same day, *The Irish Times*' social diary noted, 'Mrs Mansergh has arrived in Dublin'. Given the facts that Nicholas Mansergh was the direct liaison for propaganda visits to Ireland, that travel there was extremely restricted, and that Mrs Mansergh was an intelligent and capable confidante of her husband, it seems a possibility that Mrs Mansergh's role included that of discreet social organizer and information courier.[37]

Leslie also made lightning visits to Dun Laoghaire and Killiney – suburbs of Dublin – pursued by more autograph hunters, had tea with Professor Felix Hackett and his wife, well-known figures in Dublin, president of the Royal Dublin Society and vice-president of the Irish Red Cross respectively, and went on to an evening at the Abbey Players. The next evening, Erskine Hamilton Childers gave a party for him. Childers, later president of Ireland, was the son of Robert Erskine Childers, author of *The Riddle of the Sands* (1903), an anti-German spy story, who had been shot as a traitor by the British in 1922. Irish sympathies were quixotic.

After this exhausting round, Leslie went to stay at the house of a close friend of Lord Beaverbrook's in Killarney. This was the Right Hon. Sir Valentine Edward Charles Browne, Bt., sixth Earl of Kenmare, Viscount Castlerosse. There is unfortunately no absurd aristocratic nickname remembered for him, but he was a sociable, rumbustious type, who was well known as a gossip columnist for the *Sunday Express*, and who had also tried his hand at a few filmscripts. Lord Castlerosse is also listed in MoI files of the time as one of the sympathetic journalists to be employed in a press campaign secretly orchestrated by the ministry to direct popular hatred against the Germans.[38] His dilapidated castle, Kenmare House, in the South West of Ireland, was soon to fall into disuse, but there were still plenty of loyal retainers, and possibly Leslie and Violette tried a little countryside horse riding. On the other hand they could have visited, perhaps with Mrs Mansergh, the treaty ports of Cobh, near Cork, and Berehaven (now known as Bere Island) in Bantry Bay, both incidentally quite close to Kenmare House.

Leslie returned to the capital a few days later, where arrangements had been made for him to see the Taoiseach, Eamon de Valera.[39] Leslie would possibly have been out-charmed, and certainly out-chatted by de Valera, but their subject can never be known. However, in 1941 Churchill had secretly sent Kenneth Clark to discuss the treaty ports with de Valera. Clark could get no change, but found de Valera a sympathetic character.[40] At the end of January 1942, the first American troops arrived in Ulster for the battle in Europe. De Valera made a strong protest.

Was this one last attempt to change de Valera's mind? It could have been a coincidence that Leslie arrived at the beginning of April 1942, and the month of March 1942 had seen the greatest allied losses in the war at sea: 273 merchant ships had been sunk, including 95 in the North Atlantic.[41] In addition, the Enigma code signals for the German submarine command were suddenly no longer decipherable by the Bletchley Park code-breakers in February 1942. The German Navy had added a fourth rotor to their Enigma machines, greatly increasing the complexity of their codes and locking out the code-breakers.[42] The messages were not recovered for almost a year, and then at a great cost. At the same time, British cyphers carrying most of the Allied communications about the North Atlantic convoys were broken by German naval intelligence. The terrifying Battle of the Atlantic was at its most dangerous point.

Against this speculation is Mansergh's testimony that following Leslie's visit, the Foreign Office and Ministry of Information wanted to send him again to Ireland, because his report had been so well done. But apparently nobody thought of sending him up until April 1943, and this would suggest that whatever Leslie succeeded at, it wasn't in negotiations with de Valera.

Leslie could make no difference to the battle. But, according to the press, the legend of his charm stayed long in Dublin. At the end of his visit the *Irish Independent* commented,

> Mr Howard ... has never talked so much, or heard so much talk in so short a space as during his four days in Dublin. Between the talk and the clamour to meet and see him ... I am afraid Dublin would have been the end of him if he had not escaped to the South ... Dublin ... completely succumbed to his charm of manner.[43]

Nicholas Mansergh later praised Leslie for writing a 'sensitive' report on conditions and attitudes in Ireland, although it is hard to understand why Leslie should have found anything that Betjeman, Kenneth Clark and others who reported to Churchill, the Ministry of Information and the Foreign Office could not.[44]

By now it was the spring of 1942: Leslie had seen too much, he knew too many secrets. Most of all he had said too much. He had made enemies with his propaganda. And in the normal course of events, the most dangerous enemies are those closest at hand.

NOTES

1. BBC, Caversham transcripts (CT) of radio programmes, 16 December 1940, *Britain Speaks*.
2. CT, *Britain Speaks*, 27 January 1940.
3. CT, *Britain Speaks*, 2 September 1940.
4. CT, *Britain Speaks*, 24 November 1940.
5. Ibid.
6. CT, *Britain Speaks*, 12 August 1940.
7. CT, *Britain Speaks*, 24 November 1940.
8. CT, *Britain Speaks*, 27 January 1941, 7 April 1941.
9. Adrian Brunel, *Nice Work: The Story of Thirty Years in British Film Production* (London: Forbes Robertson, 1949), p.194.
10. CT, *Answering You*, 29 March 1942.
11. CT, *Britain Speaks*, 24 November 1940.
12. CT, *Britain Speaks*, 2 September 1940.
13. CT, *Britain Speaks*, 'The New Order', 23 December 1940.
14. CT, *Britain Speaks*, 29 July 1940.
15. CT, *Britain Speaks*, 10 November 1940.
16. Leslie Ruth Howard, *A Quite Remarkable Father* (London: Longmans, 1960), p.263.
17. CT, *Britain Speaks*, 19 August and 9 September 1940.
18. CT, *Britain Speaks*, 25 November 1940.
19. Pat Jackson, letter to author, 15 January 2006.
20. CT, *Britain Speaks*, 12 August 1940.
21. Kevin Macdonald, *Emeric Pressburger: The Life and Death of a Screenwriter*, (London: Faber and Faber, 1994).
22. Ibid., p.179.
23. Interview with Emeric Pressburger by Kevin Gough-Yates, 12 November 1970, in Kevin Gough-Yates, *Michael Powell in Collaboration with Emeric Pressburger* (London: British Film Institute, 1971).
24. Ian Colvin, *Flight 777* (London: Evans Brothers, 1957), p.55.
25. Michael Smith, *Foley: The Spy Who Saved 10,000 Jews* (London: Hodder and Stoughton, 1999), p.84, 'Colvin's contacts were so good that during the war he was consulted by the Prime Minister himself'.
26. Colvin, *Flight 777*, p.55.
27. Sidney Cole, taped interview of 9 September 1987, transcript at the British Film Institute.
28. David Niven, *The Moon's a Balloon* (London: Hamilton, 1971), p.244.
29. Graham Lord, *Niv: The Authorised Biography of David Niven* (London: Orion Media, 2003).
30. Rosamund John, taped interview in 1992, transcript at the British Film Institute.
31. See, for example, Brunel, *Nice Work*, p.191 and Anthony Bartley, *Smoke Trails in the Sky: From the Journals of a Fighter Pilot* (London: Kimber, 1984).
32. See *Oxford Dictionary of National Biography* on Lady Houston.
33. Gordon Mitchell, *R.J. Mitchell, Schooldays to Spitfire* (Stroud: Tempus, 1986), p.128.
34. *The Times*, 20 August 1942.
35. Bevis Hillier, *John Betjeman: New Fame, New Love* (London: John Murray, 2002), pp.163–4.
36. File on Leslie Howard, P2215, in the National Archives of Ireland.
37. Mrs Mansergh's role in her husband's work from Nicholas Mansergh' obituary, *The Times*.
38. Reported in Anthony Aldgate and Jeffrey Richards, *Britain Can Take It: The British Cinema in the Second World War* (Oxford: Blackwell, 1986), p.150. Report of Planning Committee on Home Morale Campaign, 21 June 1940, PRO, INF 1/849.
39. From the file, P2215, on Leslie's visit, in the National Archives of Ireland.

40. Kenneth Clark, *The Other Half: A Self Portrait* (London: Hamish Hamilton, 1977), p.34.

41. Martin Gilbert, *Second World War* (London: Weidenfeld and Nicolson, 1989), p.314.

42. Hugh Sebag-Montefiore, *Enigma: The Battle for the Code* (London: Weidenfeld and Nicolson, 2000).

43. *Irish Independent*, 17 April 1942.

44. The file on Leslie at the National Archives of Ireland was examined by the archivist. In an email to the author of 7 February 2006 the archivist describes the contents and the fact that it contains eight pages. In answer to further enquiry, in an email two days later, the archivist says that it also contains a letter or note by Leslie, with the letterhead of Kenmare House. A request to photocopy the whole file was granted, and the copies duly arrived. However they contained only six pages and no note of Leslie's. On inquiring about what had happened to Leslie's letter, the following reply was received, on 16 March 2006.

Dear Ms Eforgan,
Regarding your email below, the letter in question cannot be found at present as it may have become misfiled with another file – we are investigating the matter and will inform you of the results of the search in due course. Apologies for the inconvenience and delay caused.'
No further word was sent, so it appears that the archivist had the letter, which then became unaccountably lost.

CHAPTER NINE

1942–1943: The Gentle Sex

In November 1940 Leslie's broadcast to America, entitled 'The Female of the Species', included a chat with his spirited daughter Leslie Ruth, aged 17:

> *Miss Howard*: 'You answer me this. Why are you so concerned that women should be exposed to the dangers of war as well as men?'
>
> *Mr Howard*: 'That's an absurd question.'
>
> *Miss H*: 'I don't think so. If my brother [Ronald Howard] has to risk his life, why not me? If anything his life is more valuable than mine.'
>
> *Mr H*: 'It's not a question of that. Biologically women are less fitted for hardships than men.'
>
> *Miss H*: 'I'm sorry to have to contradict, but that is sheer masculine nonsense. Women are just as tough as men and a great deal more able to stand suffering.'
>
> *Mr H*: 'I don't think you understand. Women are the mothers of the human race.'
>
> *Miss H*: 'That's a typically masculine remark. All women are supposed to do is produce the soldiers of the future. But has it never occurred to you that no woman is ever asked to a peace conference?'
>
> *Mr H*: 'No it never had. That's an interesting thought.'
>
> *Miss H*: 'But they will take part in the next one, believe me. And in the reconstruction of the world. Unless of course the Nazis win.'
>
> *Mr H*: 'Which they won't'.
>
> *Miss H*: 'Which they won't.'[1]

(The Nazis' view of women was that they should be confined to kitchen work, looking after children and going to church.)

At the end of 1941 the British Government introduced national conscription, and this included unmarried women between 20 and 30. They were conscripted as part of the military – attached as auxiliary services to the army, navy and air force. Women were also asked to work in munitions factories, nursing, transport, on the land, in communications, or with emergency services. Much of this had previously been seen as men's work only, and many men were doubtful about women's capabilities – both physical and intellectual. By the end of 1942 women had proved themselves invaluable in all fields, their high morale and hard work giving rise to admiration, or at least a change in attitude in all but the most curmudgeonly members of the opposite sex. At the peak, 85 per cent of the women in the country of a suitable age were involved in war work.

Naturally this was encouraged and observed by the film world, which, with radio, had become part of the nation's way of talking to itself. In one of Leslie's broadcasts in March 1942, George Strauss MP commented, 'I remember one short film that had a startling success – far more than the authorities expected. It was a film appealing to women to go to labour exchanges to get work in war factories. There were enormous queues outside many exchanges, and rather to the embarrassment of the officials, more women applied than could be found work.'[2]

The reality of women's roles in the war effort had interested filmmakers in both Britain and America. Films with women as protagonists were not new, but perhaps the subject of women's own aims and aspirations was novel. Previous 'women's films' had been popular, but there was usually an impression of women being acted upon, rather than determining their own destiny. How much this was openly recognized is uncertain, but the theme was in the air. In October 1942 Pathé released *She's in the Army*, a film short about the Women's Ambulance and Defence Corps of America. In November 1942 Launder and Gilliat released *Millions Like Us*, about female munitions factory workers, followed in February 1943 by RKO's *Women at Arms*. Perhaps the most well-loved women's film of all, *Now Voyager*, was shown in Britain in April 1943. This was not so much about women's work, but the theme of an ordinary woman (well, moderately ordinary – it was Bette Davis) finding confidence and independence through her own courage, *and* keeping it, *and* providing love and support for others by doing so, was exceptionally rare.

Leslie's film, *The Gentle Sex*, which eventually premiered in March

1943, initiated, in Britain at least, some of these ideas, and both its format and its attitudes became influential for British film; the format was used time and again until it ran into the ground, from *The Way Ahead* to *Carry on Sergeant*.

The Gentle Sex originated with a young female screenwriter, Moie Charles – it was in fact her first work. She had written the script for a short documentary about women in the Auxiliary Army Corps, which she called *We're not Weeping*, and this was its title right up to the end of filming until Leslie put his foot down and changed it. Her title was a reference to a quotation from Charles Kingsley, not originally implying any misogyny. Leslie's old friend Derrick de Marney, who had acted with him in *The Scarlet Pimpernel*, tried his hand at producing, forming a company called Concanen Films (after his mother's name). He had taken up the script, and with the help of Del Giudice and with Adrian Brunel as director, had started production at the small Highbury Studios.

The first results were disappointing, and a halt was called. After some discussion with Jack Beddington, head of the MOI's film division, the whole project was forwarded to Del Giudice at Denham, and Leslie was asked to take over the direction. Adrian Brunel was upset over being replaced, but Leslie tried to soften the blow by involving him in some capacity, and Brunel was finally credited with the title of 'Production Consultant'. Main filming restarted in September 1942, after Leslie had worked over the script, making it less of a stiff documentary, and adding his own characteristic light-as-air humour. Most of all he insisted that there were to be no fairy-tale romantic endings for the girls, knowing instinctively that a film about women's newly found independence should not show them finally relapsing back on men.[3]

As it turned out, the greatest asset of the film was the gifted group of actresses that Moie Charles had helped to cast. They created great enthusiasm for the film, and a particular format emerged which was much used afterwards – the progress of a set of ordinary people formed together as a group, with the interests of all in mind, bonding and maturing both collectively and as individuals. Many of the scenes created are recognizable in more recent films, and have worked again and again to create similar interest and emotion.

In the spirit of the time the actresses actually underwent all the experiences, or most of them, of newcomers in the Women's Auxiliary Army Corps; marching and drilling together at the main training camp with real recruits, being instructed by the actual officers, and sharing the same accommodation and food. The seven female leads, Joan Gates, Jean Gillie, Joan Greenwood, Joyce Howard, Rosamund John, Lilli Palmer and Barbara Waring were all quite accepting of this, though it is difficult to imagine it happening now.

The film kept its documentary format, following the seven women through their various experiences, as Leslie provided an invisible voice-over commentary on their character and actions. The opening of the film shows a railway station, with Leslie's back to the camera above all the hurrying figures, musing in voice-over, 'women, women all over the place; the weaker sex, the fair sex, the gentle sex – let's take a closer look at some of them – a couple of armfuls perhaps'. We first see Joan Greenwood, as Leslie comments, 'now there's a dear little thing'. (And she is – the very young actress is notable in her first appearance in film.) But as Leslie comments, often ironically, about accepted male ideas on the women, he gives them all an unquestioned individuality, respect and dignity. And the plainly dressed, sensibly behaved women, minus the thick make-up, lip-gloss, stiletto heels, false breasts and surgically altered faces of modern female leads, are a revelation. The film focuses on seven particular women, all eventually travelling together in a railway carriage; 'seven characters – in search of what?' Leslie asks. That women should be in search of anything but how to get a man was something new in itself.

We see the women arrive at the camp, and in a classic scene, they are taken off the coach and formed up together for the first time as a group. Then we see a progression of scenes, including introductory talks, a first army meal, skills testing, the collection of kit. As the women put on their new uniform there is a flash of Jean Gillie's long, beautiful legs with the actress in nothing but sheer black stockings, suspenders, and her knickers – astonishing for the time, and typical of Leslie to slide it past the censor. This is contrasted immediately with a shot of Joan Greenwood looking waiflike and vulnerable in an oversized army greatcoat. As a close to the sequence, there is the 'new recruits squabbling in the dormitory' scene, again very recognisable. But the arguments here are gentle, and there is comforting advice and cheerful joking.

There is a long sequence of the actresses drilling, taking aptitude tests, training in Morse code and taking part in games and PT. In fact there is rather too much of the drill scenes, recalling the documentary origins of what should now be a feature film, but perhaps the actresses wanted all their efforts to be reflected on screen. Finally the male drill sergeant polishes them up, commenting patronizingly, but with humour and patience on the progress they have made – and this scene and characters appear to come straight from life. As we watch them marching, all the women look trim, slim and fit as a pin; and not a fad diet or session of liposuction needed. All this is enlivened by the delightful actresses, who give a fresh sparkle to the whole undertaking. Joan Greenwood and Lilli Palmer had long careers afterwards, Rosamund John appeared in sixteen films, some of them British classics. But all the actresses are interesting and sympathetic to the viewer, and it seems a pity that vehicles were never afterwards considered for them.

The women pass out of the training camp and are posted to other regiments – some just as canteen assistants, some as lorry drivers, mechanical engineers, and into the Anti-Aircraft command of the Royal Artillery. This reflected exactly the reality, and women made a significant contribution in this way, controlling the giant 'ack-ack' guns, as they were known. Officially they never actually fired the guns, although the film shows them doing just that. It also shows them being horrified at their success in bringing an enemy plane down in flames.

The girls are recognisable British 'types', except for Lilli Palmer's foreign refugee; a down-to-earth Scots woman, a chirpy cockney, a smart blonde, a sheltered middle-class girl; and they are shown finding romance with men as working equals, at a jolly and carefree dance, exchanging friendly comments and cheerful support. The romances do not end with a sexual encounter, but instead John Justin and Joyce Howard are shown philosophizing in the twilight outside the dance hall, wondering if their generation is the one that will finally succeed in establishing a different world for the future.

As a lighter contrast to this, a scene later on shows two telephonists in the middle of a bombardment, gossiping to each other about their men:

> 'He took me in his arms and then he asked me to –' (words drowned by explosion)
> 'He asked you to what?'
> 'Marry him!'
> 'Oh!' (Deeply disappointed tone).

Another more serious sequence shows the group driving a convoy of lorries full of arms to the docks for the long anticipated invasion of Europe. They have to drive non-stop, all through the night, for a journey of 400 miles. As they leave, their female officer says to them, 'and now make it a point of honour that your lorries will arrive by their own power, not at the end of a tow rope'. The film even introduces an older woman character who is discovered to have served with the Women's Auxiliary Army Corps in 1914, where she was wounded. She tells the girls, 'we women didn't know what we wanted then – but I believe you do. And I believe you'll succeed in getting it.'

The only odd note in all this determined uplift is Lilli Palmer's character; that of a foreign refugee who has some things to say which don't chime with the other girls' untroubled political views. In one scene, the women are in the guard's van of the train, overcrowded and very late:

Jean Gillie:	(the unpopular corporal): 'The Nazis are more efficient than this.'
Lilli Palmer:	'You British, you have been through the Blitz and everything else, but you still don't understand what the war really means.'
JG:	'Oh you foreigners are always getting excited. You need to keep calm.'
LP:	'My father was shot for fun, my brother tortured until he was unrecognisable. But you are right. I will stay calm.' (She breaks down in tears.)

Lillie Palmer the actress was in fact a Jewish refugee from Germany. She had no brother, but her two sisters and her mother had managed to leave the country after the Nazis came to power. In her memoirs, she remembered her father died in 1934, in despair at the rise of the Nazis. It is also known that her mother's sister, to whom she was close, committed suicide by jumping from a window when the Gestapo came for her.[4] The scene attempts to counter ideas prevalent then that the information filtering through from refugees about the Holocaust was over-exaggerated, as Jews were thought to express their difficulties in over-emotional ways, although this scrap of conversation probably did little to correct the attitude. Later in the film her character tells the others, 'hatred will help – it gives us something strong to hold on to – until the world is sane again'. In the scene where the group of girls fire an ack-ack gun and are upset to shoot down an enemy plane, this character is shown with a smile of rather macabre revenge.

The film concludes on a thoughtful note, with the future of the girls accounted for, as good wives to their male counterparts, but expected to be as strong and independent in marriage as they are now, and to play their part in the society to be renewed. Leslie speaks the final words, 'Well, there they are – the women. Our sweethearts, sisters, mothers, daughters. Let's give in and admit that we're really proud of you. You strange, wonderful, incalculable creatures!' It's a film very characteristic of Leslie in style, with its gentle, understated action, almost unnoticeable but very pointed comments interpolated, and his sly sexiness and humour. The affection and respect for the women seem to come from a lost world.

When *The Gentle Sex* was shown in April 1943, reviewers praised it as the 'First salute to women'[5] and 'The first feature film to be made about British women'. Which was all very well, but the accompanying patronizing and disdainful tone of these male critics is all too evident by modern standards. *Kinematograph Weekly* sniffed that, 'women will be enthused by it'[6] while *The Sunday Times* had managed to grasp that 'Moie Charles gives a woman's point of view'.[7] *The Star*'s critic seemed only amazed: 'Whenever I pass any member of the ATS in future I shall feel inclined to raise my hat respectfully ... They perform a hundred tasks which would have astonished their grandmothers.'[8]

Some papers commented on the documentary quality of the work, which seemed to do it no harm, and Leslie's direction was praised by all: '*The Gentle Sex* is a disarming film – the exact antithesis of *The Women* – and its general atmosphere of good fellowship and speech-day sentiment cannot blanket the quiet, persistent intelligence with which it is made' (*The Sunday Times*, 7 April 1943). And, 'Leslie Howard's direction is so adroit that the unpretentious film grips where many a million dollar production leaves the audience cold' (*Manchester Guardian*, 27 July 1943). There were a number of viewings of the film solely for ATS members, who reportedly were greatly cheered and affected by it.[9]

A photograph exists of Leslie, the actresses and the producers of the film together.[10] Leslie sits on the floor at the feet of the actresses, near Rosamund John, a jaunty cap on his head, a cigarette in his mouth, and it has to be said, with rather a smug look on his face. Away from the girls, standing at the back and looking glumly out of it are Derrick de Marney and Adrian Brunel. It was said later that Joan Greenwood had also fallen for Leslie but since the actress was never very forthcoming, and gave few interviews for the whole of her life, no more is heard of it.[11] There is no doubt that by this time in the British Studios Leslie had acquired a certain reputation for having an interest in women not wholly filmic. Rosamund John later said of him at this time,

> Leslie taught me everything I knew about film-making. I got on very
> well with him and luckily he didn't want to get into bed with me,

as he did with quite a few people he worked with ... He was an extraordinary character. I suppose one would call him amoral. He just did what he enjoyed doing. I remember one day his daughter came on the set and took out a very nice cigarette case. Leslie said, 'Where'd you get that?' 'Don't you recognise it?' she said, 'It's one Merle Oberon gave you. Mummy had the inscription removed and gave it to me.' Leslie just roared with laughter.[12]

Ronald Howard gives a much more romantic description of Leslie's relationship with Violette, who had been his mistress and companion since 1938.[13] In the main it was a loving partnership between two intelligent and attractive people. But like most relationships it was not unspotted, and neither partner seems to have been faithful at all times. Perhaps the actor's world is different. Rosamund John was living, unmarried, with Robert Donat, who was married to someone else, at the time she made her comments on Leslie. The wartime insouciance is remembered by many as a stimulant to affairs. There were reports of changing partners on some of Leslie's films, and Violette reportedly had a brief affair with David Lean during the making of *Pygmalion*,[14] although it is easy to see this as an attempt by her to even up the emotional score. It is certain that Leslie liked and loved women – perhaps all too literally.

It was at the end of filming *The Gentle Sex* that disaster struck. Both Leslie and Violette were affected by some illness and retired to their house at Monkseaton, Stoke Poges, not far from Denham Studios. Leslie recovered, believing he had suffered a bout of flu, but they were both exhausted from nearly non-stop work during the war. Violette grew worse, apparently with a boil in her nose. At last she had to be taken to hospital, where Leslie waited, agonized, to see if she would pull through. Alas, on 3 November 1942 she died, aged 34. The death certificate gives the causes as 'meningitis, thrombosed cavernous sinus and cellulitis of face'.

Leslie was shattered by her death, and was ill and depressed for many months. His wife tried to comfort him, and looked after him for some time at the family home in Surrey. Leslie turned to what consolations were possible in wartime; consulting spiritualists and, according to his family, trying to reach Violette with such messages, as if he could mentally conjure her back.[15] Violette was buried at Mortlake cemetery, and many people from the film world attended the quiet ceremony. Also present were friends of Violette amongst the Free French in London, those who had come to England to escape the German invasion of

France and who refused to acknowledge the French surrender. Leslie had known them through Violette, and according to Ronald, had sometimes attended the Free French Club off Lower Regent Street.[16]

This club, at 4 St James's Place, was started by Olwen Vaughan in response to her twin enthusiasms for films and the French. Olwen Vaughan had become secretary of the British Film Institute in its early years. She was a sociable and enterprising sort, and her club came to be frequented by such film men as Alberto Cavalcanti, Robert Hamer, Harry Watt and Angus Macphail, as well as many of the Free French. Guido Coen, Del Giudice's assistant, who also knew the club well, did not remember that Violette and Leslie appeared there very much, and Leslie did not particularly like noisy crowds of drinkers, but on the other hand, Ronald claims they went often. It is possible that Leslie and Violette attended more when they were based in London during the earlier part of the war, when Guido Coen and Del Giudice were interned as Italian refugees.[17]

Leslie had met some of the Free French at their camp when they first came over, and his broadcast of August 1940 described some of their experiences very sympathetically.[18] Much of this broadcast has been censored, presumably on the grounds that the Germans might have been able to gain information from it, and visit some vengeance on any relatives in France. It is difficult to grasp the details of this part of the story, as the Free French in Britain have not left much in the way of personal memoirs behind, and naturally they all returned to France after the war. One further difficulty is that many were in the SOE (Special Operations Executive) or knew very well those who were, and since a strict secrecy has attended the doings of that group for more than fifty years, much has yet to come to light.

Leslie now became close to some of the Free French, as they were the strongest link left to Violette, and they helped him as much as they could, even encouraging him to visit mediums and try automatic writing, and other such methods of comforting the bereaved, until Leslie could bear to face the world again. Amongst the Free French then was Josette Renee Paule Ronserail, a beautiful young woman who had enlisted in the First Aid Nursing Yeomanry, (FANY) and afterwards joined the secretive Special Operations Executive. She eventually became Leslie's new partner, some saying that she looked like Violette, and was a comfort to him for that reason.[19] She stayed with Leslie, probably from the start of 1943, until his death, when he left her in his will the house in which they had lived together. She was just 22 years old when Leslie, aged 49, met her. FANY records of her have this to say:

> We have made a search and found a trace of Josette. She was admitted to the Corps in Sept 42 in F section and apparently issued with uniform. She appears to have resigned in Dec 42, but we cannot say whether this means she went on to more clandestine work in another department, or really decided against continuing with Special Ops. This is the sum total of the papers we hold.'
>
> Joan Drummond (Captain) Adjutant, 10 May 2006 [20]

Josette's file at the National Archives shows her membership of SOE. (SOE files, File HS9 /1279/9). The chronicler of SOE, M.R.D. Foot, commented on FANY and the SOE:

> Some of these young women did indeed come from the leisured class of prewar England. They belonged to one of the least known of the women's services, a somewhat socially exclusive one, the First Aid Nursing Yeomanry (FANY) or Women's Transport Corps. Colin Gubbins (an originator of SOE) happened to know their commandant ('not what you know, but whom you know' is after all the Society's motto); and from this happy accident SOE derived a great deal of benefit, so much so that over half of FANY's total strength was devoted to its work. It did some useful work chauffeuring generals for the army, quite outside of the secret world, and a great deal more for SOE. One of the most awkward spells for agents in SOE might be the days – weeks – months spent waiting, after training was over, for the right moment to arrive to move in to action. The move might be held up by a thousand accidents of politics, weather or war. The wait was usually spent in a holding station, a secluded country house staffed and run by FANYs, who made the stay there as delectable as they could.[21]

Presumably Josette 'had decided against continuing with Special Ops' as the present adjutant puts it, when she resigned from the FANYs in December 1942. As Foot wrote,

> One other defensive point needed to be covered before agents left for the field. If it could not be handled in Group B, it could be inquired into while they were staying in safe flats in the west end of London, in the intervals between technical training courses. Did they talk in their sleep, and if so in what language? There was a devastating blonde codenamed 'Fifi' who made it her business to find out, until 1943, when SOE was able to borrow a trick from

Crockatt's MI19 and had the bedrooms in the Beaulieu houses wired for sound. After that, Fifi was only called in if a student was bright enough to find and silence the microphone.[22]

Leslie was never a great talker or revealer of secrets. But it is possible that Josette was amongst the few people with enough security clearance to be trusted. The fate of Josette Renee Paule Ronserail could not be traced past a marriage in Kensington on 27 September 1943, three months after Leslie died, to Peter Robert Jackson. A child, Claude Andre, is registered as having been born to them on 5 July 1942. These events seem to cast doubt on Ronserail's having had a genuine relationship with Leslie, and open the possibility that, working for SOE, she provided a companion whose discretion could be trusted. It is also possible that she reported back to MI5, who were in charge of all the secret services.

On the other hand, the Free French had been Leslie's close friends for a long time. Leslie was still a very desirable man and it did not need other motives for many women to be ready to take up the free space in his life. Leslie had in any case a very great sympathy with the women of SOE, who were used as the most idealistic, vulnerable and noblest of flag bearers in the battle against the Nazis, not keeping back from the frontlines of the battle, sometimes with horrifying results.

By the end of 1942 Leslie had gained a considerable reputation as a director. His style was becoming recognized. He was spoken of with warmth and admiration, known in the trade as 'Leisurely Howard' for his contempt towards strict timetables and costings. Only Leslie could have got away with this – at least during the war when the benevolent Arthur Rank was underwriting practically everything. But Leslie's skills with the most difficult of actors and technicians were considerable. There was never the slightest problem apparent on the films he directed and produced, quite an achievement given the technical difficulties, the various temperaments and the fact that the British film unions were the most intractable in the country – so bad were they that *Kinematograph Weekly* suspected that there was a 'Communist cell at the bottom of all the trouble'.[23]

Leslie also had great ambitions as a producer. By the beginning of 1943 his production company had gone through various evolutions, and he had become attached to Two Cities, as a parent company, a creation of Del Giudice's.[24] Leslie was listed as a director along with John R. Sutro (a descendant of Sutro the playwright, and great film enthusiast) Major A.M. Sassoon, and Colonel G.R. Crosfield, both veterans of the First World War, financial backers and distinguished society figures, with

Del Giudice as managing director. Leslie's daughter remembers that he was considered, or titled, production consultant, with a strong influence on the films that were to be undertaken by the company.[25] The other directors were not sleeping partners, and the supposedly humorous story was told that Major Sassoon was on duty walking the streets as an air-raid warden, as everyone of every class took their turn to do, when he was 'waylaid by a would-be screen-writer and compelled to listen to a film plot'.[26]

Leslie's long experience in the film world in Hollywood, his many contacts in all sorts of spheres, and his skills as a charming diplomat, had come to fruition. There was one project which was started due to just these skills, announced at the time but never fulfilled. At the end of August 1942, Leslie attended the official premiere of *The First of the Few*, at the Leicester Square cinema. There he met, with other film and society figures, Mr Ivan Maisky, Soviet Ambassador to Britain. Maisky was a devout Communist, of Jewish origin, but his mild charm and ability to speak a number of European languages had made him popular with politicians and diplomats, and he had become a recognized character at that time. Maisky was most anxious to do all he could to help his countrymen, at this time engaged in a desperate battle to halt the Germans in their invasion. As the film they were watching demonstrated well enough its propaganda value for Britain, it seems that Maisky considered that similar help could be got for his own country.

Several weeks later, in October 1942, Leslie received a 'fraternal message' from Soviet film workers, as a return for his own telegram of greetings and good wishes to a conference of Russian film producers and actors in Moscow, who were discussing the British and American film effort.[27] On 29 October 1942 Leslie announced the forthcoming production *Liberty Ship*, a pro-Russian propaganda film which told the story of a ship made in Canada, and its progress as it is sailed to Russia with a cargo of arms, recalling the story of *In Which We Serve*.

By the next month, the German advance had been halted for good at Stalingrad. The battle would continue for another year, although the greatest danger was over, but sadly nothing more was to be heard of Leslie's film. The Russians were at this time seen as an admired ally and it was not then anticipated that cultural links between the two countries would suffer increasing difficulties in the post-war years.

It had been Leslie's lifelong ambition to develop the British film industry, and he was now able to plan a gradual but far-reaching strategy. His motives for such an ambitious plan might certainly be thought to have included some that were personal, but the attitude of concern for the industry was a common one. Hopes were high, as cinema attendances had reached an all-time peak by the middle of 1942. Oscar Deutsch (another Jewish schoolfriend of Michael Balcon and Victor Saville) had built up an attractive and luxurious cinema chain, the Odeons, which were in place countrywide by the end of the 1930s, and the old 'flea-pits' were replaced with Art Deco attractions. They also became social centres, a venue for dances, meetings and parties as more middle-class people were drawn in, upgrading the whole business and stimulating cultural interest in cinema generally.

In particular the enthusiastic patriotism of those figures in the industry who were of Jewish background was carried almost to the point of embarrassment for the less demonstrative English. In early 1943 *Kinematograph Weekly* finally told Michael Balcon to pipe down about all the people who had left the country.[28] Balcon had also let fly about unfair American competition, and their reluctance to distribute British films in America. He now had great expectations:

> The virtual loss of our film industry after the First World War had given us, in the reconstruction period, an inferiority complex about our films, that only this war has enabled us to overcome. Therefore, at the time of our disappointment, we were inclined to attribute our failure to the fact that our product was not up to standard. That may have been so, though I am inclined to believe, while we were producing fewer films as time went on, our average standard was high enough to warrant fair competition with our American contemporaries.[29]

Meanwhile Filippo del Giudice had proposed setting up a 'League to promote British values worldwide'[30] and Alexander Korda welcomed his new British citizenship with a cheerful cry, 'to hell with bloody foreigners!' Korda was given a knighthood by Churchill in June 1942, possibly for his partially successful efforts to create a British film industry by breaking into the American market with large-scale and colourful historical 'blockbuster' films, possibly for his clandestine war work in America, and probably for his personal support to Churchill during the wilderness years.

Leslie's strategy, characteristically, was less flamboyant than Korda's, less insular than Balcon's. Instead of competing in the American market, he planned to turn to Europe. The project had been in his thoughts for some years. In 1940 he had given his views on the subject:

The British Empire and the United States speak the same language. In this simple fact lies both the weakness and the strength of English films. It is their weakness because it forces competition with Hollywood in their home market. And it is their strength because it implies the possibilities of competition with Hollywood in the American market. But I regret to say it is only a theoretical strength. We have never succeeded in invading the U. S. cinema market on a scale even remotely comparable with their invasion of ours. One is therefore forced to the unwilling conclusion that English film economics would have a sounder basis if, as in France, our language had been unique to us. Like the French, we should have built up an indigenous film industry, seeking productions which speak the idiom of our own people, consequently tending towards a higher degree of authenticity and artistry, at lower cost and with easier chances of profit, and so more attractive to finance. If there had been a difference in language, we should have been less likely to lose clever and talented people to the lure of the dollars, and above all we should not have been exposed to the crushing rivalry of some five hundred generally high quality and expensively made foreign productions each year. All the while we were commiserating with the French on their limited market, we did not realise how well off they were.[31]

It is interesting to note Leslie's mention of the Empire here, giving rise to the question of why, when the British had possession of half the world map, vast resources and a captive audience of millions, they could not manage to create a film industry, with all its attendant economic and cultural benefits, for themselves.

Leslie had the idea of making films simultaneously in two languages. This was not a new idea, but Leslie was familiar with the problems, and presumably thought they could be overcome. He had already mooted the idea with the French, of setting up a joint Anglo-French film organization where he hoped to 'produce films in two versions using bilingual artists'.[32] He also had a contact with the Italian industry, Franco Riganti, an associate of Roberto Rossellini. In August 1938 Riganti had managed to set up a company to produce and distribute films in Italy. He worked out co-production agreements with British companies, and Leslie had negotiated a film package with him.[33] Leslie had not despaired either of using his American contacts – he had the idea of starting in British film production with the backing of an American radio company. In 1938 he had announced a plan to make three films at Pinewood Studios (England) for RKO Radio.[34]

Leslie was eagerly discussing all these plans in Lisbon at the end of May 1943. He spoke to a British journalist about them, the correspondent of the *Evening Standard*, who reported in his newspaper that

> Leslie Howard had been discussing with (Portuguese) film executives his pet scheme whereby film companies would combine to use the same sets to shoot films of different languages. I understood the scheme was to shoot the scene with English artists, then without dismantling, re-shoot with French, Spanish, and Portuguese. This would avoid dubbing and have the dialogue in the language of the stars of different countries.[35]

The idea of having a film remade for each country using native well-known actors had been tried soon after the introduction of sound. But it had not worked, partly because it was too expensive, and dubbing took over for the non-English-speaking market. Interestingly, Robert Evans wrote forty years later of the remarkable breakthrough when *Love Story* was remade by Hollywood as a French movie, using French actors, writers and directors, and then in the same way, in German, Italian and Spanish, establishing American hegemony in European film once again.[36]

Michael Balcon had predicted, at the beginning of 1943, 'a new American isolationism', arguing that the US film industry would not help the British after the war, but would do their best to exclude them. He thought that the American monopoly of cinema ownership already meant that British films were not distributed in America, or only in a limited way. The American answer to this was, generally, that American audiences didn't understand British films; the accent was incomprehensible, the background cultures and values different. But American distribution seemed then to be the lifeblood of British film. Leslie was in the process of creating a different set-up; he had great experience in the film world, and many contacts internationally in addition to speaking French, German and Hungarian. Whether he could have made it work is debatable. Unfortunately, whether the scheme would have triumphed or not, it too was about to be lost.

Leslie's immersion in his plans for the film world were to be interrupted once again by wartime demands for his services as a goodwill ambassador. Leslie's views on the usefulness of his missions to the neutral countries tended towards the doubtful. He had just managed to get out of a trip to Sweden at the beginning of 1942. The situation in Sweden was then fairly odd. The Swedish government of the day swung between protesting at British aircraft flying over their country to quietly welcoming the few thousand Jewish refugees who managed to escape to them through Denmark across the Sound.[37] A propaganda battle in the country had ensued between Britain and Germany, and Leslie's friend A.G. Macdonell had visited in 1940, followed, as usual, by Kenneth Clark; Clark's memoirs say rather bluntly how dull and pointless he felt the visit was; he may well have told Leslie as much.[38] Dr Malcolm Sargent made two visits, the first in November 1942, the second a year later. Concerning this later visit, *The Times* noted,

> Dr Malcolm Sargent ... will conduct five concerts at Stockholm and Gothenburg ... including new works such as Vaughan Williams' Symphony Number Five in D and Eugene Goossens' new Symphony Number One. In addition, Dr Sargent has been specially asked to conduct two performances at the State Opera House. Since Dr Sargent's last visit to Sweden, the Germans have been making strenuous endeavours to counteract the goodwill he then obtained and have sent Furtwangler and the Berlin Philarmonic Orchestra to Sweden. Furtwangler was also sent to Portugal shortly after Dr Sargent's recent visit there. Dr Sargent's present visit has been arranged at the request of his Swedish hosts.[39]

It seems odd, sixty years on, that it might take the outcome of a battle of opposing orchestras to persuade the Swedish not to align themselves with a bunch of mass-murdering lunatics, but so it apparently was thought. Leslie took a dim view of all this, and having more important projects in mind, managed not to go to Sweden, although he was scheduled to visit, and in fact many of his friends thought he had done so. Unfortunately, he was about to get one last invitation – one that couldn't be refused.

In the meantime, however, Leslie was at work on a new project. It was a film of Monica Dickens' novel, *One Pair of Feet*. This was a newly published work in 1942 and had enjoyed a vogue, although a modern judgement of it might be slightly different. The book describes the author's experience as a trainee nurse. It is one of a series of semi-autobiographical novels in which the author's upper-middle class assumption that anyone can do manual work is disproved to her time and again. Blithely incompetent, she is sacked abruptly from every job she tries (Dickens had made an early start by getting expelled from her private school, St Paul's, age 16). The books had an interest at the time for their subversive tone, the novelty of a woman's voice describing

Figure 26. *The Lamp Still Burns*, 1943. Rosamund John looks on while comic John Laurie kisses Kathleen Nesbit.

actually working for a living, and a certain note of sulky intransigence in the telling which is still recognisable to anyone who has ever been an underling.

Two sharply told incidents remain the most memorable parts of *One Pair of Feet*, stories of patients at the hospital where the author worked. One is of a young Englishwoman whose life and mind are shattered by a car crash caused by her fiancée. Both are in the hospital, but in separate wards, not allowed to communicate. Dickens secretly takes notes from one to the other, but sees with dismay that the woman will not believe, no matter how much her partner reassures her, that she will ever be fit to marry him. This couple appear in the film, modified into a less desperate pair, played by Stewart Granger and Margaret Vyner. They have become fiancées who suffer an accident together in a bombing raid. Like Dickens' patients, they are fated to stay apart in the film, but this time because Granger falls in love with Rosamund John, playing the Dickens role.

The other patient in the book is 'Miss Klein', a Jewish refugee from

Warsaw, who gradually collapses into a mental breakdown, believing the other patients think she is a spy. Nurse Dickens is kind, but

> it was no use trying to reason with her. Small wonder that she had this persecution mania after what she had probably been through. The Warsaw from which she had fled must have been a city of spying and treachery and suspicion, of whispers in cafes and meaning glances and abusive notices mysteriously appearing on walls. How could you trust anybody when people that you knew, even your friends, appeared from one day to the next in Nazi uniform? ... For several days she lay in a huddled ball, sobbing off and on, and then early one morning she suddenly hopped out of bed, scooted for the door and was off down the passage in her crumpled night gown and bare feet before anyone could stop her. When she was brought back, struggling and shrieking in Polish, they put boards round the sides of the bed so that she couldn't get out, and she lay like a trapped animal, with only her eyes moving ... Soon after that, they took Miss Klein away; I don't know where to.[40]

It is evident that not even Leslie could manage to insert a character like this in any film, and 'Miss Klein' does not appear, the gap being filled by a couple of male patients and some knockabout joking.

In a later biography, Dickens grumbled that the film contained nothing from her novel.[41] Unlike her book, the film had to take a morale-boosting tone, but it does contain all its themes, dealt with very seriously indeed; perhaps too much so. Dickens may well have resented the film, as the issues she herself coped with by lying, evasion and sullenness are openly confronted with dignity by her film character. The petty discipline and constant humiliation of the young nurses was a strong issue in the nursing profession then, and remained so for years. The senior practitioners were determined to force nursing into a military-type, professional role, believing that this would give it dignity and prestige, and leave behind the old 'Mrs Gamp' image of former times. In some ways they were right, but behind the times. In the film Rosamund John clashes with the matron of the hospital, in bitter, overly unpleasant scenes. Matron, played by Cathleen Nesbit, is almost reptilian in her nastiness, and it seems odd that the character should be played in so unsympathetic a manner. Their clash is finally resolved when matron insists on 'rigid discipline' as being necessary for both the nurses' good name, and for the meticulously correct attention needed by medical treatment. Rosamund John has made her point, and agrees to abide by this. She is kept on as a nurse, where Dickens in real life failed and was dismissed.

The other dilemma of Dickens' book is also treated more sympathetically. At that time, no married woman was allowed to work as a nurse, which meant that the nurses, especially the senior staff, had the painful choice of abandoning their careers if they wished to marry. Again Dickens dismissed the matter scornfully, commenting of one sister who was pondering the choice, 'I thought she was mad as a brush not to get married'. In the film, the choice is put off. Stewart Granger and Rosamund John wish to marry; at the end of the film Granger says he will wait for her, 'until conditions change'. That is until married women were allowed to keep their jobs. Since the marriage bar remained a problem for senior nurses right up until the 1970s, Granger would have had to wait a little longer than anyone anticipated.

The scriptwriters were Elizabeth Baron, who had worked with Leslie on *The Gentle Sex*, Leslie's favourite, Roland Pertwee, and Charles Nelson, who added some (but not enough) light touches and humorous scenes. Leslie's sister Irene helped with casting, as usual, and the actors were an impressive list throughout, including a glimpse of Joyce Grenfell in one of her very few serious appearances.

The film's failings are perhaps that it is too static and serious. A great deal of effort had been made in exactly reproducing a hospital ward on the Denham sets, on close-up detail of medical instruments used, and the exact routines of ward rounds and operations. In that sense it succeeds so well that it could be used as a piece of medical history. The film is well balanced and holds the attention. Rosamund John has a cool attractiveness and intelligence that well matched Leslie's elegance as a director, and explains his choice of her as his leading actress in successive films.

Maurice Elvey is listed as the director, Leslie as the producer. In fact Leslie rehearsed and directed the main actors. Elvey mainly acted as assistant director, managing the crowds of extras and so on. Even worse, Rosamund John, commenting much later on Elvey, said, 'I was appalled: he had no idea of what to do or how to do it. The electricians would be shouting, "Print number three, Maurice!" He was unbelievable.'[42] Guido Coen also remembered the old silent film director as 'superannuated'. One feature in particular that spoils the film is the obtrusive background music, composed by John Greenwood and conducted by Muir Mathieson, which underlines the mood of each scene with heavy-handed emphasis. Leslie was interrupted in making the film by his trip abroad – he was due to edit the film when he came back, and could have corrected this fault.

The reviews were solemn, and sometimes accidentally comic. *The Sunday Times* wrote that, 'Cathleen Nesbit's matron admirably conveys the faintly malignant quality of a woman in authority'![43] Others praised the serious issues raised by the film, but complained that it was rather too earnest (*Manchester Guardian*, 18 January 1944). *The Times* wrote that is was marked throughout by Leslie's characteristics of understatement, lack of stridency and an appreciation of the small decencies which constitute charm; the *Evening News* praised his 'simplicity, integrity, gentle humour and firm sentiment'.

These qualities were all sorely needed. As 1942 came to a close, it became evident to those in a position to comprehend that the Nazis policy of race murder had not been abated. On 17 December 1942, a 'Joint Allied Declaration' publicly denounced the Nazi killings of Jews. The House of Commons observed a moment's silence; James de Rothschild spoke. In the House of Lords, Viscount Samuel raised the question of what could be done, saying cooperation of neutral countries might produce positive results. But no further action or statement was forthcoming.

The only other film ever to deal with this issue was to be the disastrous *Mr Emmanuel*. This was based on Louis Golding's book of the same name, published in 1939. The film was planned at the end of 1943 and shown in 1944. Sadly, it consisted of a queasily sentimental story in which an elderly Jewish man makes an unlikely return journey to Germany during the Holocaust. The grovelling attitudes of the protagonist are difficult to watch. The film recalls Charlie Chaplin's verdict on a later, supposedly pro-Semitic film, *Crossfire* (1947): '[Chaplin] stood up and became [the protagonist]: his face changed; he assumed the stance; and he gestured, "washing his hands". Inventing words to illustrate what he felt was the interpretation of the role of the Jewish victim, he said obsequiously, "why're you picking on me? I'm a nice feller, really, I'm a nice feller."'[44] Chaplin had made *The Great Dictator* in 1940, the only American film to attack the Nazis at this time.

There was a strain of incomprehension and vacillation amongst older British Jews (most younger ones were in the army). They had been so browbeaten all their lives about their inferior status as Jews that they seemed incapable of protest or action at this vital time. Louis Golding's books have this strain very strongly. The film, also scripted by Golding, was grotesquely ill-conceived. The ending had a German Jewish woman married to a high-ranking Nazi official, possibly reflecting Golding's sadly mistaken notion that the Nazis could never eradicate the Jews from their society.

C.A. Lejeune of the *Observer* criticized the film at the time for its 'falsity of action and sentiment'. Reviewing Golding's whole work in 1946, the New York Jewish writer Diana Trilling criticized it for trivializing the issues and for its moral confusion. She described his latest work, *The Glory of Elsie Silver* (1946), a description of the Warsaw ghetto uprising, as 'perhaps the most offensive of all the melodramas the anti-fascist struggle has produced'.[45] A more recent, cooler retrospective described Golding as living mostly outside the Jewish world, and 'caught between his desire to fight the racism of the Third Reich and his own confused racial attitudes'.[46]

The genesis of this film is hard to recover. It was a Two Cities production, and so chosen by del Giudice. The director, Harold French, and the producer, William Sistrom, knew little of Jewish issues. Since it must have had the sanction of the Ministry of Information, the suspicion occurs that it was made deliberately to confuse the issue at a time when the British government were anxious to put off any pressure for direct action (or any action at all) against the Nazi mass-murder. However it is much more likely that it was made quickly and thoughtlessly as a vehicle for Felix Aylmer, in the part of Mr Emmanuel, and Greta Gynt, the Nazi officer's mistress. Aylmer had recently given some impressive performances for Two Cities, including Asquith's *The Demi-Paradise* (1943). Greta Gynt, the busty blonde actress who played the female lead, was del Giudice's mistress, with whom he was besotted at the time.[47]

When Leslie had agreed to become a director of Two Cities, he had acclaimed del Giudice's competence – in financial matters.[48] He viewed the company as a parent, providing financial guidance for film-makers. Once Leslie was gone, no one seemed capable of taking on his role of making a judicious choice of subjects for serious film propaganda, or of fully comprehending contemporary events. Leslie's intelligence and understanding, his international perspective, his social contacts at every level, and his force of character, were sorely missed. The propaganda battle which Leslie had begun so defiantly with *Pimpernel Smith*, petered out blindly into a long silence.

In January 1943, Basil Dean staged a pageant at the entrance to the great St Paul's Cathedral, which had been saved from German bombs by barely a whisker. As he described the event, 'I became obsessed with the idea to use music and drama in some kind of positive assertion of the Nation's belief in itself'. Leslie was one of the many participants, and, as Dean and others described, one of the most affecting:

> Who is the frail figure suddenly seen kneeling at the top of the cathedral steps? He is dressed all in grey, with a patch over one eye. It is the ghost of Lord Nelson, come from his tomb within the cathedral to speak the prayer he gave before Trafalgar. The figure speaks his text whisper-thin above the muffled drums and trumpets – magnificent control. As he passes back into the cathedral a sigh escapes from the crowd. Yet how could they know that this was Leslie Howard's last public appearance?[49]

NOTES

1. BBC at Caversham transcripts (CT) of radio programmes, *Britain Speaks*, 25 December 1940.
2. CT, *Answering You*, 29 March 1942.
3. *Kinematograph Weekly*'s reports on the making of the film, August–October 1942.
4. Lilli Palmer, *Change Lobsters and Dance: An Autobiography* (London: W.H. Allen, 1976). Miss Palmer does not mention this film in her memoirs.
5. *Kinematograph Weekly*, 8 April 1943.
6. Ibid.
7. *The Sunday Times*, 11 April 1943.
8. *The Star*, 10 April 1943.
9. Most modern viewers accept that the film is benevolent, but inevitably of its time in its attitudes to women. There is not much modern literature about the film, but for a feminist perspective, Antonia Lant, *Blackout: Reinventing Women for Wartime British Cinema* (Oxford: Princeton University Press, 1991).
10. Adrian Brunel, *Nice Work: The Story of Thirty Years in British Film Production* (London: Forbes Robertson, 1949).
11. Boze Hadleigh, *Leading Ladies* (London: Robson Books, 1992), p.55.
12. Brian McFarlane, *An Autobiography of British Cinema as Told by the Filmmakers and Actors Who Made It* (London: Methuen, 1997), p.329.
13. Ronald Howard, *In Search of My Father: A Portrait of Leslie Howard* (London: W. Kimber, 1981).
14. Kevin Brownlow, *David Lean: A Biography* (London: Richard Cohen, 1996), p.131.
15. Howard, *In Search of My Father*.
16. Ibid., p.140. Charles Drazin, *The Finest Years: British Cinema of the 1940s* (London: André Deutsch, 1998), pp.235–40.
17. Author's interview with Guido Coen, producer Del Giudice's assistant at Denham, 8 November 2000.
18. CT, *Britain Speaks*, 5 August 1940.
19. Interview with Guido Coen.
20. Email to author, 10 May 2006.
21. M.R.D. Foot, *SOE: An Outline History of the Special Operations Executive 1940–1946* (London: Pimlico, 1999), p.75.
22. Ibid., p.88.
23. *Kinematograph Weekly*, 4 March 1943.
24. *Kinematograph Weekly*, Two Cities publicity spread, 14 January 1943.
25. Leslie Ruth Howard, *A Quite Remarkable Father* (London: Longmans, 1960), p.264.
26. *Kinematograph Weekly*, 14 January 1943.
27. *Kinematograph Weekly*, 8 October 1942.
28. *Kinematograph Weekly*, 25 February 1943.

29. *Kinematograph Weekly*, 14 January 1943.
30. *Kinematograph Weekly*, 4 March 1942.
31. CT, *Britain Speaks*, 26 July 1940.
32. *The Times*, 19 January 1940.
33. Tony Gallagher, *The Adventures of Roberto Rossellini* (New York: Da Capo, 1998), p.55.
34. *Kinematograph Weekly*, 10 November 1938.
35. *Evening Standard*, 3 June 1943, p.5.
36. Robert Evans, *The Kid Stays in the Picture* (London: Faber and Faber, 2004), pp.212–13.
37. *Anglo-Swedish Review* (London: Swedish Chamber of Commerce for the United Kingdom), November 1943.
38. Kenneth Clark, *The Other Half: A Self Portrait* (London: Hamish Hamilton, 1977).
39. *The Times*, 11 September 1943, p.6.
40. Monica Dickens, *One Pair of Feet* (London: Michael Joseph, 1942), p.28.
41. Monica Dickens, *An Open Book* (London: Book Club Associates and Heinemann, 1978).
42. Rosamund John quoted in McFarlane, *An Autobiography of British Cinema*, p.329. See also *Kinematograph Weekly* reports on the progress of the film, 4 March 1943 and 15 April 1943.
43. *The Sunday Times*, 25 October 1943.
44. *Crossfire*, 1947, directed by Edward Dmytryk, quoted in Alvah Bessie, *Inquisition in Eden* (Berlin: Seven Seas Publishers, 1967), p.267.
45. Diana Trilling, *Commentary* 1, 7 (1946).
46. Gavin Schaffer, *Immigrants and Minorities* 24, 1 (March 2006).
47. Drazin, *The Finest Years*, p.23.
48. Papers of Del Giudice, BFI. Leslie's speech on becoming a director of the company, 11 July 1942.
49. Basil Dean, *Mind's Eye: An Autobiography 1927–1972* (London: Hutchinson, 1973), pp.282–3. Nelson's prayer before Trafalgar: 'MAY THE GREAT GOD, whom I worship, grant to my country and for the benefit of Europe in general, a great and glorious victory: and may no misconduct, in anyone, tarnish it: and may humanity after victory be the predominant feature in the British Fleet. For myself Individually, I commit my life to Him who made me and may His blessing light upon my endeavours for serving my Country faithfully. To Him I resign and the just cause which is entrusted to me to defend. AMEN AMEN AMEN.'

CHAPTER TEN

April 1943: Last Trip

The origin of Leslie's trip to Spain and Portugal can be traced to a British Council idea which emerged around the end of January 1943 that Leslie could provide a propaganda-boosting visit for the Council in these countries. Leslie received a letter from Sir Malcolm Robertson, chairman of the British Council, putting the suggestion to him. When Leslie demurred, as he was in the middle of making *The Lamp Still Burns*, Sir Malcolm contacted the Ministry of Information for support. The task eventually devolved to Jack Beddington, head of the MoI's Film Division, who made a jovial approach to Leslie at Denham Studios, but met with a non-committal reply. Leslie discussed it with his family and friends, considering how best to use the opportunity. His ideas of advancing European cultural links at this time were to him just as important as a small-scale (as he thought) propaganda-boosting visit.

One friend of Leslie's with whom he had become close over the past few years was Alfred Chenhalls, his London accountant and financial advisor, well known in the film world and expert in the financial field. He was in any case a good companion for Leslie, being tall, heavily built, robust and extrovert while standing no nonsense. He was quite an attractive man also, with a military bearing (he had served in the First World War) and piercing light blue eyes. Chenhalls knew Spain well, and had business interests there in the film world. In seeking to contact the film studios abroad, and plan co-productions, Chenhalls would be vital for these discussions.

Chenhalls accordingly visited the British Council on about 18 February and spoke to a group of people, Mr Bridges Adams, Mr Kearney and Mr Braden, directors of the Council at its London headquarters. Chenhalls suggested first of all that he accompany Leslie, who did not like travelling alone. But more importantly he put to the Council the idea of a joint production of films in Spain and Portugal. He suggested it would be to Britain's advantage for various reasons, including influencing the granting of a licence, to import more British films for showing in Spain.

But Chenhalls met the same sort of attitude at the Council as Leslie had found when he first returned to Britain in 1939, and had suggested to various bored and contemptuous officials that British film-making might have some use. The opinion of the British Council officials that Chenhalls met are still extant in the form of an internal memo from the Council headquarters, preserved at the National Archives: 'I am not very impressed with this scheme for making feature films in Spain.'[1] And, 'As for Mr Leslie Howard it is not for me to express a view'. They agreed, however, that Leslie would be an effective propagandist for them, in order, as far as they were concerned, to enhance British prestige, and the internal memo notes that they will invite Foreign Office approval of the idea of a lecture tour by Leslie.

So there the matter stood. A letter from Sir Samuel Hoare, ambassador in Spain, to Anthony Eden on 1 March 1943 is also in the National Archives. The letter contains many worries about the political situation in Spain, so much so that the tone verges on the panicky at times. Sir Samuel complains that the Spanish are still not convinced of an Allied victory, and that Falangist (fascist) supporters would persuade Franco into entering the war on the German side. Propaganda would be very important at this precise time, as he says:

> There are many still in Spain, including some prominent members of the Government, who cannot bring themselves to believe in an Allied victory ... it is not fully realised in England how completely Spain has for the last five years been a *pays occupé*, infiltrated by German influence and dominated by a conviction of a German victory. As to the Press, I am not sure whether you have noticed the change that has already come over it. It is still full of unabashed German propaganda, but it has ceased its attacks upon Great Britain and the U.S.A. in recent weeks. This change is entirely due to Jordana's efforts [Spain's foreign minister]. He is at present fighting to obtain control of the foreign censorship. The battle is not decided and I will not prophesy which way it will go. He is, however, determined to get control of the foreign side of the press and you can rely upon me to do everything possible to help him.[2]

The situation in Portugal was similar, with fascist elements and German propagandists doing their best to force public opinion their way, or at least into a stultifying inaction and unhelpfulness to the Allies.

Eden was also looking about for likely propagandists, in conjunction with the British Council representatives in both countries. The British Council, an avowedly neutral, culturally orientated organization (still in existence) had, in order to remain as a trusted guest in Portugal or any other country, been separated from connection with the Ministry of Information. Leslie was a good candidate, as Britain's most committed propagandist, in addition to being well known in Spain and Portugal for his earlier films, such as *Pygmalion*. Leslie's visit to Lisbon was in fact the latest in a series of very similar tours, put on by the Council with the same intentions of indirect propaganda, or increasing 'British prestige'. From the start of the war, Britain had been concerned to ensure Portugal's good will and neutral stance, and to counter the very heavy onslaught of German propaganda in the country. Salazar, the dictator of Portugal, had complained to Anthony Eden as early as 1936 that Britain's help was needed, and that it should not neglect its oldest ally.[3] Amongst other efforts, in 1938 a British Institute was hurriedly set up in Lisbon by the British Council, and an Anglo-Portuguese Society founded in London. Visiting speakers to Lisbon thereafter included the Duke of Kent, a delegation from Oxford University which awarded Salazar an honorary degree (greatly irritating the Germans), the Astronomer Royal, the conductor Sir Malcolm Sargent, and others.

Intervention in neutral Spain was more critical, as the pro-Axis interventionists there appeared to be growing more desperate and violent, and there were several attacks by uniformed Falangist thugs on British and American embassies at this time. By mid-1943, enormous bribes laid out by Churchill to the generals close to Franco for a pro-Allied influence had been moderately effective.[4] There was also the fact that the Allies now had the military advantage. However, in a country so closed off to all communication any influence would be of use, especially one aimed at the intellectuals and other influential persons.

Leslie was still hesitant. In addition to his general exhaustion, the stress of Violette's death, and the break-up of his family for one reason or another, Leslie did not want to appear in public with any fascist contacts, diplomacy or not. He wrote a letter to Eden, outlining his worries, including the fear of a misunderstanding with his contacts in Russia, then a military ally. But Eden was determined. He replied to Leslie's fears rather lightly:

> I can quite understand your scruples about hobnobbing with Falangist leaders in Spain, but I do not think they need worry you unduly, or affect your plans for the journey. The Falangists although tiresome and influential are only a minority in Spain,

and it is I think unlikely that you will come into contact with many of them. On the other hand it is very important just now to fly the British flag in Spain and to give encouragement to our many friends there, who are to be found in all classes. On the whole I think it would be best to avoid Spanish internal politics as a subject of conversation, and to concentrate on explaining the British war effort. First hand reports on this subject are of special value in a country like Spain, where the Axis have succeeded in reducing our publicity to a minimum ...

I do not think either that you need fear that your journey will be misinterpreted by the Russians, who take a realistic view of Spanish affairs and of the importance of Spanish neutrality to the United Nations war effort.[5]

Leslie was to be instructed before he went with details of the war effort which would especially impress Spanish opinion. The Foreign Office officials concerned with the visit seemed to think it a straightforward request. Their correspondence shows that Leslie's doubts had been scorned; 'I agree that Mr Howard is making heavy weather of this. We should, I think, explain to him that the Falangists although tiresome and influential, are only a minority in Spain, that he is unlikely to come in contact with any of them and that it is very important to fly the British flag in Spain.'[6]

This was an offhand attitude to what seems in retrospect to have been a dangerous mission. However, it was open enough, on the face of it, and although it was low key, the visit could hardly be described as a secret mission from an intelligence agency. Its whole point, and its inherent danger, was in the public nature of the task. Anthony Eden's letter to Leslie concludes on a breezy note, inviting himself to dinner, 'We should certainly be delighted to dine one evening, if this letter doesn't exasperate you too much!'[7]

There is no formal note of whether Leslie dined with Eden, but it is likely to have happened. In that black spring of 1943, it is tempting to speculate what could have been discussed by the cold political fixer and the impassioned but exhausted idealist. One point to note might have been the name or names mentioned when Eden asked Leslie to 'explain the British war effort'.

So plans were duly made for Leslie and Chenhalls, under the sponsorship of the British Council, to visit Portugal for one week and Spain for two weeks, where it was thought their influence would be of more importance. They would fly to Portugal first, and travel overland to

Spain, as no Allied planes were allowed into that country. They were due to take the KLM flight, which was something of an anomaly; a passenger plane only, established during the war, flying between Bristol and neutral Lisbon. Leslie and Chenhalls arrived to take the flight on 28 April 1943.

At the airport they got their first shock. The plane they were taking, a DC3 passenger plane and therefore unarmed, showed the bullet holes and damage sustained from a German attack on 19 April, only nine days previously. The same plane, engaged in the same passenger service, had also been attacked in November 1942, but not so seriously.[8] However, there was nothing that could be done, and the plane took off for what seemed to be a tiring but uneventful eight-hour flight.

On landing at Lisbon, they stayed at the Hotel Aviz for a night, then made for the coast nearby at Estoril, a well-known and attractive holiday resort. The contrast of Portugal in the spring with dark, gloomy Britain has been described by many at that time. In addition to the cheerful people, sun, blue skies and sea and wide horizons, there was wonderful food by home standards – plentiful fresh fruit and vegetables, wines, steaks and sea food. Everyone who had the luck to visit – including the MI6 staff stationed there – indulged themselves gratefully.[9]

Leslie and Chenhalls were staying at the Atlantico Hotel, known to be full of German spies at that time, so their movements would have been suspiciously watched, but they managed to stay out of any direct confrontation. Leslie set to work, despite all this, and in the next few days had borrowed a secretary courtesy of the British Council in Lisbon, and dictated his lectures and necessary letters. The secretary, Gwyneth Williams, remained with him throughout his stay in Portugal, typing all his correspondence. Leslie also wrote letters home to his wife and children all through his stay (and presumably also to Josette Ronserail, who had accompanied him to Bristol airport to say goodbye, but these have never been recovered) enabling his son Ronald to trace his movements many years later. These letters were sent home for him in the diplomatic bag.

One of the informal contacts Leslie made was a relative of his, working at the British Embassy. This was Mrs Helen Gerassi, whose mother was related to Wilfred Noy, Leslie's uncle. It happened that her husband, Alfred Gerassi, was working for British intelligence and organizing escape routes from Lisbon for certain RAF personnel and allied agents. Leslie's briefing before the trip may have included a request for a quiet exchange of information with the Gerassis.[10]

On 2 May Leslie attended a concert at the Lisbon College of Music given by Philip Newman, the well-known violinist. This was to be one of Leslie's significant contacts in Portugal, and he was to spend some time with Newman, becoming rather touchingly close. The next day Leslie duly gave his lecture to a mainly Portuguese audience in Lisbon, using his own experiences to discuss film-making in wartime, with plenty of amusing mishaps and anecdotes to illustrate. Over the next few days he gave two more talks, on the more serious theme of *Hamlet*, and the possibilities of turning the play into a film, emphasizing his plans for joint European film-making in the future. He met Portuguese cultural figures and was entertained by the British ambassador, Sir Ronald Campbell, and Sir John Balfour, HM minister in Portugal, the cultural and press attachés and other embassy staff. There was a screening of *Pimpernel Smith* at the embassy cinema in Lisbon. At this same time, Leslie and Chenhalls managed to negotiate an extensive plan for the distribution of British war films in Portugal with Rafael Seruya of Vitoria Filme. This would include *We Dive at Dawn*, *Cottage to Let*, *49th Parallel*, and all of Two Cities' films, (not just Leslie's). Chenhalls gave Seruya and the embassy press attaché, Anthony Haigh, copies of a memorandum outlining very specific arrangements for distribution and showing. Leslie also discussed his plans for co-productions with Portuguese film-makers.[11]

Leslie created quite a sensation in Portugal. Everyone was eager to see the well-known actor, so eloquent in the anti-fascist cause. They were not disappointed. By the end of his very short trip, Leslie had made many contacts, deeply impressed many (and annoyed some by his refusal to take on every requested appointment) and was finally transformed into something approaching a myth. On 6 May, while he was still in Lisbon, a journalist described him in almost hagiographical terms:

> All eyes are focused upon a fairly tall, slim, fairish-haired man in a light grey lounge suit, the jacket set off with a white pochette. I see him in profile. Seen thus it is Greco-Roman. His hair is brushed up from his forehead, which is high and intellectual and with his eyes, an abiding place of humour and meditation ... The man in grey moves round the table to the journalists and cameramen. Flash after flash of magnesium illuminates the glasses on the table. The well-laden buffet receives scarcely any attention, so great is the news appeal of the quiet man in grey who looks so tired after his journey.[12]

On 8 May Leslie and Alfred reluctantly left their seaside hotel and travelled to Madrid by train – a gruelling, hot, twenty hours, so slow was the travel. They were met in Madrid by Walter Starkie, CMG, CBE, head of the British Institute and British Council representative in Madrid. He was a respected expert in Spanish and Romance languages and much honoured academic. But as the British grand panjandrum in Madrid, he and Leslie were set on a clashing course. On his own authority, he had arranged a long schedule of dinners, parties, press receptions and trips for Leslie, most of which would have fulfilled little purpose, as the press censor in Spain forbade any of this being publicized. It left little room for Leslie's intention of visiting Spanish film studios and arranging for what might have been much more effective – the screening of British films throughout Spain, and the forging of lasting cultural links using joint film-production.

As soon as Leslie and Chenhalls arrived, Starkie announced his schedule to them. A fierce and uncharacteristic argument ensued, as both of them realized how impossible it would be for the exhausted Leslie to appear at so many events. Starkie eventually ceded the point. He calmed down, but never overcame his resentment at the argument and Leslie's refusal to accept his authority. Immediately after the visit, he wrote a stinging report to British Council headquarters in London, which is still in existence, and publicly available at the National

Figure 27. Leslie with the British Ambassador in Madrid and guests. Walter Starkie in noticeable white suit.

Archives at Kew. Starkie accuses Leslie of only being interested in making money from the tour, and says that in any case Leslie's presence has only attracted, 'the masses of film-fans and other undesirable elements who cannot do any good to Institute cultural work'.[13]

This attitude to film was shared by many of the British Council, embassy and British government officials of the day. Luckily Spanish and Portuguese intellectuals and officials had wider horizons. Sir Samuel Hoare also seems to have been more sympathetic than might have been expected. Leslie wrote him a letter of thanks a week after his visit, with the help of his secretary in Portugal, and expressed his gratitude for the ambassador's 'personal kindness to me and my friend during our visit to Madrid', and also, 'for the help and attention which at your behest was showered upon us by the whole embassy staff. It made possible in a large measure the great amount of ground we were able to cover in the ten days.'

Leslie made clear what he thought was the most important part of the visit:

> The contacts with the Spanish people in my own profession were exceedingly cordial and will, I think, be fruitful. We visited the three principal studios and had an enormous welcome from each. We are invited to come to Spain again in connection with film-making. I think there is much to be done in this respect and hope one day we shall find the right occasion for doing so.

Leslie added that he felt the trip had also been successful as far as propaganda was concerned: 'I was particularly impressed by the fact that towards the end of my visit, evidently regarding me as quite harmless, certain official Spaniards, representing national propaganda, turismo and films, went out of their way to ask me to extend my present visit'.[14]

Leslie was being modest. His visit was a great success, and a month later the Spanish ambassador was discussing him with Anthony Eden, saying that Leslie had promised him he would make a film about Christopher Columbus, and that he wished that Britain could arrange for more visits on a cultural level, as if the promise could somehow be fulfilled by someone else.[15] But there was no one like Leslie.

Leslie did miss some of Starkie's arranged activities. On a morning after a 3:00 a.m. reception, and on the final day of Leslie's stay, Starkie had arranged an informal talk to the children of the school run by the British Institute. Leslie did not appear, and could not be traced. He later wrote to Starkie apologizing, saying that it had slipped his mind, and 'of all my shortcomings it is the one I most sincerely regret'.[16] Leslie had probably just slept in – he was notorious in the film world as a late riser. But the gaps in Leslie's schedule gave rise to some speculation, which appears to have originated from Starkie and Neville Kearney, two British Council officials – that Leslie was involved in an affair with a woman. Colvin later wove an unlikely tale of a mysterious female spy figure, although he himself described her as a composite figure, which spoils his story somewhat.[17] Ronald Howard, knowing his father rather better, hints at an assignation with the chambermaid at Leslie's Madrid hotel.

Leslie also met in Madrid a very old flame, the actress Conchita Montenegro, who had married the Spanish diplomat Ricardo Gimenéz Arnau, a senior member of the far right Falangist party. Author José Rey-Ximena interviewed Miss Montenegro, in the nursing home where she lived, just before she died in April 2007. He used her fond memories of Leslie as the basis of a book which claimed that Leslie had used her fascist connections to contact Franco, theoretically to persuade Franco to stay out of the war. The book, *El Vuelo de Ibis [The Flight of the Ibis]: Leslie Howard*, published in Spain in 2008, has yet to appear in English at this time of writing (2009). Miss Montenegro apparently gave no details of the date, time or place of Leslie's meeting with Franco. Nor did Miss Montenegro know anything further, except that she met Leslie, presumably at the film studios, just after he had been to the meeting with Franco. According to her, Leslie was 'very happy' with the outcome of the meeting, which had been to 'ensure peace with England'.[18] As to why Leslie had to convey a message to Franco, which presumably could have been given by Sir Samuel Hoare, the author of the book explains that Sir Samuel was on very poor terms with Franco at this time – in fact he was *persona non grata*, as Franco saw him as a political enemy and distrusted him entirely. There is no mention of a meeting with Franco in Leslie's final letter to Sir Samuel. But then it is not likely that such a meeting would have been openly referred to in this way.

Another topic which the book explores is the story of the mysterious 'Countess' pursued by Colvin and others. A certain Baroness von Podewils was amongst many minor Nazi underlings reporting back in Madrid. She was in charge of the beauty salon at Leslie's hotel, and had been instructed to follow his movements as closely as possible. This she did, even making a nuisance of herself at times. Later, when disaster struck, she contacted the British embassy in a panic, trying to dissociate herself from any connection to it. After all, the British might still win the war, and it was better to stay on good terms with both sides. British Council officials, still affronted that Leslie had ignored some of their celebrity ribbon-cutting schedule, made the most of the incident.[19]

Despite Starkie's grumbles, Leslie's stay in Madrid was a whirl of activity, with events on every day, and officially arranged dinners and parties into the early hours of each morning. Leslie and Chenhalls also had to arrange their own visits to the Spanish studios at San Martin. Two days after they arrived, Starkie took them to the British Club in Madrid for lunch to meet the visiting personalities. Amongst these was Wilfred Israel, introduced to him as someone making a tour of the refugee centres in Spain. Leslie apparently had a long and earnest talk with him, quite unusual for the withdrawn and reticent man Israel was. Leslie met him again in Portugal, as Israel followed him, seemingly under the spell of Leslie's talismanic charm.

Leslie attended the receptions, spoke to whoever wanted to see him, and gave his lectures on film and on his interpretation of *Hamlet*. No notes or descriptions of the lectures have survived, but since Walter Starkie long treasured Leslie's annotated copy of *Hamlet*, both Ian Colvin and Ronald Howard were able to examine and comment on it. Ronald also used it to suggest the intention of Leslie's speech – purely his own interpretation however. Ronald thought that Leslie was using speeches from *Hamlet* to subtly argue that the Spanish should not attack Gibraltar at this time, which would have greatly hampered the Allies. He suggested that the marked phrases, 'We go to gain a little patch of ground / That hath in it no profit but the name' and 'Rightly to be great / Is not to stir without great argument, / But greatly to find quarrel in a straw / When honour's at the stake', suggest this theory, although the last phrase would seem to contradict the argument. But Leslie had also marked, 'The imminent death of 20,000 men / That for a fantasy and trick of fame / Go to their grave like beds'. Colvin is less speculative, and drew no particular theory from the marked extracts. According to Colvin, who saw and handled this copy of *Hamlet*, the very last passage that Leslie marked seemed to bear no relation to Ronald's theory: It was, 'We defy augury: there's a special providence / In the fall of a sparrow. If it be not now, tis not to come; / If it be not to come it will be now; If it be not now yet it will come. / The readiness is all.'

Leslie seems to have been particularly struck by two persons he met on this trip. One was Wilfred Israel, a wealthy representative of the Jewish

Agency, resident in Britain. He had been born in Berlin, where his Jewish ancestors were well known leaders of society, and his mother was descended from Dr Nathan Adler, Chief Rabbi of Victorian England. When the Nazis came to power he did all he could to help his German Jewish countrymen, and then came to England in 1939. Here he tried to call attention to the Jewish problems, even approaching Sir Robert Vansittart personally, but he could make little headway. Israel's pleas had eventually lead to the Foreign Office making use of him by giving him a number of visas to British-controlled Palestine for the refugees in Spain, who were annoying Franco (which Sir Samuel Hoare wanted to avoid) and giving the Falangists cause for complaint. He had also a number of visas for Portuguese refugees. Leslie met Israel in both countries, and there is evidence that they had some long talks – but only at public receptions. Israel was to be a passenger on the plane with Leslie on his last flight home.

The other person with whom Leslie formed an attachment was Philip Newman. Newman was the most remarkable character of all in his way, although his adventures have now been forgotten. He was at that time professor of music at the Lisbon Conservatorio, and a celebrated concert violinist, but he was of British origin, born in Manchester in a Jewish family. He had studied abroad for some years in the 1930s, including two years in Germany from 1932 to 1934, and knew that language well. The outbreak of war found him in Belgium, but instead of returning home, he had for some reason taken refuge in Portugal by May 1940. By the personal intervention of Salazar, he was able to remain, give recitals, and was given the status of professor, despite German efforts to remove him. He gave many celebrated concerts for charity, to support the Portuguese Red Cross, for the refugees and other causes. He was a very public figure, playing at all the Lisbon hospitals and prisons, at patients' bedsides, including the incurable and contagious wards. He also visited British merchant ships in Lisbon harbour, giving many concerts to British seamen during the war years. He later made a tour of all the mines in Portugal, organizing an orchestra entirely from the miners and their families. He was given the Portuguese Order of Merit. He was attached throughout the war to the British Council, who praised him for combating German cultural propaganda in the country. Given these facts, he was also possibly one of British Intelligence's contacts in Portugal.

Leslie attended two of Newman's concerts, and by the second occasion was accompanying him in his car, patting his hand to soothe pre-concert nerves, according to Colvin's evidence. There are several photographs of them together, the most affecting showing their last meeting, Newman in his car seemingly upset, with Leslie crouched down, waving a last goodbye.[20]

Again, what Leslie discussed, in public or private, with Newman is not known. The fate of European Jewry concerned Leslie, Newman and Israel. All were doing what they could, according to their abilities and opportunities, but were mainly helpless in the face of events. It may be that in this sheltered moment for all of them, they said little of their greatest fears and talked of hopeful plans instead. But it is evident that Leslie had become, in a very few days, a light of hope for both the other men and for many others whom he met, a harbinger of Allied victory and a breath of sanity in their troubled world.

Leslie and Chenhalls returned to Portugal from Spain on 20 May, this time with no official engagements ahead of them, and greatly in need of a holiday. They returned to Estoril for a few days, but Neville Kearney, the Films Director of the British Council, visited them to ask if they could send for a copy of *The First of the Few*, and attend a showing. This would take a further few days, and would delay their return. Leslie agreed, and so enjoyed more Portuguese hospitality. On 30 May they gave a beach party for all the friends and contacts who could attend, which many remembered afterwards with great fondness. Leslie was photographed on the beach in just a pair of shorts, looking rather skeletal. With him is Chenhalls, incongruously dressed in city clothes, and looking reproachfully at Leslie, as if he wanted to get back to business.[21]

The film finally arrived and was shown on 31 May, and Leslie and Chenhalls returned to Lisbon, ready to fly home, staying a last night at the Hotel Aviz. There they lunched with Calouste Gulbenkian, the wealthy oil mogul, who had taken a suite at the hotel for the duration of the war. The Aviz was a luxurious place, run by two Gibraltarians who were staunch supporters of Britain, and who refused to take in Italians and Germans throughout the war. Gulbenkian's son Nubar, in his autobiography years later, was carefully vague about his father's business in Lisbon at that time, describing Calouste as having 'quite a lot of important social engagements ... which meant getting in touch with either high Portuguese officials or members of the American or British Embassies. He overcame his inherent reluctance to social life and played his part.'[22]

On the last night, Leslie was given a dinner after the film showing, after which the Portuguese minister made a speech and presented Leslie with a gold medal for the finest film of 1942. Leslie made a last speech, and his official obligations were over. The assistant press attaché at the embassy later remembered that this evening was another great success:

> Leslie, who was after all thoroughly accustomed to star treatment, was himself surprised by the strength of emotion and the enthu-siasm he aroused in the Portuguese, and was interested in our explanation of it. Someone suggested it was because he was not only a great actor but because he fitted so precisely the Portuguese idealised picture of the perfect Englishman. Leslie laughed at this and said, 'I suppose we do not have to tell them that I began as Hungarian'. This was certainly the first I had heard of his Hungarian origin and I could hardly believe it, though I know I have since read it.[23]

Next morning, for once having to get up early, Leslie and Chenhalls proceeded to Lisbon airport for the 9:30 flight. A lot of their acquain-tances got up too, and accompanied them to the airport to say good-bye, including embassy officials, Portuguese friends and some press photographers. As Leslie and Chenhalls had decided to take this flight at the last moment, some other passengers were 'bumped' for them, as they had priority. This proceeding was very common, and sometimes lead to ruffled feathers, as one official or another had to give way to someone thought more important or influential. This time the bumped passengers would only remember the incident with wondering relief.

The airport was simply arranged – passengers walked out openly on to the tarmac and climbed into the plane. Press photographers, German mechanics at the airport and any observers or spies would have been able to take note of the fuss and crowds as Leslie and twelve other passengers got into the plane. It seems that information proceeded from there to German sources, but whether it was directly acted upon will never be known.

NOTES

1. Internal memo of the British Council, 24 to 26 February 1943. National Archives, BW 1/20.
2. Letter of Sir Samuel Hoare to Anthony Eden, National Archives, FO 954/27.
3. Glyn Stone, *The Oldest Ally: Britain and the Portuguese Connection, 1936–1941* (London: Royal Historical Society, 1994), p.50.
4. David Stafford, *Roosevelt and Churchill: Men of Secrets* (London: Little, Brown, 1999).
5. Letter of Anthony Eden to Leslie Howard, 20 April, 1943. National Archives (NA), FO 954 27.
6. Reply of J.H. Roberts to K.T. Gurney, Foreign Office minutes, 16 April 1943, NA, FO 954 27.

7. Letter of Anthony Eden to Leslie Howard, 20 April 1943. NA, FO 954 27.
8. Ronald Howard, *In Search of My Father: A Portrait of Leslie Howard* (London: W. Kimber, 1981), p.175, and Ian Colvin, *Flight 777* (London: Evans Brothers, 1957), pp.96–109.
9. Philip Johns, *Within Two Cloaks: Missions with SIS and SOE* (London: Kimber, 1979).
10. The story of Alfred Gerassi's bravery is told in the BBC's magazine *Prospero* in the July 2009 issue. There is a photograph of Leslie and Helen Gerassi having a drink together, with Chenhalls, in Ronald's book, *In Search of My Father.* Mrs Gerassi is mislabelled as 'Madame Thais', Calouste Gulbenkian's secretary. An unknown man also at the table is wrongly labelled as Gulbenkian. Information from Mr Patrick Gerassi, Helen's son.
11. Howard, *In Search of My Father*, p.182.
12. *Anglo-Portuguese News*, 6 May 1943.
13. Report of Walter Starkie to British Council, London. NA, BW 1/20.
14. Letters of Leslie Howard to Sir Samuel Hoare and Lady Maude Hoare, Cambridge University, Templewood Papers XIII: 5 (25–6). With thanks to Cambridge University Library for permission to quote the letters.
15. Letter of Anthony Eden to Sir Samuel Hoare, 21 June 1943. NA, FO 954/27.
16. Howard, *In Search of My Father*, p.205.
17. Colvin, *Flight 777*, pp.130–6.
18. José Rey-Ximena, *El Vuelo de Ibis [The Flight of the Ibis]: Leslie Howard* (Madrid: Facta Ediciones, 2008), p.172. This book read for the author in the original Spanish by John Wainwright, former Librarian of the Taylorian Library, Oxford, and well-known Spanish scholar, and his Spanish wife, Laura Wainwright. Both enjoyed the book, and declared they had been convinced that Leslie met Franco.
19. Ibid., p.121.
20. Photograph and information about Philip Newman in the collection of the archives of The Royal Northern College of Music, reference no. PN/223. With thanks to the archivist, Mrs Mary Ann Davison, for her help in supplying this material.
21. Howard, *In Search of My Father*, illustrations.
22. Nubar Gulbenkian, *Pantaraxia: The Autobiography of Nubar Gulbenkian* (London: Hutchinson, 1965), pp.207–8.
23. Quoted in Howard, *In Search of My Father*, p.214.

CHAPTER ELEVEN

June 1943: Lost Actor

Leslie returned from Lisbon on the BOAC flight number 777 on 1 June 1943, at 9:35 a.m. On board with him were twelve other passengers, including two children, and four KLM staff. The passengers were: Carolina Hutcheon, aged 1½ years; Petra Hutcheon, aged 11 years; Mrs Violet Hutcheon, their mother; Mr Leslie Howard; Mr Ivan Sharp, mining engineer; Mr Francis Cowlrick, representative of a British engineering firm in Spain; Mr Gordon MacLean of the Foreign Office, then inspector-general of His Majesty's consulates; Mr Wilfred Israel, representative of the Jewish Agency; Mr Kenneth Stonehouse, Washington correspondent of Reuters news agency; Mrs Evelyn Stonehouse; Mrs Cecilia Paton, foreign language secretary; Mr Alfred Chenhalls; and Mr Tyrell Shervington, general manager of Shell Oil Company in Portugal. The crew were Captain Quirinus Tepas, pilot; Mr D. de Köning, first officer; Mr Cornelis van Brugge, radio operator; and Mr Engbertus Rosevink, flight engineer. This regular, unarmed passenger plane had flown the same route for about three years. At 12:54 p.m., over the Bay of Biscay, it was attacked by a squadron of eight German military aircraft, Junkers 88s. The plane was shot down, and there were no survivors. It fell into the sea in the Bay of Biscay, and no trace of it was ever recovered.

The deaths caused a sensation at the time, and since it was a civilian airliner, questions were asked in parliament. Such investigations as were possible then, and much research later, even up to the present time, have led nowhere in particular. Two researchers who managed to unearth as much original evidence as possible were Ian Colvin, the enterprising reporter who went round Germany and Portugal and used his knowledge of the country and contacts in intelligence to produce his book, *Flight 777*, in 1957; and much later, Ronald Howard, Leslie's son, who spent years of his life writing his own book on the incident, *In Search of My Father*, finally published in 1981.[1] Many others have since contributed their opinions.

Both Colvin and Howard found the documentary record of the incident in Luftwaffe reports of the time, in the Bundesarchiv. Colvin and others found some of the pilots involved and reported brief testimony from them. The accounts of the pilots are conflicting. One of the main documents recovered, the log book of one of the pilots, said to be Bellstedt, the pilot in charge of the flight, has since gone 'missing' from the archives of the Dorsetshire Regiment, now the Devon and Dorset Light Infantry.

Adding to the confusion are the forests of nonsense that have surrounded the facts, and which are to be found in every account of the incident. Neither Colvin nor Howard could resist adding to the tale the supposed premonitions of those involved, together with gypsy warnings, visions of deaths' heads, ghost phone calls, meaningful quotes from *Hamlet*, haruspications about thirteen at table, beautiful but unidentifiable female spies, SOE codes, the Ultra secret and even Leslie's magically evanescent personality. After half a century all this has coalesced into a minor legend in the manner of the *Mary Celeste*, in which all who become concerned believe they have something new to add, and that their evidence will confirm their own personal theory.

Flight 777 from Lisbon, a DC3 run by KLM, the Royal Dutch Airline, under BOAC and with the supervision of the Air Ministry, took off from Lisbon at 9:35 a.m. The record of what happened to the flight was kept at Whitchurch by KLM and was written by Captain Dirk Parmentier, who was in overall charge of the Lisbon group. The plane had radioed its position at 10:20, 11:20 and 12:20. After three hours flying, at 12:54 a.m. according to the record of the flight, the radio operator signalled twice to the Whitchurch control tower in England, 'an unidentified aircraft follows me' and then, 'am attacked by enemy aircraft'. There was nothing further.

The plane, apart from being a distinctive type of civilian aircraft, had civilian markings – the upper surface was camouflaged with a 'temperate land scheme' colouring – dark green and dark earth; the under surface was silver. The upper surface of the wings had two-feet high civil registration letters underlined with red and blue stripes, each six inches wide, red stripe immediately below the letters, which were in black. The under-surfaces of the wings and the fuselage had exactly the same identification. The fins had vertical red, white and blue stripes, eight inches wide. The aircraft carried the additional marking of a Union Jack on each side of the fuselage, approximately six feet by three-and-a-half feet.[2]

According to German records from the Bundesarchiv, the following report was written soon after the attack (the original document is quoted, retaining minor grammatical mistakes):

> Einsatz von aufklaerungsflugzeugen gegen England und einsatz fuer Atlantikaufgaben an 1. 6. 43 –
> 8 Ju 88 (start 10:00 UHR) Seenotsuche und enge sicherung W Brest –Atlantik Fuer 2 Eigene U-Boote. U-boote nicht Gesichtet. Seenotsuche wegen schlechtwetter abgebrochen –
> 12:45 UHR Qu 24 W. / 1785 1 Douglas DC 3, Kurs no.
> 12:50 UHR 6 Angriffe von Hinten und rechts vorn auf Douglas DC 3 Brand rechter flaechenbehaelter und Rumpf, absprung von 4 mann. 2 Fallschirme geoeffnet, davon einer in der luft verbrannt – der andere nach aufschlag sofort untergangen. Senkrechter absturz des flugzeuges.[3]

The report says the squadron were to provide cover for two U-boats, which however were not sighted. The squadron flew on, and at 12:45 a.m. the DC3 was sighted. At 12:50 a.m., five minutes later, it was attacked by six of the eight planes in the Staffel (squadron), one after the other. The plane burst into flames and four men jumped from the aircraft. The Junkers were equipped with cameras and took photographs of the plane as it went down. Although the report says that no U-boats were found, the squadron flew on west, away from their base, further west than they normally did, until they met the DC3.[4]

This squadron was the Vth gruppe of the Kampfgeschwader (Coastal Group) 40, based at Kerlin-Bastard airport near Bordeaux. Major Alfred Hemm was their Kommandant until September 1943. Presumably he wrote the above report. But Major Hemm has never been located. From BOAC/KLM records, according to both Colvin and Howard, Whitchurch control tower received the signal at 12:54 a.m., nine minutes after German records note the sighting, from the DC3, 'am attacked by enemy aircraft'. No men could have jumped from the aircraft, as it was not possible to open the heavy doors in flight while the plane was being shot at and exploding in flames. As Ronald Howard supposes, they were blown out by the force of the explosion. No parachutes were kept on board.

The only direct testimony ever found was given to Ian Colvin by one of the pilots of the squadron, Peter Friedlein. It reads as follows:

> The time was almost noon. The position near 46 degrees North and 9 degrees West. Our Staffel was on patrol from Lorient in

Brittany. I suppose I've been in a hundred patrols in the Biscay and Channel area. Our practice was to fly out in echelon to latitude 14 degrees West and then work to a chessboard pattern southwards. If we located crippled U-boats, we gave them umbrella. On these patrols we have fought Liberators, Whitleys, Sunderlands, Catalina, Lancasters, Wellington and Halifax bombers. I remember that day. The bay was rough ... We came out of cloud, at the tail-end of our patrol, and it was Flight-Lieutenant Bellstedt of Bremen, I think, who sighted the aircraft in the sun ... about 1000 feet above the cloud. Lieutenant Bellstedt was in a good position to attack, and he went in at once. My aircraft, the second in the third pair, did not have time to attack. It was over very quickly ... I think he went in to attack immediately, because the aircraft was so close and right in the sun, so he couldn't see the markings.[5]

Friedlein further told Colvin, 'Lieutenant Bellstedt is dead now. All the officers of that flight were killed.' Another anomaly occurs in the evidence, with Friedlein telling Colvin that a pilot officer called Necenany was part of the squadron that shot down the DC3. Friedlein says he was killed soon afterwards; this name occurs in later records as belonging to a different squadron in May 1943.[6]

Colvin also found in Germany, at the time he researched his book, a Colonel Robert Kowalewski, whom he was told was commodore of the Bordeaux Coastal Group in 1943. This was odd, because other records show no such person in this position. In the list of Kommodoren for this group, Oberst Martin Wetter is shown, serving from January to September 1943.[7] Kowalewski, whoever he was, added nothing helpful to the enquiry. He suggested that the planes were protecting a blockade runner trying to approach Bordeaux with a cargo of rubber. This is a doubtful story, as the Staffel's own report says that they were protecting U-boats and they had flown out over 400 miles from Bordeaux to the Bay of Biscay, and finally Colvin's research confirmed that the Board of Admiralty was certain that no blockade runner was approaching Biscay in that week.

Both Friedlein and Kowalewski separately stated that there was 'a lot of talk when we got back to base because we had shot down a civil aircraft' and 'there was a great fuss about it all'. Friedlein's statement, given in the 1950s, seems a giveaway – if there was a fuss as soon as they got back to base, it must have been the pilots themselves who already knew that they had shot down a civil plane. The official German News Agency, according to Reuters, had first announced that the plane was missing, and 'must have met with an accident', before it became generally known that the pilot was able to radio 'am attacked by enemy aircraft' before being shot down.[8]

There is one further piece of evidence. This was an album from one of the German pilots or crew members of the flight, recovered by the Dorsetshire Regiment, in 1944 or 1945 from the German home of one of the Junkers crew; it has been suggested that this was Lieutenant Bellstedt's house.[9] Copies of this were sent by the Air Ministry, first to BOAC, and by them to the relatives of all who had perished on the plane. All the same, it did not add much. There were some fuzzy photographs of the DC3's destruction (the Junkers 88s were equipped with cameras) and a note by the owner about the plane's passengers. It said, 'Leslie Howard was not only a film actor but a manufacturer of aircraft parts and a member of the Intelligence Service. Further, the Director of Shell Co in Lisbon, who was at the same time Chief of Secret Service in Lisbon, was on board.'

This looks like a rationalization of what happened, with some truth in it, although of course garbled. Presumably the 'manufacturer of aircraft parts' referred to Leslie's playing of R.J. Mitchell, the Spitfire designer. Since the Germans had never seen *The First of the Few*, they would not have recognized the source of this rumour. The original documents, from which copies were taken, have now been lost.

Long afterwards, another rather curious statement emerged in a book by Chris Goss, military historian. The book, *Bloody Biscay*, was published a few months after Ronald Howard died, in December 1996, and Howard was the expert on the incident, having studied it for years. A certain Hintze then emerged, claiming that he and not Bellstedt had been the Staffel leader, and that the whole incident had been a complete accident. As to why they had shot down the plane, Hintze says only that the markings were not visible. Hintze had not been heard of before 1997 when the book was published. No record shows his name connected with the squadron. In addition, Friedlein, the only eyewitness who gave personal testimony, stated that all the officers of the Staffel were dead. On the other hand Friedlein does not actually say that Bellstedt was in command, only that he attacked first.

Hintze's story, and in fact any claim that the shooting down of the aircraft was an accident, taken with what is on record, amounts to this: six planes, carrying six experienced pilots, and their eighteen crew members (Junkers 88s had a crew of three) failed to recognize, in broad daylight near noon, in brilliant sunshine since the DC3 was flying well above the cloud layer, a plane whose flight path, distinctive aircraft shape, type and very distinctive civil markings as described above, were well known to them – the DC3 had been flying the same route for three years. The Junkers 88s flew towards the DC3 and had it in view for five minutes (according to German records) or nine minutes (according to KLM records). The aircraft was shot down by mistake because the markings were not visible, and/or the aircraft was in the sun. Only a combat pilot of those times will be able to judge how likely this version is.

There have been three main theories, besides complete accident, put forward by people who wish to have the deaths explained. These are: first, that the Luftwaffe had been searching for Churchill, who was flying home from the Algerian Conference at that time. Second, that Leslie himself was the target, for various reasons, including the belief that he was a spy, or that he was connected in some way with Jewish refugees, of which there were a number in neutral Lisbon throughout the war. The third theory is that the plane was shot down with intent, but a number of factors combined to put it in jeopardy as a quasi-legitimate target at that time.

The Churchill theory was widely believed in Britain after the incident became known. Not only that, but Churchill himself and his family believed so, as do contemporary RAF personnel to this day. Churchill was at this time trying his best to persuade his allies to take decisive action to end the war quickly. He did not want a long, uncertain ending, with the Nazi regime able to hang on and possibly reconstitute itself. On 25 May 1943, Churchill was in Washington with Roosevelt. They gave a joint press conference in the afternoon and told the press, 'the day and night bombing of Germany by United States and British aircraft was achieving a more and more satisfactory result'. This statement was greeted by approving laughter from the surrounding pressmen.[10]

There is some evidence that the Germans were angry with this, which was reported back to them quickly and mentioned in their press. Goebbels' paper, *Der Angriffe*, carried an article on 27 May, stating that Churchill was in Washington and headed, '*Churchill's klare schuld – Luftterror eine rein englische erfindung*'. In other words, that the terror civilian bombing then happening in Germany was Churchill's personal fault. Churchill flew to Algiers from the conference on 27 May, stopping at Newfoundland and Gibraltar, where he was joined by Eden, the French prime minister, and Generals Alan Brooke, Marshall and Eisenhower. He flew to Tunis on 1 June. He flew back to Gibraltar on 4 June, and back to Britain on the same day.

Just to show that anyone can get the Leslie mystery garbled, Sir Martin Gilbert, Churchill's authoritative biographer, added this to his history of the time:

> Because of the bad weather, the flight from Gibraltar had continued in the Liberator, instead of the more comfortable Boeing Clipper flying boat to which they had intended to transfer. Another Clipper was flying from Lisbon to Portsmouth that same day (4 June) along a similar flightpath. This unarmed plane was shot down, and all its passengers killed, amongst them the British actor Leslie Howard.[11]

Here both the date and the flight are mistaken.

All the same, Churchill afterwards believed himself to have been the target. In his own history of the time he wrote,

> Eden and I flew home by Gibraltar. As my presence in North Africa had been fully reported, the Germans were exceptionally vigilant, and this led to a tragedy which much distressed me ... The regular commercial airline was about to start from Lisbon ... Although these passenger planes had plied unmolested for many months between Portugal and England, a German war plane was ordered out and the defenceless aircraft shot down.[12]

His daughter Diana wrote to him two weeks later, saying, 'we have been rather anxious about you since they got Leslie Howard'.[13]

More evidence was added to the story in a biography of Wilfred Israel by Naomi Shephard, published in 1984.[14] Israel was one of the passengers on the DC3. He had been concerned with funding the Jewish refugees in Lisbon and trying to arrange passage to safe countries for them (Portugal tolerated their presence but would grant no legal entry to their country).

Naomi Shepherd gives her source as James Langley, second-in-command at MI9, the escape and evasion branch of intelligence, during the war. Mr Langley, interviewed thirty-nine years after the event, told her three things: first, that he had heard from an MI9 colleague, who had it from a German pilot whom he had known before the war, that the Germans were planning to shoot down every plane between Portugal and Britain which might have had Churchill on board. Second, that Langley flew on the BOAC route Lisbon-Bristol the day before the downing of the DC3, and his plane was also attacked. Thirdly that 'when the Luftwaffe squadron leader responsible was taken prisoner later in the war, "it was decided not to prosecute him as a war criminal"', because trying to kill Churchill was a legitimate target.[15]

This evidence, some of it hearsay and all of it given thirty-nine years after the fact, doesn't quite make sense. Bellstedt was the officer concerned. According to the German Luftwaffe personnel, he was not disciplined at the time or later. He was killed, not taken prisoner, during the war. If anyone else had been tried, the matter would almost certainly have become widely known, as the relatives were likely to be informed and there was tremendous press interest. And it is not clear why the Germans should attack 'every plane between Portugal and Britain' when Churchill flew from Gibraltar.

One further piece of evidence is the loss of a Sunderland flying boat which next day searched for any survivors from the DC3. This belonged to 461 squadron, Royal Australian Air Force, originating from Pembroke Dock, South Wales. There were nine Australians and two British crew, normally looking for U-boats, but this time with this additional search duty. Very near the site where the DC3 had been shot down, it was attacked by a squadron of Junkers 88s (some claim the same squadron that shot down the DC3). The Sunderland crew claimed to have shot down three of the Junkers 88s in the ensuing battle, and damaged two more. However, the Sunderland itself was badly damaged, one man being killed, and it just managed to return to base.[16] Although this was an epic battle, its significance for any particular theory is not clear. The bitter air battle in the Bay of Biscay continued, even after it was known that Churchill had returned home, and according to some accounts, June 1943 did not even see the worst of the fighting there.

The second theory is that Leslie himself was aimed at. There is not a scrap of direct evidence for this, and many other factors indicate it is unlikely. Leslie's mission in Portugal was reasonably open – Anthony Eden summarized it in his letter to Leslie. The mission was to promote the idea that the Allies were prevailing in the war, and to promote friendly feeling in as many contacts as possible amongst the figures in cultural, business and possibly political high society whom Leslie would meet. Leslie was also promoting British films, and his own interests, trying to set up contacts for the distribution and screening of films, using the suggestion of Spanish and Portuguese historical themes. Very probably he would be 'debriefed' when he returned, with as much information as possible on attitudes, conditions and morale in both countries. But there were plenty of other agents who would have been able to do this. In fact Leslie was one of a series of official visitors in the cultural and artistic field who were sent to Spain and Portugal for propaganda purposes (for once Kenneth Clark followed Leslie instead of preceding him in his own visit to Lisbon).[17]

There is no other mission that Leslie could have carried out. As far as is known, he did not meet Salazar, who in any case was in contact with the British government as an old ally of this country and was most concerned to keep himself and his regime in place, as was Franco, dictator of Spain. Ronald Howard stated in his book that Goebbels was particularly concerned with Leslie, and that after his death Goebbels' paper, *Der Angriff*, carried the headline, 'Pimpernel Howard has made his last trip'. In fact there is not a single word about Leslie in *Der Angriff*, either at the date of the incident, or at any other time during June 1943. It was a daily newspaper and therefore would have been unlikely to start a discussion on the matter much later, when the world's press had been describing it at the time. There is also nothing about Leslie in Goebbels' daily diaries of the date, nor is there any other reference to Leslie in them.[18] It was likely that Goebbels had a great deal more to worry about at this time than a British propagandist who was little known in Germany.

One more secret purpose has occurred to some minds – the Jewish refugees who were in Lisbon. There is some evidence that attitudes in modern Portugal tend to connect Leslie with this. A letter from Joan Croft de Moura, a contact of the British Council in Lisbon, in answer to an inquiry about what is now remembered about the incident in Portugal, ended with the information that some people in Lisbon still believed the Leslie had come to Portugal to aid Jewish refugees.[19]

According to historical records, there was a population of about 4,000 Jews who had managed to find temporary wartime refuge in Portugal. The numbers remained constant, even though some managed to escape elsewhere from time to time. They were mostly in seaside camps at Caldas da Rainha and Ericeira. There was a very small native population of Portuguese Jews in Lisbon, those who remained after hundreds of years of the Inquisition, and who did what they could for the refugees. By 1943 there were few places the refugees could escape to, and even Wilfred Israel could do little for them. Since Leslie was not connected with any Jewish agency, and had no funds or entry visas to other countries to offer, there was nothing he could do either.[20]

Wilfred Israel had not only a small number of visas to Palestine for Spanish and Portuguese Jewish refugees, but also wider plans to try to coordinate the rescue of Jews throughout Europe. For Spain he had of course been instructed by the British Foreign Office, who were anxious to rid Franco of some of the troublesome refugees in Spain in order to keep his goodwill. For Portugal he had no backing at all, and was trying to act entirely on his own initiative. Since the Germans were obsessed with the Jews to the point of insanity at this time, and since his activities were very likely to have been monitored, Israel makes just as likely a target as Leslie. Also, given that Leslie had been entrusted with a government mission, it has to be said that if he had aided the Jewish refugees in any way he would have been acting contrary to official policy and attitudes at this time.

The third theory is that a number of circumstances combined to make the plane a military target. These include the intelligence situation in Portugal, the background of the other passengers, evidence from MI9, the precise turn of the war at that date and the situation of the German pilots themselves. There is also the fact that there had been previous attacks on the plane in November 1942 and April 1943, when of course Leslie was not on board.

British intelligence in both Spain and Portugal was limited during the war. In Spain the British ambassador, Samuel Hoare, insisted that any such activity might lead to Franco abandoning his neutrality and coming in on the Axis side, especially if British agents were found allied to opponents of Franco's regime. These were often Communists, abhorred by both Franco and Salazar. In Portugal there was the additional problem that hardly any British people knew the language. Both regimes allowed certain Allied operations to take place – particularly finances to pay for Allied armed forces escape routes through France and Spain. There was an MI6 presence in Lisbon, together with other branches of intelligence. It was limited, but according to Nigel West, managed to extract information from refugees escaping from occupied Europe and the local Anglo-Portuguese community.[21] Philip Johns, head of the MI6 staff in Lisbon until 1942, also describes the atmosphere in his memoir of the time.[22]

It is plain that Lisbon was full of spies on both sides, and that the ordinary Portuguese also participated, making as much money as possible from all sides. It was well known, for example, that the head waiter at the Hotel Aviz, where Leslie stayed, 'did a profitable round after lunch each day, reporting on who was lunching with whom and recounting snatches of conversation he had overheard. He went to the PIDE, the Portuguese secret police, then to the German Legation, the

American and British Embassies and finally to his own Italian Legation.'
(His name was Rapetti, of Italian origin.)[23]

Philip Johns does however state quite openly that Tyrell Shervington,
director of Shell in Portugal, and passenger on the DC3, was a major
source of information in Portugal for MI6. Similarly Ivan Sharp,
another of the passengers on the downed plane, had been touring
the country reporting on tungsten mining for the British government.
Tungsten was a vital component in the manufacture of steel, and both
sides were desperate to obtain supplies and prevent their enemies from
getting access to this element. Luckily Sharp's report had gone ahead of
him, so his information was not lost. Both men were at least as important as Leslie for intelligence purposes in Lisbon, and probably more so.

Another well-known contemporary, Airey Neave, was working for
MI9 at this time. In his memoirs he states that military personnel often
used this plane, dressed in plain clothes;[24] Colvin reports the same
information. If this was the case, it is hard to argue that the plane was
completely out of bounds by the rules of war. Instead the British seemed
to have been criminally irresponsible as to who was allowed to travel,
quite openly, on this route.

Another attempt to link Leslie directly with spying activities was
made in the *Journal of Contemporary History* in 1983. This article
reports that the Germans could easily have obtained information on
who was due to fly on Leslie's plane, and argues that the downing of the
plane, together with pressure from the British government, prompted a
law against spying to be passed by the Portuguese authorities.[25] But
Hinsley's authoritative history of intelligence in the Second World War
makes it plain that, at this date, considerable pressure was brought to
bear on the Salazar regime by the British, but on other accounts than
Leslie's. The most obvious instance was the de Menezes case in May
1943, where a member of the Portuguese Embassy in London was
caught spying and sentenced to death. In return for his reprieve, and
MI6's evidence of other Axis spy activity, the Portuguese government
arrested a number of agents identified by MI6, including the head of
the SD or German secret police in Portugal on May 25.[26]

This speculation that the plane had been spied on had actually been
confirmed long before. The *Evening Standard* had a permanent correspondent in Lisbon, probably also passing on information to various
authorities. On 13 December 1943 a small paragraph appeared in the
Evening Standard stating that,

Ever since the airplane carrying Leslie Howard was shot down over the Bay of Biscay, the Portuguese police have been investigating the affair. The time of departure of airplanes [from Portugal], their destination and their passenger lists are always kept secret, and the police set out to find how the Germans got wind of the date and hour and route of the Howard airplane.

They discovered that a message was sent by the Baron von Weltzen [*sic*] who, in Lisbon was reputed to be a wealthy German manufacturer with trade interests in Portugal. To avoid international complications, the Herr Baron has been politely escorted across the Portuguese border with instructions not to enter the country again.

Confirmation of this story is found in the files at the National Archives, Kew, where this newspaper article has been cut out and pasted into one of the Intelligence Services files on enemy agents abroad.[27] Underneath the article is a scribbled conversation between Sir David Petrie, then Director General of MI5, and his deputy, Dick White:

David Petrie: Is this Weltzien 'one of ours' and is his departure a fact? [Quotation marks in original.]
Dick White: Yes, Weltzien was expelled by the Portuguese and is now working in Paris.
David Petrie: Good.

MI5 at this time, although they were the home security service, and not responsible for foreign affairs, did maintain agents abroad. They had been involved with the well-known 'Double Cross' operation, developed under David Petrie's supervision, of turning German agents. Von Weltzien has not since been named as such an agent. The *Evening Standard* revealed his name in 1943. But the fact that MI5 knew the spy was only released at the National Archives in 2005. What exactly was meant by the phrase, 'one of ours'? Presumably Petrie meant that this German spy was well known to them and had already been marked down. If MI5 knew the man, they must have known his conditions, his background – was he a low-level watcher, like the doorman at the Hotel Aviz? Or was he a more sophisticated person, with influence, at a higher level of command? Was he in a position to send an order for the plane to be attacked? It seems that MI5, at any rate, knew more than they ever deigned to tell the relatives of the dead.

The progress of the war meant that the Germans were fighting with increasing desperation in the Bay of Biscay at this time, having just lost the Battle of the Atlantic at the end of May 1943. On 24 May Admiral Dönitz withdrew most U-boats from the main routes, and directed the majority of them to an area southwest of the Azores to attack convoys on the US-Gibraltar route. A few submarines were left to attempt to deceive the Allies about the abandonment of the main routes. This might account for the observation that aircraft activity in the Bay dropped off after the beginning of June, as there were few U-boats left to protect.

One final point indicating the vulnerability of flight 777 is a minor one, and concerns the German pilots' own world: the Staffels of the KG 40 group were apparently competing for the honour of flying their five-hundredth mission. In order to catch up with another squadron, which achieved this tally on 21 May, the squadron which shot down the DC3 took off on 1 June.[28] All these facts combine to suggest that the flight was vulnerable for a number of reasons besides Churchill's flights at the time and Leslie's propaganda activities.

No doubt more speculation, and possibly more evidence, will emerge, but it can never be conclusive. But the thought has occurred that if the Germans had successfully targeted Churchill, they might have managed, not to win the war, but perhaps to avoid losing it. Churchill's plane to the Algerian conference also transported Anthony Eden, Generals Alexander, Ismay and Alan Brooke and Air Marshal Tedder and General Marshall (USA). It was Churchill who was cajoling the Allies to follow through in Europe. Without him they would surely have seen off the Japanese – but would they have interfered so decisively in Europe? The future might have been dark indeed if the Germans had succeeded in finding and destroying the right plane. And if Leslie had known this, haunted as he was by his failure of resolve in the First World War, it might have comforted him to be at least part of one sacrifice for such a cause.

In the chaos of war, Leslie was just one more casualty. Ten days later, as it began to be understood that he, like many others, would not be returning, *Kinematograph Weekly* published a quiet epitaph, the final judgement of his peers: 'His temperament took the form of apparent casualness, but it invariably inspired a loyalty and devotion in sharp contrast to the more assertive methods of others. His qualities of kindness, patience and receptiveness were not poses, but realities, and no one who knew him, however slightly, could do anything but surrender to them.'[29]

Lisbon 1943 ... 'I started as Hungarian'... Leslie didn't have to step out of hiding – he was always in plain sight. He was not Jewish, by any law or by upbringing. Instead he fought Nazi propaganda on principle, at one point knowingly risking bankruptcy and wrecking his own career to do so. Yet he did not, like many others, disconnect from what was Jewish in his own background. In the face of a terrifying threat, his bravery and balance were remarkable. Perhaps it was because he had no early training in prejudice of any sort that he had the courage to speak out very simply against racism. It didn't occur to him that a decent man could do otherwise. He was someone who finally was not afraid, who had conquered his fears, who was free and at peace.

May he rest and remain so.

NOTES

1. Ronald Howard, *In Search of My Father: A Portrait of Leslie Howard* (London: W. Kimber, 1981). Ian Colvin, *Flight 777* (London: Evans Brothers, 1957).
2. Information from P.J.V. Elliott, senior keeper at the RAF Museum, Hendon, in a letter to the author, 29 October 2001.
3. Translation: 'German Atlantic Archives of 1st June 1943. Starting at 10:00 hours, 8 Junkers 88s flew west from Brest (France), their tasks being air-sea rescue and protection of two U-Boats. They found nothing. At 12:45 hours that day they sighted a Douglas DC3 [Leslie's plane]. At 12:50 it was attacked by 6 of the Junkers 88s, one after another. Four men were seen to jump from the aircraft. Two parachutes were seen. The plane caught fire and fell into the sea. No survivors were seen.' (In his examination of this report Ronald Howard notes that there were no men jumping from the plane, with or without parachutes – the plane was simply blown to pieces by the attack and fell immediately into the sea. Howard, *In Search of My Father*, pp.218–23.)
4. With thanks to Chris Goss, author of *Bloody Biscay* (Manchester: Crecy Publishing, 1997), for providing a copy of this document.
5. Colvin, *Flight 777*, p.188.
6. Chris Goss, *Bloody Biscay*.
7. Website of Michael Holm of Denmark: http://www.ww2.dk/air/kampf/kg40.htm.
8. *Evening Standard*, 3 June 1943.
9. By Chris Goss.
10. Martin Gilbert, *Winston S. Churchill*, vol. 7, *Road to Victory 1941–1945* (London: Heinemann, 1986), p.414.
11. Ibid., p.426.
12. W.S. Churchill, *The Second World War*, vol. IV, *The Hinge of Fate* (London: Cassell, 1948–1954), p.742.
13. Churchill Archives, Churchill College, Cambridge, Char 1/375/3–4.
14. Naomi Shepherd, *Wilfred Israel: German Jewry's Secret Ambassador* (London: Weidenfeld and Nicolson, 1984).
15. Shepherd, *Wilfred Israel*, p.251.
16. Rowan Matthews website: http://www.n461.com/howard.html.
17. Kenneth Clark, *The Other Half: A Self Portrait* (London: John Murray, 1977), pp.96–7.
18. Elke Frohlich, *Die Tagebuch von Joseph Goebbels* (Munich: K.G. Saur, 1993).
19. Extract from a letter from Joan Croft de Moura, head of the British Historical Society of Portugal, to the author, 6 March 2002.
20. Shepherd, *Wilfred Israel*, and Paul Bartrop, 'From Lisbon to Jamaica', *Immigrants and Minorities* 13, 2 (1994).
21. Nigel West, *MI6: British Secret Service Intelligence Operations, 1909–1945* (London: Panther Books, 1985), p.305.
22. Philip Johns, *Within Two Cloaks: Missions with SIS and SOE* (London: Kimber, 1979).

23. Nubar Gulbenkian, *Pantaraxia: The Autobiography of Nubar Gulbenkian* (London: Hutchinson, 1965).
24. Airey Neave, *Saturday at MI9* (London: Hodder and Stoughton, 1969).
25. Douglas Wheeler, 'In the Service of Order: The Portuguese Political Police and the British, German and Spanish Intelligence 1932–45', *Journal of Contemporary History* 18, 1 (1983), pp.1–25.
26. F.H. Hinsley and C.A.G. Simkins, *British Intelligence in the Second World War*, 5 vols (London: HMSO, 1970–1990).
27. National Archives, Public Record Office, KV 2/1930.
28. Goss, *Bloody Biscay*, p.67.
29. *Kinematograph Weekly*, 10 June 1943.

Finally, concerning certain rumours that the codebreakers of Bletchley Park ignored their knowledge that the civilian airliner would be shot down in order to save the Enigma secret. I received the following letter from Mrs Mavis Batey, decoder at Bletchley Park during the Second World War, on 20 July 2002:

> Dear Miss Eforgan, I have received your letter via Christ Church [College, Oxford] about the death of Leslie Howard and a possible connection with Bletchley. There is of course from what you say no direct evidence that Bletchley was involved in intercepting and decoding the fatal message. Instructions to shoot down the plane, if you say it was done on purpose, could have gone out from German HQ speedily by telephone or teleprinter securely.
>
> There are several rumours about action not being taken on Ultra Intelligence (as the Bletchley information was called) for fear of disclosing the Enigma secret – the worst being the raid on Coventry, which we know is absolutely untrue. Churchill did not say that the raid must go on to its known target for the 'sake of Enigma'. After all we were regularly breaking the traffic which enabled raids to be diverted from major cities: it was just very sad that the Air Force section were unable to break the code on the night of Coventry. As far as I know (this from reading the histories as we told nothing at the time) there is only one occasion when commanders in the field had to decide not to act on Ultra information fully as it would have been obvious that knowing the actual landing place would have made the enemy know that their message had been broken and that was Crete. There were usually means of covering up. The Ultra information provided for the Battle of Matapan gave the actual rendezvous and time for the Italian fleet's appearance and reconnaissance planes were sent out in advance to the actual spot before Cunningham's guns opened fire. Of course the next day the newspapers claimed a great triumph for reconnaissance. Now whether or not Bletchley decoded a message about the plane you are interested in, I think you can be sure that it was not ignored to 'save Enigma'.
>
> Air flights for passengers in wartime were always extremely dangerous. I remember being saddened by the news of Leslie Howard's death. He was one of my favourite actors.
>
> With all good wishes,
> Mavis Batey

Leslie Howard's
Theatre and Film Work

EARLY THEATRE IN LONDON 1917–1920

June 1917. *The Tidings Brought to Mary (L'Annonce Faite à Marie)*, Paul Claudel. Strand Theatre. Actor: played Apprentice.

February 1918. *The Freaks*, Arthur Pinero. New Theatre. Actor: played Ronald.

March 1918. *Romanticismo*, Gerolamo Rovetta. Comedy Theatre. Actor: played Marquis Giacomino D'Arfo.

July 1918. *The Title*, Arnold Bennett. Royalty Theatre. Actor: played John Culver.

April 1919. *Our Mr Hepplewhite*, Gladys Unger. Criterion Theatre. Actor: played Lord Bagley.

January 1920. *Mr Pim Passes By*, A.A. Milne. New Theatre. Actor: played Brian Strange.

February 1920. *The Young Person in Pink*, Gertrude E. Jennings. Prince of Wales's Theatre. Actor: played Lord Stevenage.

February 1920. *Kitty Breaks Loose*, Kingston Stack. Duke of York's Theatre. Actor: played Jack Wilson.

June 1920. *East is West*, Samuel Shipman and John B. Hymer. Lyric Theatre. Actor: played Billy Benson.

July 1920. *Rosalind of the Farmyard*, Mary Pakington. Shaftesbury Theatre. Actor: played Captain L'Estrange.

EARLY SILENT FILMS IN ENGLAND 1917–1921

1914. *The Heroine of Mons*. England, Clarendon Company. Actor: unnamed.

1917. *The Happy Warrior*. England, Harma Company. Actor: played Rollo.

1919. *The Lackey and the Lady*. England, British Actors Company. Actor: played Tony Dunciman.

1920. *Bookworms*. England, Minerva Films. Producer, actor: played Richard.

1920. *The Bump*. England, Minerva Films. Producer.

1920. *£5 Reward*. England, Minerva Films. Producer, actor: played Tony Marchmont.

1920. *Twice Two*. England, Minerva Films. Producer.

1920. *Too Many Cooks*. England, Minerva Films. Producer.

1921. *The Temporary Lady*. England, Minerva Films. Producer.

THEATRE IN LONDON, 1920–1943

January 1921. *On the Brink*, Stanley J. Holloway. Ambassadors Theatre. Director.

January 1921. *The Voice in the Street*, E. Thornley-Dodge. Ambassadors Theatre. Director.

January 1921. *The Five Wishes*, Laura Leycester. Ambassadors Theatre. Director.

November 1921. *The Faithful Heart*, Monckton Hoffe. Comedy Theatre. Stage Director.

July 1926. *The Way You Look At It*, Edward Wilbraham. Queen's Theatre. Actor: played Bobby Rendon.

June 1928. *Tell Me The Truth (A Bit of Tomfoolery)*, Leslie Howard. Ambassadors Theatre. Author.

August 1928. *Her Cardboard Lover*, Valerie Wyngate and P.G. Wodehouse, adapted from Jacques Deval. Lyric Theatre. Actor: played André Sallicel.

March 1929. *Berkeley Square*, John L. Balderston and J.C. Squire. Lyric Theatre. Producer, actor: played Peter Standish.

October 1933. *This Side Idolatry*. Talbot Jennings. Lyric Theatre. Producer, actor: played William Shakespeare.

July 1934. *Elizabeth Sleeps Out*, Leslie Howard. Whitehall Theatre. Author. (First performed in June 1928 as *Tell Me The Truth*).

May 1938. *Here's to Our Enterprise*, Edward Knoblock. Lyceum Theatre. Actor. (Henry Irving Centenary show, with participation from every well-known actor in London.)

25 September 1942. *Cathedral Steps*, Clemence Dane. Pageant, with 500 artists, staged on St Paul's Cathedral steps. Actor: solo speech as Lord Nelson. Final public appearance.

THEATRE ON BROADWAY 1920–1936

November 1920. *Just Suppose*, A.E. Thomas. Henry Miller's Theatre. Actor: played Sir Calverton Shipley.

October 1921. *The Wren*, Booth Tarkington. Gaiety Theatre. Actor: played Roddy.

December 1921. *Danger*, Cosmo Hamilton. 39th Street Theatre. Actor: played Percy Sturgess.

March 1922. *The Truth About Blayds*, A.A. Milne. Booth Theatre. Actor: played Oliver Blayds-Conway.

August 1922. *A Serpent's Tooth*, Arthur Richman. Little Theatre. Actor: played Jerry Middleton.

November 1922. *The Romantic Age*, A.A. Milne. Comedy Theatre. Actor: played Gervase Mallory.

December 1922. *The Lady Cristilinda*, Monckton Hoffe. Broadhurst Theatre. Actor: played Martini.

February 1923. *Anything Might Happen*, Edgar Selwyn. Comedy Theatre. Actor: played Hal Turner.

May 1923. *Aren't We All*, Frederick Lonsdale. Gaiety Theatre. Actor: played Hon. William Tatham.

January 1924. *Outward Bound*, Sutton Vane. Ritz Theatre. Actor: played Henry.

August 1924. *The Werewolf*, Gladys Unger, from the play of the same name by Rudolf Lothar. 49th Street Theatre. Actor: played Paolo Moreira.

January 1925. *Shall We Join the Ladies?*, J.M. Barrie. Frohman Theatre. Actor: played Mr Preen.

January 1925. *Isabel*, Curt Goetz. Frohman Theatre. Actor: played Peter Graham. (Double Bill with *Shall We Join the Ladies?*).

Septembe 1925. *The Green Hat*, Michael Arlen. Broadhurst Theatre. Actor: played Napier Harpenden.

March 1927. *Her Cardboard Lover*, Valerie Wyngate and P.G. Wodehouse, adapted from Jacques Deval. Empire Theatre. Actor: played André Sallicel.

September 1927. *Murray Hill*, Leslie Howard. Bijou Theatre. Author, actor: played Wrigley.

October 1927. *Escape*, John Galsworthy. Booth Theatre. Actor: played Matt Denant.

September 1929. *Candlelight*, Siegfried Gayer with P.G. Wodehouse. Empire Theatre. Actor: played Joseph.

November 1929. *Berkeley Square*, John L. Balderston. Lyceum Theatre. Producer, director, actor: played Peter Standish.

August 1930. *Out of a Blue Sky*, Hans Chlumberg, translated by Leslie Howard. Booth Theatre. Director.

January 1932. *The Animal Kingdom*, Philip Barry. Broadhurst Theatre. Producer, actor: played Tom Collier.

March 1932. *We Are No Longer Children*, Leopold Marchant, book adapted by Ilka Chase and William B. Murray. Broadhurst Theatre. Director.

January 1935. *The Petrified Forest*, Robert E. Sherwood. Broadhurst Theatre. Producer, actor: played Alan Squier.

April 1936. *Elizabeth Sleeps Out*, Leslie Howard. Comedy Theatre. Author. (Originally seen as *Murray Hill* in 1927.)

November 1936. *Hamlet*, William Shakespeare. Imperial Theatre. Producer, director, actor: played Hamlet.

FILMS IN HOLLYWOOD AND ENGLAND, 1930–1943

Films in which Leslie was solely the narrator have been omitted.

1930. *Outward Bound*. Warner Brothers. Actor: played Tom Prior.

1931. *Never the Twain Shall Meet*. MGM. Actor: played Dan Pritchard.

1931. *A Free Soul*. MGM. Actor: played Dwight Winthrop.

1931. *Five and Ten*. MGM. Actor: played Berry Rhodes.

1931. *Devotion*. RKO. Actor: played David Trent.

1932. *Service for Ladies*. Paramount British. Actor: played Max Tracey.

1932. *Smilin' Through*. MGM. Actor: played Sir John Carteret.

1932. *The Animal Kingdom*. RKO. Actor: played Tom Collier.

1933. *Secrets*. United Artists. Actor: played John Carlton.

1933. *Captured*. Warner Brothers. Actor: played Captain Fred Allison.

1933. *Berkeley Square*. Fox. Actor: played Peter Standish.

1934. *Of Human Bondage*. RKO. Actor: played Philip Carey.

1934. *The Lady is Willing*. Columbia. Actor: played Albert Latour.

1934. *British Agent*. Warner Brothers. Actor: played Stephen Locke.

1934. *The Scarlet Pimpernel*. London Film Productions. Actor: played Sir Percy Blakeney.

1936. *The Petrified Forest*. Warner Brothers. Actor: played Alan Squier.

1936. *Romeo and Juliet*. MGM. Actor: played Romeo.

1937. *It's Love I'm After*. Warner Brothers. Actor: played Basil Underwood.

1937. *Stand-In*. United Artists. Actor: played Atterbury Dodd.

1938. *Pygmalion*. MGM. Actor: played Professor Henry Higgins.

1939. *Intermezzo: A Love Story*. United Artists. Associate Producer, actor: played Holger Brandt.

1939. *Gone with the Wind*. MGM. Actor: played Ashley Wilkes.

1941. *From the Four Corners*. Ministry of Information. Actor, presenter.

1941. *Pimpernel Smith*. British National Films. Producer, director, actor: played Professor Horatio Smith.

1941. *49th Parallel*. Ortus Films. Actor: played Philip Armstrong Scott.

1942. *The First of the Few*. British Aviation Pictures. Producer, director, actor: played R.J. Mitchell.

1943. *The Gentle Sex*. Two Cities Films. Director, narrator. (Glimpsed at beginning of film, his final screen appearance.)

1943. *The Lamp Still Burns*. Two Cities. Producer.

Bibliography

Agate, James, *A Short View of the English Stage, 1900–1926* (London: H. Jenkins, 1926).

Aldgate, Anthony and Jeffrey Richards, *Britain Can Take It: British Cinema in the Second World War* (Oxford: Blackwell, 1986).

Allen, David Rayvern, *Sir Aubrey: A Biography of C. Aubrey Smith, England Cricketer, West End Actor, Hollywood Film Star* (London: Elm Tree Books, 1982).

Anonymous, *British Security Coordination. The Secret History of British Intelligence in the Americas 1940–1945* (London: St Ermin's, 1998).

Astor, Mary, *A Life on Film* (London: W.H. Allen, 1973).

Balcon, Michael, *Michael Balcon Presents . . . A Lifetime of Films* (London: Hutchinson, 1969).

Bankhead, Tallulah, *Tallulah: My Autobiography* (London: Gollancz, 1952).

Bartley, Anthony, *Smoke Trails in the Sky: From the Journals of a Fighter Pilot* (London: Kimber,1984).

Behlmer, Rudy (ed.), *Memo from David O. Selznick* (New York: Viking Press, 1972).

Beider, Alexander, *A Dictionary of Jewish Surnames from the Russian Empire* (Teaneck, NJ: Avotaynu, 1993).

Beller, Stephen, *Vienna and the Jews 1867–1939. A Cultural History* (Cambridge: Cambridge University Press, 1989).

Bessie, Alvah, *Inquisition in Eden* (Berlin: Seven Seas Publishers, 1967).

Blumberg, Sir Herbert Edward, *Britain's Sea Soldiers: A Record of the Royal Marines During the War 1914–1919* (Devonport: Swiss, 1927).

Bolchover, Richard, *British Jewry and the Holocaust* (Cambridge: Cambridge University Press, 1993).

Breitman, Richard, *Official Secrets: What the Nazis Planned, What the British and Americans Knew* (London: Allen Lane The Penguin Press, 1999).

Breitman, Richard, *U.S. Intelligence and the Nazis* (Cambridge and New York: Cambridge University Press, 2005).

Brewer, Susan, *To Win the Peace: British Propaganda in the United States during World War II* (Ithaca, NY and London: Cornell University Press, 1997).

Brown, Frederick, *Zola: A Life* (London: Macmillan, 1996).

Brownlow, Kevin, *The Parade's Gone By* (London: Secker and Warburg, 1968).

Brownlow, Kevin, *David Lean: A Biography*, (London: Richard Cohen, 1996).

Brunel, Adrian, *Nice Work: The Story of Thirty Years in British Film Production* (London: Forbes Robertson, 1949).

Butler, Ewan, *Mason-Mac: The Life of Lieutenant-General Sir Noel Mason-Macfarlane: A Biography* (London: Macmillan, 1972).

Cave Brown, Anthony, *The Secret Servant: The Life of Sir Stewart Menzies, Head of Intelligence* (London: Michael Joseph, 1988).

Cazenove, H., *Northamptonshire Yeomanry 1794–1964* (Northampton: Belmont Press, 1966).

Chandler, A.R., *Alleyn's: The Coeducational School* (Henley-on-Thames: Gresham Books in partnership with Alleyn's School, 1998).

Churchill, W.S., *The Second World War*, vol. IV, *The Hinge of Fate* (London: Cassell, 1948–54).

Clark, Kenneth, *The Other Half: A Self Portrait* (London: Hamish Hamilton, 1977).

Cline, Sally, *Radclyffe Hall: A Woman Called John* (London: J. Murray, 1997).

Cockin, Katherine, *Women and Theatre in the Age of Suffrage: The Pioneer Players* (Basingstoke: Macmillan, 2001).

Cohn, Michael, *Jewish Bridges: East to West* (Westport, CT and London: Praeger, 1996).

Colvin, Ian, *Flight 777* (London: Evans Brothers, 1957).

Constanduros, Mabel, *Shreds and Patches* (London: Lawson and Dunn, 1946).

Cooper, Diana, *The Light of Common Day* (London: Hart Davies, 1959).

Courtney, Marguerite, *Laurette* (New York: Atheneum, 1955).

Cull, Nicholas, *Selling War: The British Propaganda Campaign against American 'Neutrality' in World War II* (New York and Oxford: Oxford University Press, 1995).

Danischewsky, Monja, *Michael Balcon's 25 Years in Film* (London: World Film Productions, 1947).

Davies, Marion, *The Times We Had: Life with William Randolph Hearst* (London: Angus and Robertson, 1976).

Dean, Basil, *Seven Ages* (London: Hutchinson, 1973).

Dickens, Monica, *One Pair of Feet* (London: Michael Joseph, 1942).

Dickens, Monica, *An Open Book* (London: Book Club Associates and Heinemann, 1978).

Doherty, Edward, *The Rain Girl* (Philadelphia, PA: Macrae, 1930).

Drazin, Charles, *Korda: Britain's Only Movie Mogul* (London: Sidgwick and Jackson, 2002).

Duff Cooper, Alfred, *Old Men Forget: An Autobiography of Duff Cooper* (London: Hart-Davis 1957).

Dunkel, W.B., *Sir Arthur Pinero: A Critical Biography With Letters* (Chicago, IL: The University of Chicago Press, 1941).

Ellis, L.F., *The War in France and Flanders 1939–1940* (London: HMSO, 1953).

Errington, Col. F.H.L., *The Inns of Court Officers Training Corps During the Great War* (London: Printing Craft, 1922).

Evans, Robert, *The Kid Stays in the Picture* (London: Faber and Faber, 2004).

Eyles, Allen, *Oscar Deutsch Entertains Our Nation: Odeon Cinemas* (London: Cinema Theatre Association, 2002).

Fairbanks Jnr, Douglas, *The Salad Days* (London: Collins 1988).

Fairbanks Jnr, Douglas, *A Hell of a War* (London: Robson, 1995).

Foot, M.R.D., *SOE: An Outline History of the Special Operations Executive 1940–1946* (London: Pimlico, 1999).

Foot, M.R.D. and J.M. Langley, *MI9* (London: Book Club Associates, 1979).

Frohlich, Elke, *Die Tagebuch von Joseph Goebbels* (Munich: K.G. Saur, 1993).

Gallagher, Tony, *The Adventures of Roberto Rossellini* (New York: Da Capo, 1998).

Gannon, F., *The British Press and Germany 1936–1939* (Oxford: Clarendon Press, 1971).

Gargan, William, *Why Me? An Autobiography* (New York: Doubleday, 1969).

Gifford, Dennis, *The British Film Catalogue*, 3rd edn (London: Fitzroy Dearborn, 2001).

Gilbert, Martin, *Winston S. Churchill*, vol. 5, *Prophet of Truth 1922–1939* (London: Heinemann, 1976).

Gilbert, Martin, *Winston Churchill: The Wilderness Years* (London: Macmillan, 1981).

Gilbert, Martin, *Winston S. Churchill*, vol. 7, *Road to Victory 1941–1945* (London: Heinemann, 1986).

Gilbert, Martin, *Second World War* (London: Weidenfeld and Nicolson, 1989).

Gilbert, Martin, *In Search of Churchill: A Historian's Journey* (London: HarperCollins, 1995).

Golden, John, *Stagestruck* (New York: S. French, 1930).

Gordon, Lois, *Nancy Cunard: Heiress, Muse, Political Idealist* (New York: Columbia University Press, 2007).

Goss, Chris, *Bloody Biscay* (Manchester: Crecy Publishing, 1997).

Gough-Yates, Kevin, *Michael Powell in Collaboration with Emeric Pressburger* (London: British Film Institute, 1971).

Gough-Yates, Kevin, 'The European Film-Maker in Exile in Britain, 1933–1945' (PhD diss., Open University, 1990).

Gough-Yates, Kevin, *Somewhere in England: British Cinema and Exile* (London: I.B. Tauris, 2009).

Guiles, F.L., *Marion Davies: A Biography* (London: W.H. Allen, 1973).

Gulbenkian, Nubar, *Pantaraxia: The Autobiography of Nubar Gulbenkian* (London: Hutchinson, 1965).

Hadleigh, Boze, *Leading Ladies* (London: Robson Books, 1992).

Hamilton, Cosmo, *Unwritten History* (London: Hutchinson, 1924).

Hamilton, Cosmo, *Four Plays* (London: Hutchinson, 1925).

Harris, M.J. and D. Oppenheimer, *Into the Arms of Strangers: Stories of the Kindertransport* (London: Bloomsbury, 2000).

Hayes, Helen, *On Reflection: An Autobiography* (London: W.H. Allen, 1969).

Hepburn, Katharine, *Me: Stories of My Life* (London: Viking, 1991).

Hillier, Bevis, *John Betjeman: New Fame New Love* (London: John Murray, 2002).

Hinsley, F.H. and C.A.G. Simkins, *British Intelligence in the Second World War*, 5 vols (London: HMSO, 1970–90).

Holroyd, Michael, *Bernard Shaw: The Lure of Fantasy* (London: Chatto and Windus, 1991).

Houseman, John, *Run-Through: A Memoir* (New York: Simon and Schuster, 1972).

Howard, Leslie, *Murray Hill: A Comedy in Three Acts* (London: S. French, 1934).

Howard, Leslie Ruth, *A Quite Remarkable Father* (London: Longmans, 1960).

Howard, Ronald, *In Search of My Father: A Portrait of Leslie Howard* (London: W. Kimber, 1981).

Howard, Ronald (ed.), *Trivial Fond Records* (London: W. Kimber, 1982).

Israel, Lee, *Miss Tallulah Bankhead* (London: W.H. Allen, 1972).

Johns, Philip, *Within Two Cloaks: Missions with SIS and SOE* (London: Kimber, 1979).

Kelly, Andrew, Richards, Jeffrey and Pepper, James, *Filming T.E. Lawrence: Korda's Lost Epics* (London: I.B. Tauris, 1997).

Keyishian, Harry, *Michael Arlen* (Boston: Twayne, 1975).

Kotsilibas-Davis, J. and Loy, Myrna, *Myrna Loy: Being and Becoming* (London: Bloomsbury, 1987).

Lasalle, Michael, *Complicated Women: Sex and Power in Pre-Code Hollywood* (New York: St Martin's Press, 2000).

Lawrence, V. and Hill, P., *200 Years of Peace and War: A History of the Northamptonshire Yeomanry* (London: Orman, 1994).

Leber, Annedore, *Conscience in Revolt: Sixty-four Stories of Resistance in Germany* (London: Vallentine Mitchell, 1957).

Leiter, Samuel L., *The Encyclopaedia of the New York Stage 1930–1940* (New York and London: Greenwood, 1989).

Lester, Elenore, *Wallenberg: The Man in the Iron Web* (Englewood Cliffs, NJ: Prentice-Hall, 1982).

Lillie, Beatrice, *Every Other Inch a Lady* (London: W.H. Allen, 1972).

Lipstadt, Deborah, *Beyond Belief: The American Press and the Coming of the Holocaust 1933–1945* (New York: Free Press, 1986).

Lockhart, Robert Bruce, *Friends, Foes and Foreigners* (London: Putnam, 1957).

London, Louise, *Whitehall and the Jews 1933–1948: British Immigration Policy, Jewish Refugees and the Holocaust* (Cambridge: Cambridge University Press, 2000).

Lord, Graham, *Niv: The Authorised Biography of David Niven* (London: Orion Media, 2003).

Low, Rachael, *The History of the British Film, 1906–1914* (London: George Allen and Unwin, 1973).

Low, Rachael, *Film Making in 1930s Britain* (London: George Allen and Unwin, and the British Film Institute, 1985).

Lumet, Sidney, *Making Movies* (London: Bloomsbury, 1995).

Macdonald, Bill, *The True Intrepid: Sir William Stephenson and the Unknown Agents* (Surrey, British Columbia: Timberholme Books, 1998).

Macdonald, Kevin, *Emeric Pressburger: The Life and Death of a Screenwriter* (London: Faber and Faber, 1994).

McFarlane, Brian, *An Autobiography of British Cinema as Told by the Filmmakers and Actors Who Made It* (London: Methuen, 1997).

Madsen, Axel, *The Sewing Circle* (London: Robson, 1996).

Manchester, William, *The Caged Lion: Winston Spencer Churchill, 1932–1940* (London: Michael Joseph, 1988).

Mangan, Richard (ed.), *Gielgud's Letters* (London: Weidenfeld and Nicolson, 2004).

Mason Brown, John, *The Worlds of Robert E. Sherwood, Mirror to His Times* (New York: Harper and Row, 1962).

Matthews, A.E., *Matty: An Autobiography* (London: Hutchinson, 1952).

Meltzer, Albert, *I Couldn't Paint Golden Angels: Sixty Years of Commonplace Life and Anarchist Agitation* (Edinburgh: AK Press, 1996).

Mitchell, Gordon, *R.J. Mitchell, Schooldays to Spitfire* (Stroud: Tempus, 1986).

Montgomery Hyde, H., *Secret Intelligence Agent* (New York: St Martin's Press, 1982).

Morgan, William J., *Spies and Saboteurs* (London: Gollancz, 1955).

Neave, Airey, *Saturday at MI9* (London: Hodder and Stoughton, 1969).

Nicholson, Michael, *Raoul Wallenburg: The Swedish Diplomat Who Saved 100,000 Jews* (Watford: Exley, 1989).

Nicolson, Nigel (ed.), *Harold Nicolson: Diaries and Letters 1907–1964* (London: Weidenfeld and Nicolson, 2004).

Niven, David, *The Moon's a Balloon* (London: Hamish Hamilton, 1971).

Norwich, John Julius, *The Duff Cooper Diaries 1915–1951* (London: Weidenfeld and Nicolson, 2005).

Orczy, Baroness, *The Scarlet Pimpernel* (London: Greening, 1905).

Palmer, Lilli, *Change Lobsters and Dance: An Autobiography* (London: W.H. Allen, 1976).

Pascal, Valerie, *The Disciple and His Devil* (London: Joseph, 1971).

Persico, Joseph, *Piercing the Reich: The Penetration of Nazi Germany by OSS Agents during World War II* (London: M. Joseph, 1979).

Peterson, Theodore, *Magazines in the Twentieth Century* (Urbana, IL: University of Illinois Press, 1964).

Pincher, Chapman, *Their Trade Is Treachery* (London: Sidgwick and Jackson, 1981).

Pinero, Sir Arthur Wing, *The Freaks: An Idyll of Suburbia, In Three Acts* (London: William Heinemann, 1922).

Pound, Reginald, *Arnold Bennett: A Biography* (London: Heinemann, 1952).

Pritchard, Michael, *Sir Hubert von Herkomer and His Film-Making in Bushey 1912–1914* (Bushey: Museum Trust, 1987).

Quayle, Anthony, *A Time to Speak* (London: Barrie and Jenkins, 1990).

Quirk, Lawrence J., *Claudette Colbert: An Illustrated Biography* (New York: Crown, 1985).

Read, Anthony and David Fisher, *Colonel Z: The Life and Times of a Master of Spies* (London: Hodder and Stoughton, 1984).

Reed, Nicholas, *Camille Pissarro at the Crystal Palace* (London: London Reference Books, 1987).

Rey-Ximena, José, *El Vuelo de Ibis: [The Flight of the Ibis] Leslie Howard* (Madrid: Facta Ediciones, 2008).

Richards, Jeffrey and Anthony Aldgate, *Best of British* (Oxford: Blackwell, 1983).

Rose, Norman, *Vansittart: Study of a Diplomat* (London: Heinemann, 1978).

Rosza, Miklos, *Double Life. The Autobiography of Miklos Rosza* (Tunbridge Wells: Midas Books, 1982).

Schenkar, Joan, *Truly Wilde* (London: Virago, 2000).

Sebag-Montefiore, Hugh, *Enigma: The Battle for the Code* (London: Weidenfeld and Nicolson, 2000).

Shepherd, Naomi, *Wilfred Israel: German Jewry's Secret Ambassador* (London: Weidenfeld and Nicolson, 1984).

Smith, Michael, *Foley: The Spy Who Saved 10,000 Jews* (London: Hodder and Stoughton, 1999).

Smith, R. Harris, *OSS: The Secret History of America's First Central Intelligence Agency* (Berkeley, CA: University of California Press, 1972).

Stafford, David, *Roosevelt and Churchill: Men of Secrets* (London: Little, Brown, 1999).

Stafford, David, *Churchill and Secret Service* (London: Abacus, 2000).

Stone, D., *Responses to Nazism in Britain, 1933–1939. Before War and the Holocaust* (Basingstoke: Palgrave Macmillan, 2003).

Stone, Glyn, *The Oldest Ally: Britain and the Portuguese Connection, 1936–1941* (London: Royal Historical Society, 1994).

Tabori, Paul, *Alexander Korda* (London: Oldbourne, 1959).

Tarkington, Booth, *The Wren: A Comedy in Three Acts* (New York: S. French, 1922).

Taylor, A.J.P., *Beaverbrook* (London: Hamish Hamilton, 1972).

Taylor, Philip M., *The Projection of Britain: British Overseas Publicity and Propaganda, 1919–1930* (Cambridge: Cambridge University Press, 1981).

Thorold, Anne (ed.), *The Letters of Lucien to Camille Pissarro, 1883–1903* (Cambridge: Cambridge University Press, 1993).

Thwaite, Ann, *A.A. Milne: His Life* (London: Faber and Faber, 1990).

Tomlinson, David, *Luckier than Most: An Autobiography* (London: Hodder and Stoughton, 1990).

Vane, Sutton, *Outward Bound* (London: S. French, 1924).

Vizetelly, Ernest Alfred, *With Zola in England: A Story of Exile* (Leipzig: B. Tauchnitz, 1899).

Wasserstein, Bernard, *Britain and the Jews of Europe 1939–1945* (London and Oxford: Institute of Jewish Affairs and Clarendon Press, 1979).

Watts, Stephen (ed.), *Behind the Screen: How Films are Made* (London: A. Barker, 1938).

Wearing J.P. (ed.), *The Collected Letters of Sir Arthur Pinero* (Minneapolis, MN: University of Minnesota Press, 1974).

Wearing, J.P., *The London Stage, 1910–1939: A Calendar of Plays and Players*, 3 vols, (Metuchen, NJ and London: Scarecrow, 1990).

West, Nigel, *MI5: British Security Service Operations, 1909–1945* (London: The Bodley Head, 1981).

West, Nigel, *MI6: British Secret Intelligence Service Operations, 1909–1945* (London: Weidenfeld and Nicolson, 1983).

West, Nigel, *Unreliable Witness: Espionage Myths of the Second World War* (London: Grafton, 1984).

West, Nigel, *Secret War: The Story of SOE, Britain's Wartime Sabotage Organisation* (London: Hodder and Stoughton, 1992).

Whitehouse, Arthur George, *The Fledgling* (London: Vane, 1965).

Who's Who in the Theatre (London: Pitman, 1912–81).

Wistrich, Robert, *The Jews of Vienna in the Age of Franz Joseph* (Oxford and New York: Published for the Littman Library by Oxford University Press, 1990).

Wright, Peter, *Spy Catcher* (New York: Dell, 1988).

Wyman, David S., *The Abandonment of the Jews: America and the Holocaust 1941–1945* (New York: Pantheon Books, 1984).

Young, Kenneth (ed.), *The Diaries of Sir Robert Bruce Lockhart* (London: Macmillan, 1973–1980).

Index

N